This book is dedicated to Frank Albert Stubblefield, member of the US House of Representatives from Kentucky's first district (January 3, 1959–December 31, 1974).

I will always be grateful for taking a personal interest in me during such a critical point in my life. I owe whatever success I have in my life to him and Odessa, his wife.

# CONTENTS

Foreword ..................................................................................... 7
1. Parnell, Kentucky, 1940–1945 ............................................. 11
2. "Number One" Community, 1946–1948 ............................ 25
3. Sardis, Kentucky, 1946–1948 ............................................... 31
4. Columbus, Kentucky, 1949–1950 ........................................ 37
5. Hornbeak, Tennessee, 1951–1956 ........................................ 40
6. Elbridge, Tennessee, 1956–1958 .......................................... 47
7. Washington, DC, 1958–1962 ............................................... 54
8. Murray State University, 1962–1965 ................................... 78
9. Marine Corps Reserve Active Duty, September 1965–March 1966 ................................................................. 86
10. Memphis, Tennessee, 1966–1971 ......................................... 89
11. Memphis, Tennessee, 1968–1971 ......................................... 98
12. United States Secret Service Headquarters, 1971–1977 ...... 108
13. Louisville Field Office, 1977–1988 ..................................... 150
14. Post–Secret Service Career .................................................. 192
15. Entering into the Totally New World of Politics ................. 194
16. Kentucky State Senate Campaign, 1990 ............................. 222
17. Kentucky State Treasurer Campaign, 1991 ........................ 226
18. My Most Disgusting Political Race ..................................... 232
19. Kentucky State Auditor's Race, 1995 .................................. 234
20. US Congress Race, 2000 ..................................................... 241
21. Kentucky Lieutenant Governor Race, 2003 ....................... 248
22. Life After Being a Candidate for Political Offices .............. 253
23. Life in Florida ...................................................................... 255

# FOREWORD

The purpose of the contents in this book is to leave my life story behind for my family and friends. I also wanted to document the trials and tribulations of just an average young kid who did not want to end up in poverty for the rest of his life. I expect that many individuals will have very little interest in reading this book. This book is not only about my career as a special agent with the United States Secret Service, but about all the facts regarding how someone born into the lowest financial class in our country could navigate around and through the great white sharks in life without remaining in the lowest class as a human being on this earth. My personal faith and sheer fear of failure kept me going. I never had two good choices as I traveled through life. I always had only one choice. For example, when I stepped into the airplane for my first airplane ride to Washington National Airport on June 8, 1958, my other choice was to remain in Elbridge, Tennessee, and have a career in a local feed mill, making five dollars a day. Well, as I saw it, I had only one choice, and that was to leave home and take the lowest-paying job in the United States government as a clerk in the Federal Bureau of Investigation, in Washington, DC. I thank J. Edgar Hoover every day for giving me the $2,960-a-year job. He gave thousands of poor young kids, and others, from the rural areas of our country the opportunity to see a whole new world.

In addition, I wish to profusely thank US Congressman Frank Albert Stubblefield, who saw something in me that caused him and his spouse, Odessa, to go above and beyond to make arrangements for me to attend Murray State University, Murray, Kentucky. Congressman Stubblefield represented the First Congressional District of Kentucky. The longer I live, the more I realize how much they did for me as a young kid in Washington, and later as friends, while assigned to our headquarters, in DC. I think about their kindness almost daily. They were among the nicest people I have ever known. I dedicate this book to them.

I also wish to mention how much I appreciate Maurice Miller, the Secret Service agent in charge of the Memphis, Tennessee Field Office. He saw something in me that caused him to push Secret Service Headquarters hire me as a Secret Service agent. I will always be grateful to him.

My spouse Stephanie and our children, Becky, Greg, and Brian, had to hang in there with me during my absence while on assignments with the Secret Service. I always managed to bring them a gift when I returned home. Sometimes, while on extended assignments, I would become emotional thinking about them as I sat in my hotel room, because I missed them so much. I have done the same thing today, after my little grandchildren leave for home. I have never mentioned this to anyone.

Oh, I almost forgot all those political campaigns as a candidate for all those offices, knowing that my chances for victory were almost zero. I sometimes forget how much stress and agony that I put my family through. Looking back, I simply do not know how I withstood all this activity, which was horrible, at times. I never mention this side of my life to anyone, except those who already knew that I was a candidate for many political offices. I was in the big leagues as far as being a candidate for Congress, etc. Most of our friends here in Vero Beach know nothing about that side of my life. Trust me, I was up close and personal to the darkest side of politics. I saw it from the national level, right down to the lowest level. As you read this book, you will understand what I am talking about. I did my best to be very descriptive, in view of the fact that I have not mentioned various names since many of the subjects remain alive, today. I do not want to say anything to embarrass their children.

I wish to emphasize that I have not done anything great in the eyes of most people, but I thought that I would inform anyone who reads this book that I was someone who believes in the power of one. I wanted to experience many things in my life other than being a Secret Service agent, although I am very grateful that I was able to experience a career with the Secret Service. So these writings are about my overall experiences in life. I accidentally became a Secret Service agent for which I am thankful. I wanted to experience as many things throughout my life as possible, BECAUSE I want to be tired at the end, realizing that I have eternity to rest.

# PARNELL, KENTUCKY
# 1940–1945

Show me a person with no enemies and I will show you a person with no MISSION, no PURPOSE, no PASSION, and no COURAGE. Having a few enemies is EVIDENCE you are actually alive and not dreaming.

On May 17, 1940, a very tired and aggravated stork was making its last stop at the end of the day, flying around looking for a house to drop me off. However, it took revenge on me and left me in the most God-forsaken place on earth, Parnell, KY, the ass-end of civilization. Man, that stork must have been really tired at the time, due to its unusually very busy day.

My grandmother Maggie Bell was the midwife that brought me into this world on May 17, 1940. The only medical device present at this birth was a pan of hot water located on the old wood-burning cooking stove and some rags. We could not afford anything else. My grandmother Cole, on my mother's side, was a full-blooded Cherokee Indian, and a midwife. Her parents were part of the Trail of Tears march from North Carolina to Oklahoma. Along the way, they dropped out of the march and settled in Clinton County, Kentucky, which borders the state of Tennessee. This was the route that the Cherokee's were forced to take as they marched to Oklahoma. President Andrew Jackson, who hated American Indians, was responsible for relocating the Cherokees. Both my grandmothers traveled all over the area delivering babies. I do not believe they received any money for their services. Someone may have given them a chicken or eggs, etc. I was a very stubborn and determined young baby. While being held by someone, I would grab a head of hair and never let it loose until someone pried my hand open. No matter how hard my hand would be hit or slapped, I would not let go.

My house was located in a God-forsaken place called Parnell, Kentucky. An old wood railing fence was built alongside the slate road. Horse-drawn buckboard wagons filled with parents and children, bouncing up and down, would travel down the road. Every now and then, a vehicle would go back and forth on the so-called road. Even into the 1990s, the county school superintendent told me that he had to send two buses to Parnell, in order to keep the Parnell students from fighting the other kids. My house had an open hallway, and it was put together with old logs and boards with cracks between them, which let snow blow into the rooms during a snowy, cold winter night. I slept on a homemade straw mattress at the foot of a bed, with my two brothers at the head.

One night the kids of a family that lived in the same area that had straw mattresses kept feeling something moving under them, inside the mattress. The next day, the father cut into the mattress, and to his surprise, a family of copperhead snakes had made their home inside the straw. The mattress with the snakes was taken outside and burned. Straw mattresses were common for most of the poor families because they were inexpensive to make. We had no electricity and no inside or outside bathrooms. NOT EVEN AN OUTHOUSE!

One day, while I was taking a crap in the field, my brother Otis started throwing rocks at me, which caused an unpleasant interruption. He had always gotten some type of pleasure out of throwing rocks for whatever reason. To this day, I have a scar on my forehead that was caused by one of the rocks that Otis threw that connected with my head. On those cold, winter nights you could piss off the front porch, since there was an open outside hallway, but if you had go the bathroom, you had to bare your butt in the yard, or in the open field behind the house, if you could call it a house with less than a thousand square feet.

There would be no heat in the house after everyone went to bed. The old wood-burning stove that was used for heat would go out because it took too much wood to keep it burning throughout the night. We had to sleep under as many quilts as possible in order to keep from freezing. The only wallpaper we had were pages from magazines and Sears and Roebuck catalogs, etc., that were given to us at Stearns Grocery Store. There were eleven children and two parents, who survived in this dwelling. I guess I did survive, which beats the hell out of me. We never wore shoes from May or June until September. One pair of shoes had to last until you wore them out, or until your foot got so big that the toe of the shoe had to be cut, in order to let your toes expand beyond the cut out part of the shoe. In other words, as an old Hank Williams song went, the shoe soles got so thin that if you stepped on a dime, you could tell if it was heads or tails.

Sometimes my oldest brother Eldon had to walk to school in the snow, with old rags wrapped around his feet due to the fact he either had no shoes at that time, or because his old pair of shoes were absolutely too small to walk the five miles to school. I can remember always being hungry. We ate meat, which was a chicken, on Sundays, once a month if we were lucky. Once a year, again, if we were lucky, meaning that if our father could find a hog to kill, we could eat pork. My parents, along with my brothers and sisters, would make lye soap and hominy in borrowed big black kittles sitting over a wood-burning fire in the yard. We ate a lot of cornbread and milk. I never remembered eating beef until I was much older while living in another area. We never had store-bought milk or bread. I remember to this day, the first time I ate store-bought bread. One loaf had to feed at least ten of us. It tasted so good that I could have eaten the whole loaf in five minutes. I was always hungry, and food was the most important thing in my life at that time. Sociologist Abraham Maslow's Hierarchy of Needs were physiological (food, water, shelter); safety (personal, financial, health); love-belonging (friendship, intimacy, family); esteem (self-respect, respect from others); self-actualization (accomplish everything that a person can to become the most that one can be, such as causes, etc.); and self-transcendence (giving itself to some higher goal outside oneself, such as altruism and spirituality).

Well, it seemed that it took forever for me to reach the second need, which was safety. I was always consumed with getting food.

Our Christmas gift consisted of an apple and an orange in one of my mother's old worn silk stockings. I never remembered receiving an actual toy for Christmas. All the drinking and household water was carried from a spring, which was located down a hill from our house. I had a two-pound lard bucket that I carried, and my older brothers and sisters had larger lard buckets for their water. During the day, we continually went back and forth from the house to the spring with our buckets, looking like piss ants crawling in a line.

My grandmother Bell was extremely stingy. She would not share the apples on her apple tree with anyone. When my sisters Chris and Pauline went to the spring to get their bucket of water, they would pass the apple tree and pick one or two apples and then put them in their bucket of water in order that grandmother Bell could not see them. That was their way of hiding them due to the fact she would take them away from my sisters. Back at the house, we kept one pail of water with a dipper or gourd in it, as the drinking water. All of us drank out of the same dipper. We lived in rattlesnake and copperhead country, and during the summer, in our bare feet, we had to dodge these snakes. In other words, we had to walk softly and carry a big stick and run like hell.

Life was unbearably unpleasant living in the middle of nowhere, with no electricity or any inside or outside bathrooms. We always felt like we had received a bonus when, for whatever reason, we did not have to go to church service on a Sunday night. During this period of time, after dark, my older sisters would attempt to scare the crap out of us by covering their body with white sheets and running around outside making noises like ghosts. I was four or five years of age and being out in the middle of nowhere with no electricity, the darkness seemed unusually dark. They did a good job scaring us. Since I grew up around seven sisters, who were tough as nails, I had no doubt that females were the dominate sex. My sister Chris could throw a haymaker that would stun Mike Tyson. I firmly believe that women can take more punishment than men. Most men that I know are whiners who are dominated by women. They are generally weak! Remember, the strongest force on earth is a rich, good-looking woman.

# STRUGGLE TO ZERO

During the winter months, we felt like we were freezing to death, and during the summer we walked around with no shoes, always on the lookout for rattlesnakes and copperheads. I can still hear our neighbor Tom Alley screaming and cussing his mule, Tob, as he broke new ground in the field around his log cabin. Man, did he ever use vile language, which included using the name of God in every sentence. I felt sorry for Tob. When you are four or five years of age, Tom Alley's log cabin looked normal in size. Tom's log cabin has been designated as an historical site today. It was just a short distance down the road from our old cruddy house. The cabin remains there today, and one of our family reunions was held there in the yard several years ago. As I entered the cabin to look around, did it ever look small inside? How did a family with children, especially the females, have any privacy inside such a small living space? All I can say is that the frontier families had no privacy inside their tiny homes. The only way you could have any quiet time or privacy would be in the outhouse, if there was one. As we grow older, things shrink, I guess.

These Bell family reunions brought together some the most unusual and sometimes classless people on earth. Where did some of these people come from? An example was Carlos Holder, the brother of the ex-spouse of my sister Ollie. I never really knew Carlos and never laid my eyes on him anywhere, except at one or two of our reunions. Carlos had led a sorry life. He had done time in prison for reasons unknown. However, he really tried to "shine" and present his best image at the reunions. Apparently, he had a set of false teeth made while doing time many years prior. He wore these teeth only when he came to the reunions. They did not fit his mouth, and when he opened his mouth, you needed to have your sunglasses on in order to prevent blindness from his unbelievably white teeth.

At one of the reunions Carlos's wife brought a photo of a copperhead snake stretched out on their bed. She stated that when she walked into her bedroom one day, she immediately knew that a copperhead was in her room due to the fact copperhead snakes give off an odor similar to a cucumber. She began looking for that snake in her bedroom and finally found it. She shot and killed the snake and laid it on her bed in order to photograph it. As I previously mentioned, Carlos Holder was not the best human being on earth, and due to the fact he and his wife fought all the time, she finally had enough, so she loaded her pistol one day and opened up on him, thus, killing him on the spot in their house. Carlos was so mean to her that she was never charged with any crime. The sheriff was happy to get rid of him. Damn, I can still see those white, bright, prison made teeth, today, due to the fact they looked so unusual and bright in his mouth.

My brother Eldon told me about an incident that happened regarding one traveling preacher that stayed at our house while he and our father went around together, preaching the Word. The "guest" preacher would always have the first choice of food on the table during meals and the kids would end up with what was left. Sometimes, when these preachers found a home that would let them stay for long periods of time, they took advantage of this situation. Anyway, Eldon got tired of this setup, so one night, he and his buddies located a skunk. While the preacher was asleep, they took his trousers and enticed the skunk to leave its great smelling scent on the trousers. Well, when the preacher woke up and attempted to put on his trousers with the skunk odor, he left our house as fast as he could and never came back.

The area of Parnell, Kentucky, was so out of main stream compared to other parts of the United States that it was pathetic. The people in that area were so far behind culturally that they thought they were first. A relative of mine, Strongie Bell, had never seen himself in a mirror. So he had no idea how he looked to other people. One day, he and his family traveled to Burnside, KY, to catch the train for Cincinnati, Ohio. Burnside was the closest train station, which was located many miles from Parnell. While on the train Strongie had the urge to go to the bathroom. He finally located the door handle to the bathroom. However, he could not figure out how to open the door. As he was pulling on the door handle, he looked to the right and saw a man trying to get the door to the bathroom open also. However, what Strongie saw was himself in the long floor to ceiling mirror located right next to the bathroom door. Due to the fact that Strongie had never seen himself in his life, he did not recognize himself as being the man in the mirror. Man, you had to be backward to have never seen yourself in a mirror when you were in your thirties.

During 1938, as a two-year-old, my brother Garvin became sick with what was called the old flux, an intestinal illness. He could not keep food down, and as a result he was on the edge of death. His eyes had already sunk in, plus, he could not move. Our father stayed at his bedside, around the clock for two weeks and dropped water that was squeezed from a rag down his throat. He frantically tried to find a cure, and finally, the only old doctor in the county stated that the only cure was sheep tallow. After many attempts to find someone who would give him a sheep, one poor soul gave him one, which was slaughtered. The tallow was prepared and dropped into Garvin's throat. He slowly got better and survived.

Actually, his condition was caused by the lack of food. Back then, due to the hard times, generally speaking everyone was stingy with their possessions, including giving up one of their sheep. My sister Flonnie weighed less than two pounds at birth but survived without doctors or hospitals. She was so small that my father could hold her in one hand. No baby milk bottles were available, and milk would be dropped into her mouth by squeezing it from rags. Our home remedy for the croup (a very hoarse cough) was a teaspoon of sugar with two or three small drops of coal oil (kerosene) mixed with the sugar. In the middle of the night, my father would come to our bedside with an old coal oil lamp in one hand and the teaspoon of sugar containing a few drops of kerosene in the other. Down the hatch this "great" tasting remedy would go. The taste was so horrible that it scared the croup out of our system. However, it apparently worked. Other great tasting home remedies were cod liver oil and mineral oil. I almost puke when I think about the taste of these remedies.

As a four-year-old, I recall many things very clearly, such as hoping that I could find a perfect forked tree branch that could be used to make a sling shot. How I longed for a perfectly made sling shot. A piece of rubber cut from an old rubber inner tube was used as part of the sling shot. I would dream about having toy cars to play with. Also, during the day, I would always stay outside the house during the summer months running up and down the hills. Sometimes, I would get so tired that I would have to lay down on the ground to rest, without thinking about those copperhead snakes. We had lunch, which was called dinner, during the middle of the day. This was customary for families. We would usually have nothing to eat but a piece of cornbread, maybe poke salad, pinto beans, or sometimes milk. I learned to like pinto beans because if I would not eat them, I would go hungry. We never had any glass windows or screens. Therefore, flies were everywhere during the summer months. So while we were eating this "gourmet food," one of us would have to stand up at the table with a tree branch and fan the flies away. My mother and I were clean freaks; therefore, those flies never had any luck in landing on our food. Once a week, we would take a real bath in two old round tubs, which were used for washing clothes. Out of all this misery, my mother was a stickler for cleanness. In fact, all of us kids later on in life would always make certain that we were clean. We were always the cleanest children in the area. I am this way today. I believe that the very least anyone can do for themselves is to always have a clean body and clean clothes, regardless as to how poor they are. Water and soap can do wonders for people. I believe that cleanliness shows the true character of an individual. Many thanks go to the person who invented soap.

We had an old battery-operated radio that made it very difficult to understand what the person was saying. Gabriel Heater, the World War II commentator, would give his nightly update on the war. "Ahhh, there's a bit of good news, tonight" was his opening sentence when there was a bit of good news to report. My oldest brother Eldon was in the war from 1940–1945, which was called the duration. He was at Pearl Harbor when it was bombed and on Wake Island when it was attacked. Then he was shipped to the European theater as a tail gunner flying numerous bombing missions over Germany, the last being over Dresden. He stated that his plane always drew fire on the missions. One time the plane was shot up so badly that when it touched on the ground in England it broke completely in two sections. Since he was in the tail as the tail gunner, he survived, but other crew members were killed. He was in both the Pacific and European theater. He made it through five years of fighting without any injuries. After the war, he settled down in the Detroit, Michigan, area.

Prior to going to the War, when Eldon was either seventeen or eighteen years of age, he ran around in the county with a group of five or six boys. They were tough and did things, such as working a local constable over after he took their beer from them that they had just bought across the Tennessee state line. The constable would wait on the road for those who came along with their beer in their car. He would take the beer and keep it for himself. However, Eldon and his buddies made up their minds that he would not take their beer, so they roughed him up and left him not in good shape on the roadside. The boys had guns, and one evening as they were playing around shooting at tree trunks, etc., a bullet accidently hit one of the boys. The parents were contacted and his body was laid out in an old wooden homemade casket, thinking that he was dead. After hearing about the shooting, members of my family went to his house. Everyone thought he was dead, but my sister Ollie put her hand on his face and she said that it felt warm. Back then there were no doctors or hospitals available. Anyway, he was buried. Proper medical care may have kept him alive. No charges were brought against any of the boys. This part of Kentucky was similar to the Wild West.

My father was born in 1897, and somehow he missed out on serving in World War I. Maybe it was because he was so poor that the Army would not have him. To his defense, he did fall backward while on a ladder, breaking his back.

My parents did not start having children until 1922, when my brother Eldon was born. From 1922–1947, a new baby made its appearance into this world almost every two years like clockwork, except the last, Glenna, who was born in 1947. Our grandmothers delivered ten out of the eleven of us at home. Old Dr. Mosley, from Kuttawa, KY, crossed the Cumberland River on a ferry boat to be at Glenna's birth. She was the only one out of eleven who had a doctor present at birth. During 1925, my father, mother, and brother Eldon (three years old) went to Cincinnati, Ohio, where my father got a job with the Proctor and Gamble Corporation. However, the lure of

God-forsaken Parnell, KY, kept calling for him to come back there and suffer for the rest of his life. He moved back, and the rest of us suffered until we finished school and moved away as soon as possible.

While back in Parnell, our father got a "calling" from GOD to be a preacher. He traveled around the area preaching to anyone who would listen, hoping to make a buck. He was lucky if he made a dollar, which had to be used to feed twelve of us. Times were hard during the depression and during my younger days. A few bucks would buy a lot of groceries even during the first years of my life. Currently, in certain parts of Kentucky, there is this unexplained, surreal, mystic, strange lure to remain there, suffer, and live from hand to mouth in the hollows, hills, and mountains, for the rest of your life.

Life in the area did improve after Lake Cumberland was created by the TVA. Lake Cumberland was a HUGE person made lake. It was my luck that through eminent domain the lake was able to come into existence AFTER I moved from this area. This was one of the good reasons for eminent domain. Presidential candidate Donald Trump would have been pleased with this project, which created Lake Cumberland due to the fact he stated that eminent domain does serve a good purpose in certain cases.

During the 1920s, '30s, and '40s, many men who were looking for an easy way to make a dollar became self-proclaimed preachers. They would declare themselves as having a calling from God. Then they would get a Bible and go here and there preaching, taking up collections, hoping that someone would throw a penny or a dime into the collection hat. No one had a spare dollar to give. Bo Flag, one of these traveling preachers came to my grandparents Holy Roller Church to preach. He was running my grandfather Bell down, because he would not give him a percentage of his eggs, and other food. My uncle Orville was outside the church on his horse, being back for a visit from Michigan, where he lived and worked at that time. Bo Flag was in the pulpit trying to get the Holy Spirit from on high into his soul, yelling, "Strychnine won't poison me, and lightning won't strike me, because I have such strong faith in Jesus."

At that time, uncle Orville opened the very wide, side church door and, while remaining on his horse, ran up to Bo Flag, grabbing him by the shirt collar, yelling to him, "Damn you, strychnine may not poison you, and lightning might not strike you, but damn you, I can hit you." Uncle Orville hit him and knocked him halfway out of the church, picked him up at the door, and knocked him the rest of the way out. After making his point, Uncle Orville left the church and headed back to Michigan in his car. Uncle Orville was noted for having a mean streak in him.

My father was there and watched the entire incident. My father told me that during these periods of time it was not unusual to have someone during the church service suddenly stand up and start cussing, for whatever reason.

My grandmother and grandfather Bell were Holy Rollers who attended the local small Holiness Church, which was located a long walking distance from our home. My father eventually broke away from their church and became a Methodist. My grandmother would go into her bedroom and get worked up in a trance, talking in "unknown tongues." One night, my grandfather had a terrible nightmare. He dreamed that he opened the front door to the local Holy Roller Church, and as he opened it, he saw nothing but huge flames of fire inside, which indicated to him that if you went inside a Holy Roller Church, you would go to hell. The nightmare was so scary to him that the next day he made up his mind to never enter the door of a Holy Roller Church. Prior to his death, he lived with us while we resided in Columbus, Ky. I remember him very well. He never entered a Holy Roller Church as long as he lived. However, my grandmother continued with her Holy Roller Church beliefs until she died in 1947.

My grandfather Frank Cole died during 1936 at his home, which was located a few miles from our log/plank shack. He was my mother's father, who was born in 1865. He and my grandmother were married during 1882, in Clinton County, Kentucky, which was the next county over from where I was born. Due to the fact my grandmother was a Cherokee Indian, my grandfather Cole had to post a $100 bond, which committed him to remain married to my grandmother for one year. That $100 was equivalent to $1,000, today. My grandmother Cole was energetic, but my grandfather was lazy. They lived in an old log house and had to depend on my grandmother to keep things going. Their log house was better than the darn old shack that my family lived in. I believe that our log house/shack was probably the worst living abode in the area. Damn, it was bad! Grandmother Cole would throw an old gunny sack on her shoulders and head for the woods looking for wild roots and other edible foods. Also, she was a midwife who traveled throughout the area delivering babies.

The only thing Grandfather Cole did to make any money was to take eggs and wood that he had chopped into town to sell them. One day on their way to town in their old buckboard wagon with eggs to sell, which were placed on the floor in a box, the wagon unexpectedly hit a large bump in the road, causing the eggs to break. Grandfather Cole went out of his mind with anger, realizing that the hens could not replace all those eggs in one day. You know, a photograph of Grandfather Cole does not exist today. The only photograph of him was hanging on the wall in my sister Ollie's sorry little one room shack, which was put together practically in the yard of our house. Ollie's shack burnt down, along with the only photo of my grandfather that existed. Hell, we had no wall space on the walls in our sorry house to even hang his picture.

On the date of his death, Grandfather Cole's body was laid out in the bedroom in their house, which was customary. There was only one funeral home in the county, and it was located many miles away. Also, my grandparents could not afford to use a funeral home. My sisters Ollie, Chris, and Pauline, were standing at the old front gate when an old black car zipped by them, stopping in front of the house. Two men got out with their buckets and small hoses and went inside the house. The kids had to remain outside the gate, but they observed these men coming in and out with their buckets, pouring liquid in the yard. The liquid was, of course, grandfather's blood from the embalming. This was the only way that embalmings were carried out in these God-forsaken, rural areas. In addition, nickels were laid on grandfather's eyes in order to keep them shut, after death. My sister, Ollie, who is still living (eighty-seven years old), was present when grandmother Cole noticed that one of the two nickels was missing from grandfather's eye. A search for that nickel was conducted high and wide inside and underneath the house due to the fact there were cracks between the planks used as a floor. She accused my sister's Ollie and Chris of taking the nickel. Boy, did she ever get mad. However, she changed her tune when she determined that her son Everett was the one that took the nickel.

My father would go away for days at a time looking for places to preach the Word. He would leave our mother at home to take care of the ten children at home. To this day, I cannot understand how our mother did not end up in a mental institution. The living conditions were worse than terrible. Not enough food to eat, no electricity, and carrying all the water from the spring, which was some distance from the house, etc. My mother made my sisters dresses out of twenty five-pound flour sacks. As a four- and five-year-old, my brothers and I would search the area for wild strawberries and mulberry trees for food. Man, were we ever happy whenever we located some ripe berries, which were very small and on a small plant.

One time as I was standing under a mulberry tree, a big snake dropped from the tree, barely missing my head. I did not like that. My butt sucked wind. My father believed in the literal interpretation of the Bible, meaning that if you spared the rod, you would spoil the child. Therefore, he would not spare the rod when it came to his children. He let his misguided interpretation of the Bible make our home life an unpleasant existence. We never knew when the wrath of the "rod" would come after us. This verse should never have been in the Bible!

Later on in life, when we were in high school, he continued to not spare the rod. In addition, if we had a friend over for a visit, he would always come into the room and sing religious songs. Then he would get down on his knees and pray. It was totally an embarrassment to us. Thank goodness, none of us ended up with any mental problems or turned against faith later on in life.

Finally, after completing a prescribed set of correspondence courses for aspiring Methodist ministers offered by Emory University, Atlanta, GA, my father was given five small Methodist churches as their minister. Until 1965, when my father retired, he never made more than $3,000 a year. His standard of living increased in retirement. Remember, this was in the 1930s and 1940s, not 2016, so do not get the idea that all Methodist ministers were illiterate. Life was a rough row to hoe. It was TOUGH where we lived! The Pilgrims had a better life than most of the people in the Parnell area. The rules were different back then for becoming a minister. Today, the Methodist ministers have a good standard of living and are basically taken care of as long as they are connected with the church. I think of myself as a Methodist, not a United Methodist.

# "NUMBER ONE" COMMUNITY
# 1946–1948

During 1946, we moved from Parnell, KY, to another location in the same county, which was closer to the county seat, Monticello. The community was called Number One. (What a name!) I turned six years of age and started school. I would totally rebel against wearing short britches to school. Every now and then, I would take an apple to school as part of my lunch, which was normally piss-poor.

After I ate the apple down to the core, several of the students would beg me for the core to eat. My brother Otis continued to enjoy throwing rocks. One day, he threw a rock and hit me on my forehead. To this day, I have a scar from that zinger. My brother Eldon and his spouse, Pat, came for a visit from Dearborn, Michigan, right after the War. He was driving a new-looking, slick-back, black 1939 Ford. He would take us for a ride into Monticello to get an ice cream cone, and boy, I thought I was really something sitting there next to the window hoping that people would see me. It made me feel like I was ten feet tall. What a feeling! However, it did not take long for me to come back to reality.

Living at Number One was a step up from that hellish Parnell, KY. During 1991, while campaigning for state treasurer in the adjoining county, I was talking with a Kentucky State Police trooper, and when I mentioned that I was born in Parnell, he gave me a second look and stated that its reputation has not changed over the years. However, on Sunday nights during the summer months there in Number One, and while church services were in progress, a group of rowdies would congregate in front of the church, which was literally located right next to our house. They would fight, yell, and throw rocks on top of the church, which had a tin roof. They would be there every Sunday night. Therefore, the county sheriff, or a deputy, would come to our house and sit in a chair on the front porch and wait until they started disturbing the church services.

Harassing church services was a form of entertainment for the rowdies in the county. When this happened, the rowdies would be taken to jail. The memories are so vivid to this day, that I can see us walking across the yard, with the sheriff sitting on our front porch waiting on the rowdies to cause trouble outside the front door to the church. Another form of church service harassment during the colder months was for the rowdies to cover the coal burning stove pipe on top of the church and wait for everyone to run out of the church to get air when it would fill up with smoke. We remained at Number One for two years. If someone in our community became very ill and bedridden, neighbors would start a twenty four hour prayer vigil or death watch. They would come and go twenty four hours a day, bringing food and praying for this ill person. The praying would last until the person died.

My father married many couples in our house. The marriage ceremony would take place in our living room. All the children would be shooed out of the room while the ceremony took place. It was not uncommon for the bride to be fourteen years of age. Also, a few young girls got married at thirteen years of age with their parent's consent. My father never married anyone this young. It was not uncommon for certain country music stars to marry a girl thirteen years of age. When country music star Loretta Lynn was thirteen years of age, she married a twenty-five-year-old man. Today, in many countries, girls as young as nine are given away by their parents to marry some old, hairy, dingle-berried, stinking-assed man. My, how screwed up the world has been and is today, regarding the relationship between a man and woman. Just thinking about these young girls getting married at such a young age makes me sick to my stomach, especially, in view of the fact I have an eleven-year-old granddaughter.

Grandmother Cole taken in front of her cabin along with my sisters and aunt.

Grandmother Cole (Cherokee Indian) with family members during 1938.

Me being held by my mother in our yard at my birthplace.
My brothers and sisters are also in the photo.

My family taken in Hornbeak, TN. I am approximately fourteen years of age.

Me with my father and mother siting on the front porch of my grandfather's log cabin.

My father when he was approximately thirty years of age.

## Marriage Bond.

### THE COMMONWEALTH OF KENTUCKY.

Be it Known, That we, H. W. Cole as principal, and A. J. Latham as surety, are jointly and severally bound to the Commonwealth of Kentucky in the sum of One Hundred Dollars.

The Condition of this Bond is as Follows:

That, whereas, Marriage is intended to be solemnized between the above bound H. W. Cole and Miss N. C. Latham

Now, if there is no lawful cause to obstruct said marriage, this Bond shall be void, otherwise it shall remain in full force and effect

Dated at Albany Clinton County, this 5 day of September, 1882

H. W. Cole
A. J. Latham X
              mark

Attest:
C. B. Parrigin
By J. J. Leslie, Clerk Clinton County Court.

A copy of my grandfather and grandmother Cole's marriage license dated 1882. Due to the fact my grandmother was a Cherokee Indian, my grandfather had to put up a $100 bond to get married.

# SARDIS, KENTUCKY
# 1946–1948

My father's next stop was Sardis, Kentucky, a rural community located in the western part of Kentucky. We kept moving west, toward the Mississippi River. Then, Sardis was located near the Kentucky Lake Dam. Every now and then, we would go fishing right below the dam, but never caught enough fish for a decent meal. One of my father's churches was located next to our house along with a two-room school consisting of eight grades that was sitting practically in our yard. Also, a small country grocery store was located close to the school. On the moving day, going from Number One, to Sardis, we loaded up all our belongings in an old truck that belonged to one of our church members and hit the road to Sardis. Eight of us were stacked in our old car, which was driven by our father. We followed the moving truck and crossed the Cumberland River on a ferry boat and continued to head west. On the way, our car broke down, and thank goodness, a Good Samaritan helped find someone who could repair it for free. The ride was totally miserable with eight people in that car with our arms and legs sticking out the windows. We looked like Ma and Pa Kettle heading to the dustbowl during the depression in the 1930s. Anyway, we made the trip to Sardis, which was well over one hundred miles.

My father always had four or five churches because he was at the very bottom of the totem pole in the Methodist Church hierarchy. Again, his screwed up interpretation of the Bible continued to make our lives miserable. He was particularly rough on my two older sisters. My mother would step in on occasion when she felt that he became too rough on us. I have absolutely no use for any religious fanatic's viewpoint, such as the one who has a total misguided view and interpretation of the Bible. In fact, I truly believe that these religious extremists will be responsible for the downfall of western civilization. The majority of churches and denominations appear to be nothing but a business. Sadly, it appears to me that the primary concern of far too many churches today is to be a money-raising machine, not being truly interested in the down trodden, and people in need of spiritual healing.

However, I believe that churches serve a good purpose in most cases, whether they are run as a business or not. The religious extremist can be one of the most dangerous persons on earth, if they justify all their actions in the name of God. There are dangerous religious extremists in many religions. Therefore, we must be very vigilant in order to prevent these extremists from hijacking sensible, good religions. How many Americans would continue to support their church if their monetary gifts were not a tax deduction? This would be one way of determining who is TRULY a religious person. I believe in true religious inner faith. Most, not all, public prayers make me feel a little uncomfortable. Now, DO NOT BELIEVE THAT I AM AGAINST CHRUCHES OR RELIGION! There is an appropriate place for certain public prayer. I am speaking in general terms. Sometimes I feel that certain individuals use public prayer for the wrong reasons. Faith is a personal thing, and I believe that prayer should be conducted in silence, or in a closet, as mentioned in the Bible. My inner faith and silent prayers kept me going, because I never had but one choice. If I had not made the correct choice, which was only one at a time, my life would have been a total disaster.

For example, if I had not looked at a pamphlet containing information regarding employment as a GS-2 clerk with the FBI, in Washington, DC, during my senior year in high school, I would have ended up working in a feed mill or on a farm picking cotton, etc. I could not imagine being able to attend college because I had no financial means. As a college graduation gift, my parents did give me $50. This was the ONLY MONEY that was ever given to me. I worked to pay for my college and everything else. I consumed many cans of Campbell soup while in college. I always had faith that a better life was ahead of me. Therefore, I had to take advantage of every opportunity that came along. If ever there was one person on this earth who should have been turned completely against organized religion, it was me. I saw the darkest side of organized religious extremism and how weak-minded people could be taken advantage of by these fake, so-called preachers and churches.

I truly believe that the perfect church would be one that does not collect money, except to help individuals who need financial help on an immediate basis. In other words, no money should be paid to anyone in the form of a salary. Everything should be voluntary, including the minister or church leaders. However, I have not given up. I continue to attend church due to my strong inner faith and past religious beliefs. One may call it "fire insurance," but I had rather believe in a supreme being than to not believe in any life after death. I realize there is a chance that I could be wrong. So I want to build up as much "fire" insurance as possible. Please understand that I have an unusual interest in these religious extremists due to the way I was reared. I was close and personal with individuals who had unusual religious beliefs. Therefore, I tend to zero in on this subject with good reason and knowledge.

Getting back to my days living in Sardis, Kentucky, which is now called the Land between the Lakes due to the fact it is located between Lake Barkley and Kentucky Lake. When I lived there, from 1948–1950, Lake Barkley was not in existence. Lake Barkley was named after vice president of the United States Alban Barkley, who was President Truman's vice president. Of course, at that time I had no clue that later on in my life, as a young person in Washington, DC, that I would be attending a dinner in honor of Vice President Barkley's wife, which is mentioned later in another chapter. In order to get to the two closest towns, Eddyville and Kuttawa, we had to cross the Cumberland River on a ferry boat. The state penitentiary was located in Eddyville. Executions were carried out, plus, the building was, and is today, scary-looking, being made out of those large, gray stones. Man, every now and then, in the middle of the night, a loud whistle would blow, indicating that a prisoner had escaped.

I cannot understand how, but for some reason, my father was able to buy me a single shot J. C. Higgins BB gun. I thought I was going to be able to go out and bring food home to be put on the table. Hell, the BBs did not have enough force to go in a straight line. I soon learned that I could not hit the side of a barn, but I was happy, anyway, with the gun. The two-room school was so close to our house that it was just an extension of our yard. It housed eight grades, with two teachers, Ms. Penninger and Ms. Wright. An outhouse was the shared bathroom for both boys and girls. I was so bashful that I would not raise my hand to go to the bathroom during class.

One day I just sat there and wet my britches. During the fall, and after the leaves had fallen, the school kids would build these long A-frame leaf tunnels in the woods during recess, which was always fun. These tunnels were very long. A little Yates boy would, for whatever reason, enjoy biting the head off these green beetle-type bugs. Also, we would use sticks as pretend horses and race around and around the school building during lunch and recess. After the weather turned cold, J. R. Stafford, an eighth grader, would walk past our house on his way to the schoolhouse to build a fire in the old Warm Morning stove. That job always went to an eighth grader. During those days, when the kids were not in school, they would always run around outside instead of sitting around in the house. We never spent much time around or inside the house. We were always on the move.

Jeanette, one of my classmates when I was eight years of age, liked me. Her father ran a small grocery store nearby. When I would go there with my father, I would sit on a one hundred–pound sack of feed. She would quietly sneak around and sit beside me. I was so bashful and miserable in a good way because I really liked for her to sit next to me, but I never said anything or tried to move away. At that point, I guess I realized that I was seriously heterosexual. Rowena and Jacob Payne owned a small grocery store next to the schoolhouse. Rowena was a rotund lady who had a VERY visible, stubby beard. Whenever I was given a nickel or dime (never a quarter of half-dollar), I would run to Rowena's store and buy a twelve-ounce bottle of Pepsi Cola and a bag of peanuts or a candy bar. I would pour the peanuts in the Pepsi and drink it. I never bought a Coca-Cola because their bottles contained only six ounces. The Ne Hi orange/grape drinks, RC Colas, and Pepsis were big twelve-ouncers.

I would have dreams quite often of finding dimes on the floor throughout our house. I loved dimes. In fact, they are my favorite coins today. As an eight-year-old, I remembered the talk among older boys about a certain woman in the neighborhood who was very lax with her sexual desires. I did not know what all the conversations meant. My knowledge in this area was a zero. I never mentioned this to my father, for obvious reasons. The young kids would talk, but nothing unusual was thought about this. Life continued to be the grinding, boring, church life, as usual. One day we got word that one of our neighbor's son's had been killed in the Korean War. I remember him as being a tall chubby young man, not in good physical shape. The military draft took every male, including some that had no business going to war due to their poor physical condition. This fellow's poor physical condition may have been a factor in his death. Anyway, his death had an impact on my viewpoint of death in the military.

Sadly, the highlight of a Sunday was when a favorite church member invited us to their home for Sunday dinner (lunch). I knew exactly which church member would have fried chicken, which was my favorite, or darn old dry meat loaf, which sucked. Those hour-long-plus sermons were sheer torture. The hard wooden seats in the churches would wear thin on a young child's rear end. You did not dare go to sleep because your rear would come into contact with a preacher's hand afterward.

From birth, until I left home, living at home was somewhat similar living in a prison, with one exception, in prison you did not get roughed up as often. Sometimes, my father would preach three times on certain Sundays, and once during the week. The Methodist Church moved him from Sardis, due to the fact that certain church members thought he was too rough on us kids. So again, we headed farther west, ending up in Columbus, Kentucky. We had finally reached the Mississippi River, which was as far west as we could be while remaining in Kentucky. The Methodist Church was very kind to my father, and I am very grateful for that. Throughout my life I have known very few Methodists that were radical religious fanatics. Most have always been very reasonable people. Wait until a religious extremist comes to your doorstep.

My son became a casual friend of a nice Muslim girl in one of his college classes. She invited him to her birthday party in her home here in Vero Beach. While at her small birthday gathering, one of her male relatives casually told him that he would take a machete and behead him if this relationship progressed any further. My son got the hell out of there. So this is the type of danger that lies within some of these fanatic religions.

# COLUMBUS, KENTUCKY
## 1949–1950

Here we go, again, from Sardis, Kentucky, to Columbus, Kentucky, which was located right on the banks of the Mississippi River. We were as far west as you could get, in Kentucky. We landed in Columbus during the summer of 1950. I liked Columbus better than any of the other places we had lived. It was a very small town that had a grocery store, a filling station with a jukebox and a pinball machine right next to the Methodist Church. Young boys and men would hang out, talk, and wrestle, etc. During the summer months a moving picture show would be set up under a tent next to the filling station on certain Saturday nights. For ten cents, you could see a cowboy movie such as *Red Ryder and Little Beaver*, *Rex Allen*, *Allen Rocky Lane*, *Gene Autry*, etc. I always preferred my cowboy heroes to wear two pistols, not one, as Tim Holt did. The closest movie theater was located ten miles away, in Clinton, KY.

    Maybe, twice a year someone would take me to see a western movie, which cost twenty-five cents. After seeing *Alan Rocky Lane* fighting the bad guys, I would walk outside and feel as if I could whip the world. I would flex my muscles, feeling like Charles Atlas. As an eleven-year-old, I had my first encounter with cigarettes. I was given a cigarette from time to time, and I would sneak behind an old car garage in our yard, light up and puff on it. I never got the hang of smoking. If my father had caught me, my ass would still be red to this day. Another thing that happened while living in Columbus was that these small, triple-X-rated *Dagwood and Blonde*, *Mutt and Jeff*, cartoon drawing, sex books were making their rounds among the young boys. Were they ever XXX-rated and very, very, graphic?

The grown-ups in the community apparently never got wind of these books due to the fact nothing was ever said about them as they were being passed from one young boy to another. Kids can be extremely deceiving and secretive as most parents realize.

Alma Feasel, our neighbor across the narrow street from our house, was our telephone central operator. The switchboard was located in her living room. We had party lines; therefore, you could listen in and learn the details of your neighbor's everyday living. Whenever we got word that a big steamboat would be coming up the Mississippi River, I, along with my brothers and friends would run down the long hill to the river and watch the boat as it traveled northward. At that time, the river water was clean enough for commercial fisherman to make a living catching fish from the river. They would catch these huge catfish, sixty-pound buffalo fish, and carp. The river was dangerous for the fishermen due to the numerous whirlpool currents.

These currents would take you and your boat under the water, thus, drowning you. Alma Feasel's brother-in-law, a commercial fisherman, was drowned in one of these whirlpools. At one time, many years ago there was talk, only in Washington, DC, that due to the fact that Columbus was located on the Mississippi River right in the middle of the United States, it would be a good location for our nation's capital. At that time, the city of Columbus was located right on the river, but later, the whole city sank into the Mississippi River. So much for the nation's capital talk.

Columbus was the home of Belmont State Park, a nice state of Kentucky, Civil War Park. I roamed all over the town during the daytime. I never hung around the house. Whenever we got word that a truckload of watermelons would be coming up the long, steep, river bank, we would run down there and try to get a watermelon from the long, slow-moving, truck, which was loaded down with watermelons from Missouri. We very seldom had any luck. All vehicular traffic came across the river in a ferryboat. There were no bridges.

As a fourth-grade student in the Columbus Elementary School, I was a good speller. Myself, and a girl, tied for the county elementary school spelling bee championship. We never misspelled a word. She was given the blue ribbon and a blue ribbon was promised to me at a later date, but it never arrived. I was disappointed, but I learned to accept it. This was my first lesson in tolerance and disappointments. I had to attend four churches, one being the Mt. Zion Methodist Church, which was located near Columbus. Mr. Cosby, who lived in Columbus was a member of this church and was someone that I recall vividly, to this day. He was a very nice person who was sincerely religious. He sang in the choir, and 100 percent of the time when the song "Amazing Grace" got to the third verse, "when we've been there ten thousand years, bright shining as the sun," Mr. Cosby would stand up and start shouting praises to Jesus in a very loud voice, such as, "Lord, I am coming home," "save us from our sins," "halleluiah," "praise be to God," etc. He would continue until the end of the song. So as a young ten-year-old kid, I always looked forward to having a church member request the song "Amazing Grace." HEY, as a nine- or ten-year-old kid who had to attend church several times a week, you had to take whatever entertainment you could get! So do not condemn me too much.

# HORNBEAK, TENNESSEE
# 1951–1956

After two years in Columbus, Kentucky, the Methodist church moved our family to Hornbeak, Tennessee, which is located in the northwestern part of the state approximately one hundred miles directly north of Memphis. Actually, some of the church members did not agree with my father's theory of the "spare the rod" philosophy, as it related to my sisters Flonnie and Pauline.

This was 1951. Hornbeak was located six miles from Reelfoot Lake, a twenty thousand–acre lake formed by the earthquake of 1812. Cotton was the cash crop in this area. There were one hundred–acre cotton fields in Lake County, with rich soil and flat land that was located along the Mississippi River. Our county, Obion, had eleven schools, and all county schools started in July. They would let out for one month during September so that the students could pick cotton to make a little money for clothes, etc. My father, myself, and my sisters and brothers would get into our old family car and travel to Obie Moore's farm in Lake County to pick cotton in these huge cotton fields. My lunch consisted of bologna sandwiches, Hostess Cup Cakes, and a jug of ice tea. We arrived at the cotton fields around 7:00 AM, when the dew was still on the cotton boles. The boles had very sharp ends, and these sharp ends would stick under the quick on my fingernails, which was VERY uncomfortable.

Some mornings, I would be extremely tired due to the fact that the night before, when I was in the eighth or ninth grade, I would practice basketball, hoping to earn a basketball suit on the team. While picking cotton, I had a nine-foot cotton sack, and when it was full of cotton, I would take it to the wagon located in the middle of the field so that Obie Moore could weigh it and record the weight.

Horace, an African-American cotton-picking buddy of mine would pick cotton alongside me. We would sing, and he taught me how to do the hambone. He would also tell me about his weekends in Tiptonville, Tennessee, where he would go to drink whiskey and beer, plus mess around with the women. I would pick cotton with Horace a month at a time during cotton-picking season, which was in September. I learned a lot from him as a young kid. Sometimes, I would get so tired and sleepy that I would lie down on my cotton sack and take short naps. Oh, how I would look forward to eating that bologna sandwich and chocolate Hostess Cup Cake for lunch. They were larger and better tasting than they are today. I would get under the cotton wagon in the shade and eat lunch.

Horace and his family were indentured servants who lived in horrible shacks located on the farmers' land. These shacks were terribly built on stilts, with chickens running under the floor. I could definitely relate to a sorry-built house, because I was born in one. Whenever another farmer needed help on their farm, this farmer would pay off the debts, of say, Horace's family, and Horace's family would move and become indentured servants to that farmer. This was definitely a form of slavery, which was an awful existence for these poor souls. If I did not pick cotton for three cents a pound, I would go without a new pair of Levi's, and other clothes that I wore to school that year. The most cotton that I picked in one day was 309 pounds. At 3 cents a pound, I made $9.18. I really felt like a rich fellow who was financially secure.

Bruce Cashion owned the Hornbeak cotton gin. The most disliked job I had was chopping the weeds out of corn and cotton fields. I would start at 6:00 AM and finish at 6:00 PM, with an hour off for lunch. I would usually earn $4 a day, but in many cases I would be paid only $2 per day. I needed money so badly that I probably would have taken fifty cents a day. There were no unions to protect you against these low wages. I would usually wear no shirt while working in the fields; thus, my back would sunburn and huge blisters would appear all over my shoulders. However, after a few days the blisters would disappear and your shoulders and back would develop a tan. I never heard of sun screen.

My brother Garvin would drive Bruce Cashon around on Saturday nights so that he could drink his beer. He was very tall, six-foot-seven. Constantly, he was being asked, "How is the weather up there?" Finally, he got tired of this question and came up with the standard answer, "I have a phone in my butt, dial me up and find out."

As a twelve- to sixteen-year-old boy, what do you do for entertainment in a town of two hundred people? During that period of time, our small house had to house our large family. We definitely had close quarters. My father continued to believe in the biblical passage, which stated that sparing the rod would spoil the child. In other words, he continued to not spare the rod every now and then. We lived in Hornbeak longer than anywhere else. This was because of our ability to play basketball. Listening to my father preach the gospel continued to be extremely boring. How awful.

So what did you do for entertainment during church service as a young kid? Well, your entertainment consisted of laughing whenever someone in the seat beside you, or in the seats in front of you passed gas or had a very loud Tony the Tiger stomach growl when it was quiet, such as during a prayer. I was aware that the Sunday school superintendent was running around the night before, which was Saturday night, getting drunk and hanging out with women other than his wife at Red Boyette's night club in Samburg. His wife was doing the same thing separately. Here I sit in church, painfully listening to my father repeat himself for one-plus hours and over to my left were these church members who had been out the night before, pleasing the devil with their sins.

My brother Garvin, who was four years older than me, was "messing around" with the superintendent's wife. In other words, these church members were screwing, boozing, and cleansing their soul, all within one twenty-four-hour period. We never let our father see us laughing or cutting up during church services, because we would pay for it dearly afterward. Man, I hated to go to these four churches and listen to my father preach.

# STRUGGLE TO ZERO

Every year, a small carnival would come to Union City, the county seat, and set up shop for a few days. The workers were the usual greasy, tattooed, strange-looking human beings. One of the attractions had a good-looking female, maybe in her mid-twenties, come out and dance around. The admission was twenty-five cents. You stood at a rope line inside a tent while she danced. She was wearing short shorts. If you wanted to touch her, it would cost you an additional twenty-five cents. I stared in amazement because this was the first time I had seen anything like this. I was only thirteen years of age. During the 1950s, a young person had to learn the facts of life from your peers in school and from older men. Sometimes during the evening I would be at Bob Pitts, Pure (name of the gasoline) gas station, just hanging out. A customer would come in and ask for some "night gowns." I asked Bob what "night gowns" were. He told me they were "rubbers." I never heard of a parent educating their children about the facts of life.

Can you imagine my father or mother teaching me about the birds and bees? Extremely close to the gas station was a house with a huge ground level window across the side next to the gas station. The lady who was residing in the house died, and her corpse was laid out in the living room, as was customary. A horrible rain and lightning storm came up suddenly. As several people were sitting around the casket, suddenly, a huge black dog jumped through the window and landed right there in the living room. The lightning storm had frightened the poor dog so badly that it ran full force and jumped through the window. The poor people inside jumped up, ran, and screamed because this was a very scary moment. There were very few dull moments in Hornbeak, except while in church.

The fifties were wide open for young people growing up. The community never mentioned anything about these "hootchy Kootchy" shows, etc. The young boys had on the job training. My two older brothers, along with other high school boys, would get into a car and then travel via ferry boat across the Mississippi River, to Caruthersville, Missouri, to a whorehouse. They would more or less line up and wait their turn, just like in the movie, *Porky's*. Luckily, no one ever got into any trouble. However, they certainly were taught the facts of life. I was always too bashful to participate in any of these type activities. I never participated in any of these activities. I was too chicken, I guess, or maybe I was too concerned that I would get caught and face the consequences at home. WHATEVER!

Hornbeak had a gas station that we called "The Tavern." No alcohol was sold in the county, or at the Tavern, but the tavern had a jukebox and a pinball machine. Ray Chilton and his brother ran the gas station, plus, they would work on cars. They also sold cheap thirty-cent rag bologna sandwiches, which usually consisted of an added flavor of car grease or motor oil on the white bread. Anyway, the high school boys, and others, would congregate at the tavern on Saturday nights because there was nothing else to do. Sometimes fights would break out and balloons filled with water were tossed on passing cars.

I would work for my basketball coach, Ralph White, while I was in the eighth, ninth, and tenth grades. I helped him bale hay, lifting those 120-pound bales with snakes cut in half, hanging out of the bales. This was extremely hard work, but I thought I had to do it, if I was going to get suited out on the basketball team. The coach's mother, Lillie White, would ask me to help her in her flower beds. She would usually pay me fifty cents, regardless of the time it took to complete the job. She was stingy. Her nice house was located on the main highway, and I was always afraid that someone would see me working in those damn flower beds, pulling weeds. I always attempted to hide my face whenever a car passed on the road.

While in the eighth grade, I became a self-employed, businessperson. I bought a shoe-shining business for five dollars, from Willis Reagan. It was located in Tince Covey's, one man barbershop, in Hornbeak. I shined shoes on Saturdays, getting fifteen cents a pair. Sometimes, I would make anywhere from three, to possibly, four dollars a day. I never made over five dollars a day. This was my first venture in business. I would listen to all the stories, or lies, of the men who would come in for their sixty-cent haircut. Many of the men who went to Detroit for work would save their haircuts for Tince Covey's sixty-cent haircut, when they came back over a long holiday weekend. They had been away, for say, three months, but when they came in for their haircut, they had a northern brogue.

Man, I would hear about all the money they were making, and their good fortunes. Norris Cranford came back after three months with a northern brogue. While in the barber chair, he stated with his northern brogue, "Gee, are onions ripe, yet?" Well, idiot, onions are ALWAYS ripe. Many years later, Norris was elected the Obion County judge executive. In addition, on Saturday mornings various farmers would kill rattlesnakes and copperheads and bring the dead snakes to Hornbeak and hang them in front of the bank and grocery store. They would usually bring the longest and biggest snakes in order to show them off.

I learned to swim in a cow pond, which had six inches of mud on the bottom that would "squish" between your toes. I was determined to learn to swim, even though snakes and turtles were also swimming around within a few feet of where I was swimming. I would always have a friend with me when I went swimming, because I was afraid of those darn snakes.

One of the county magistrates, who lived a short distance from our house had been a Night Rider during the early 1900s. The Night Riders tortured the black Americans, and sometimes hung them from trees for no reason at all. What an awful period of time. I was never told about any of the details as a young boy, and many years later I learned about the significance of this terrible period in our history. There is a community near Hornbeak, called N—— Kingdom. This area, today, is known by the older residents for its terrible treatment of the black Americans. Many hangings took place in that community. I was personally shown this area while back there visiting in my later years. Learning the history of this area almost made you sick to your stomach. Can you imagine, as a parent or young child, always having the constant fear of a group of men on horses (no cars) suddenly riding up to your house, storming through the door, grabbing your father, with all the family members screaming and crying. Your father would disappear, and later, his body would be located hanging on the end of a rope tied to a tree limb, dead. These cowards, who had their heads covered, would operate only at night and then go back to their jobs during the day. Thus, the name, Night Riders, came into existence.

I watched TV for the first time while living in Hornbeak. Mr. Smith, a neighbor, bought the first TV set in Hornbeak. Out of kindness, I suppose, he would invite me to his house on Friday nights to watch the Gillette Cavalcade of Sports boxing matches. Jersey Joe Walcott, Ezzard Charles, Joe Louis, etc., were some of the fighters that I watched. Lord, I enjoyed watching these Friday night fights. Probably, the only reason we remained in Hornbeak, Tennessee, for five years was because my sister, Joyce, myself, and my two older brothers played basketball. Also, we were well known in Hornbeak, if for nothing else, because of our father's reputation of not sparing the rod to get his point across. In addition, it could have been due to the fact that we were considered to be good looking children really. We were the cleanest, neatest, human beings in our school. My Levi's were always ironed, with a crease in the legs. There were never any dirty spots on our clothes. We were clean freaks.

# ELBRIDGE, TENNESSEE
# 1956–1958

Well, during June 1956, it was time to move on, again. My sister Flonnie, and two brothers, Otis and Garvin, had graduated from Hornbeak High School. My sisters Joyce and Glenna and I were the only children left at home. The Methodist Church moved us to the big city of Elbridge, Tennessee, population twenty, which was eight miles from Hornbeak. My father had four churches assigned to his "charge" or circuit. The parsonage and one church were located in Elbridge, a very small community which had one bank, two grocery stores, and a gas station. That was it.

My high school, named Cloverdale, was located approximately two to three miles down the road in the middle of a corn field with only eighty students in the high school. The grammar school was next to the high school. "Bear" Hargett, the principal, lived in a house that was on the high school grounds. He resembled the big bear that was in one of the Disney musical cartoon movies. My sister, Joyce, was one of the best girl basketball players in the state of Tennessee. Therefore, Cloverdale had one of the best girl basketball teams in the state. I made the boys basketball team, as an average player who had a deep desire to be on the team. Due to Terry Gardner being a very good center, we were the county champions one year. Get this, our county, Obion, had eleven high schools. Each small community had its own high school. Being the county champion was a big deal. Union City, which had its own school system, was the county seat. I won almost every honor Cloverdale High had to offer, such as the best dressed, the best this, or the best that. I won so many of these useless honors that I felt bad for the other boys. However, due to the fact that I had nothing on my mind but girls, I did not win any honors that counted, such as the smartest, most studious, etc. I honestly do not know how I earned two college degrees with practically NO high school education, other than the social education part of high school. The only explanation is that I must have had some hidden intelligence inside my brain housing that I never knew existed.

During May 1956, I got my driver's license. For some unexplained reason, my father did not resist my getting the license. Also, he did not resist my going out on a date in our old black, 1956 Chevrolet. My first date after getting my license was with Elizabeth Sharpe, who lived in Troy, Tennessee, located approximately ten miles away. I stopped at a gas station and bought $1 worth of gas (16 cents a gallon), picked up Elizabeth, and headed for the drive-in theater, in Lake County, Tennessee. Admission for both of us was $1, and during the movie, at intermission, I bought two cokes and two bags of popcorn, for a total of $1. So for a grand total of $3, I bought gas, paid for the movie admission, plus bought food and drinks. However, while watching the movie, I was so bashful that after I finally got up enough nerve to put my arm around Elizabeth's shoulders, I was too bashful to take it down.

Darn, my arm fell asleep and I was in total misery. Adding to my misery, I was so nervous that my stomach would start growling loudly. I was totally embarrassed. She was as shy as me, which did not help. Man, I wished that she would have grabbed me and gave me a big hug, or something, just to relieve my tension. We just sat there like two knots on a log afraid to move. How miserable! I thought the reason my stomach growled was because of something that I ate prior to going on the date, such as ice cream, etc. Therefore, prior to going on future dates, I would constantly change my diet, hoping that my damn stomach would not growl. This was just one of those small things that I put up with due to my being so damn bashful around girls. Most girls during this period of time had to stay by the phone on Saturdays, waiting on that phone call from a boy asking them for a date. Many a girl had to go to bed disappointed on Saturday nights because they never received a phone call. Good grief, how things have changed.

During the summer of 1957, between my junior and senior year in high school I was selected by the American Legion to attend Volunteer Boys State for one week at the Castle Heights Military Academy, Lebanon, Tennessee. The purpose of this week-long event was to learn about local and state government, such as running for various offices, etc. I was elected to the position of County Surveyor (WOW). Lamar Alexander was elected to the position of governor, which was the highest office. He later became Governor of Tennessee, and currently, he is a United States senator from Tennessee. In addition, Randy Tyree, from Carthage, Tennessee, was also in attendance. Randy will play a significant role later in my life, during my years in Washington, DC, from 1958 to 1962. During the 1980s, he became the mayor of Knoxville, Tennessee, during the period of time he was responsible for bringing the World's Fair to Knoxville.

Photos of me as a young boy.

Me and my brother Garvin, taken in our yard in Hornbeak, TN.

My Cloverdale High School class photo taken in 1958.

Photo taken in 1957 at Volunteer Boys State, a week of learning about our Tennessee state government and political system. The event was located at the Castle Heights Military Academy, Lebanon, TN. I am the one holding the "2" card, front row middle.
The event was sponsored by the American Legion.

My 1957–1958, senior year at Cloverdale High School was more or less uneventful. I was on the baseball and basketball team. However, I was just a very average player. I had a girlfriend, Linda Sellers, who was a good basketball player. The girls' team always rode on the bus with the boys, and played the same school as the boys. We always sat together on the bus, going to and from these games. There was a little male/female, togetherness, after the games, in the dark, on the bus heading home. My "togetherness" consisted of sitting together only.

During my senior year at Cloverdale High, Warren Hearn, the Dyersburg, Tennessee, FBI resident agent, left a brochure at the school regarding being hired by the FBI, in Washington, DC. After reading this material, I then phoned the number on the brochure and stated that I wanted to apply for a job. After an extensive background investigation, I received a letter prior to graduation, telling me that I had been hired as a GS-2, clerk, at FBI Headquarters in Washington, DC. My reporting date was June 9, 1958. I was excited beyond belief. Man, was this something? You can imagine, here I was, living in the middle of nowhere, with my high school being located in a cornfield with eighty students, and I was going to Washington, DC.

My neighbors would say, "An FBI agent came by today asking about you." This was definitely a leap of faith. I had no idea how my life was about to change, hopefully, for the better. In order to be hired by the FBI, a security clearance background investigation was conducted, and I had no idea that from that time, until the present time, fifty years of my life consisted of having high-level security clearances. My total faith that things would be better kept me going. I had never been away from home, except for short visits with my sisters. Washington was nine hundred miles from Elbridge, Tennessee. The letter from J. Edgar Hoover (actually, Ms. Gandy, his administrative aide signed it) told me that my starting salary would be $2,960 annually. I had to bring enough money to last one month due to the fact I would not get paid for one month. As it turned out, my two-week take-home pay was $90. I had to live on $45 a week, which could be a challenge. I later determined that J. Edgar Hoover liked to hire these young kids from rural areas due to the fact they obeyed orders and worked very hard without realizing it. I will always be grateful to J. Edgar Hoover for hiring kids from these rural areas of the country, which included me.

# WASHINGTON, DC
# 1958–1962

I made arrangements to fly to Washington National Airport on Sunday, June 8, 1958, in order to report to work at 9:00 AM, in the old post office building, Twelfth and Pennsylvania Avenue (currently a Trump hotel). My family and my girlfriend, Linda Sellers, got into our 1956 Chevrolet and drove to the very small airport in Union City, Tennessee. This was definitely a bitter-sweet occasion. I boarded a Southeast Airlines DC-3 with one stewardess, which was the only airplane flying out that day. As I recall, I was the only passenger. The plane made several stops on the way to Nashville, where I boarded an American Airlines DC-6, for a nonstop flight to Washington National Airport. I truly hated to leave my family and girlfriend.

Everyone was lined up at the chain-link fence as the plane left Union City. I kept looking out that small window until everyone disappeared. A year or two later, the same airplane crashed near Johnson City, TN, and everyone on the plane died, including the Stewardess that was on the plane that I was on when I left for Nashville, TN. I still have a vague image of her in my mind, today, after 58 years. As soon as the plane got into the air my attention then turned to being on my first airplane ride and the stewardess, as we puddle jumped from Union City, to Nashville, Tennessee. I was really impressed with the DC6 plane ride from Nashville to Washington, meaning, being impressed with the food and the good looking stewardesses serving me food and drink. I had never been in a situation like this in my life. Lord, I wish the flight attendants looked that good, today.

# STRUGGLE TO ZERO

At 11:30 PM, Sunday night, my plane arrived at Washington National Airport. LAFAYETTE, I AM HERE! However, I had no place to stay due to the fact that I forgot to phone ahead and make hotel reservations. I made a phone call from the airport to the FBI Headquarters housing unit, and the weekend employee on duty finally found me a hotel room in a very small, rowhouse–type hotel, almost on the George Washington University campus. Even though the hotel was very small, a desk clerk was on duty.

After I was inside my room and to my horror, I had forgotten to bring an alarm clock with me. So every hour I would go downstairs to check the time. Needless to say, I did not get any sleep due to the fact I certainly did not want to be late for work. I checked out and left the hotel very early. I had no idea which electric powered trolley would get me to Twelfth and Pennsylvania Avenue (currently a Trump hotel). I had to ask strangers for directions, and finally, I arrived at my correct destination. The first day consisted of filling out forms, obtaining a badge photo, and being advised of the dos and don'ts. Each employee was given a list of boarding houses to contact in order to rent a room until we found an apartment. I chose Matt Kane's Guest House, located at Thirteenth and Massachusetts Avenue, NW. The monthly $60 rent, included a bed, breakfast, and dinner. Most of the boarders were FBI employees, such as me. However, Matt Kane, the owner, had to discontinue serving bread from the table because these hungry young men were breaking the bread bank. If you wanted bread, you asked for it individually.

I walked to my FBI work location, which was the FBI Identification Division, Second and D Street, SE. The walk was very long and hot during the summer. I would walk down below the US Capitol Building, facing west toward the Washington Monument. Immediately off the Capitol grounds was a shanty-type town area, which consisted of old one story apartment-type buildings. People were actually living in these buildings. A few of these apartments on the ground floor level had dirt floors. My job in the FBI Identification Division was to search fingerprint cards through the criminal files. I had to attend a six week fingerprint classification school before I was qualified to actually search fingerprint cards through the criminal and civil files. This was during the summer and fall of 1958.

Prior to the end of my first month at Matt Kane's Guest House, me, Randy Tyree, Bob Gabler, and Larry McCain, got together and located a two-bedroom apartment near Boling Air Force Base, in the Congress Park Apartment Complex. The total rent was $120, monthly, which was split four ways, for a total of $30, each. My total two-week take-home pay was $90. We pitched in $5 a week for food, and $20 would buy a lot of food in 1958. Bob Gabler was the only one of us that had a car. Therefore, he hauled our butts to work in his '56 Ford. During my first year, I saved $600, and bought a '56 Chevrolet from the Dwight Blackley Chevrolet Dealer in Hornbeak, Tennessee. I still marvel at myself for being able to save $600, during my first year in Washington, DC. I was extremely frugal with my money. I knew every trick in the trade on how to save money. I was a tightwad. However, maybe my main motivation for saving money was that I REALLY WANTED A CAR! I was also VERY tired of walking two or three miles to work each way and riding with other employees with cars.

In addition to this misery, I felt like I needed to write my high school girlfriend, Linda, a damn letter every day, telling her how much I missed her. Man, was this misery, in that my writing hand felt as if it was totally separated from my arm. After a month or so, I had to stop writing these letters because all this writing was causing problems with my hand. During my second visit back home, I finally broke off this relationship because of all the misery in trying to come up with new subject matter each day to write about, while in DC. My writing hand remains forever grateful for stopping all the writing to my high school girlfriend.

One evening, I received a phone call from Max Parr, a high school friend who stated that he was in the Congressional Hotel on Capitol Hill. Max had rolled in on a Greyhound bus at Twelfth and New York Avenue, from Union City, Tennessee. While inside the bus station walking around, someone stole his wallet containing all his cash and driver's license, etc. He phoned his father, tacted his US Congressman Fats Everett, who m to get him a hotel room. Max needed a place to s and I went to the Congressional Hotel and rescu in with us, which made a total of five young men in the two-b room apartment. Max had a job in DC, under the patronage of US Senator Estes Kefauver, as an elevator operator on the Senate side of the US Capitol Building. Actually, Max remained with us as a roommate until he got married. Prior to getting married, he became a US Capitol police officer. In those days, the training period of time for a Capitol police officer was one day at the pistol range.

Congressman Robert A. "Fats" Everett was my congressman during the years that I resided in Tennessee, prior to going to Washington, DC, as an FBI employee. "Fats" was a huge man, six-foot-four, and weighing 350–400 pounds. During the late 1930s, he taught school at my high school, Cloverdale High. He never married, and his mother lived with him until her death. However, while in Washington, he resided in the Congressional Hotel on Capitol Hill with his mother. On two occasions, 1960 and 1961, he had me over for New Year's Day dinner. The dinner was the very traditional black-eyed peas and hog jowl. It was rumored that this menu would bring you good luck throughout the coming year. In addition, "Fats," as everyone called him, would occasionally take me to the Army/Navy Club for dinner. He had an extremely loud, booming voice, when he talked. He was extremely popular as a congressman on Capitol Hill. President Lyndon Johnson truly relied upon him to get certain legislation through the House of Representatives. He was always in his office by 5:00 AM every day.

On one occasion, I was in his residence in the Congressional Hotel waiting on him to get ready to go for dinner at the Army/Navy Club. Ureka! Here he walks out of the shower with his towel around him, drying off, and asking about his Jack Daniels whiskey. He always drank the green label. The infamous Bobby Baker's brother from South Carolina, a capitol police officer, was also in the room. One or two other individuals were also present.

Bobby Baker's job title was secretary to the majority leader, which was Senate majority leader Lyndon Johnson. Baker wielded enormous nationwide power in this position, which later got him into serious trouble with the law. Anyway, here was Congressman "Fats" Everett, walking around nude, drying off with his towel, with his voice booming about his Jack Daniels whiskey. What a sight. When you gaze upon a 350–400 pound, six-foot-four, naked man standing there drying himself off, with all that excess fat hanging down, it was, to say the least, attention getting. "Fats" died at the age of fifty-two, due to diabetes, gout, etc. Several years later and prior to his death, while visiting "Fats" at his office in Union City, Tennessee, with my spouse Stephanie, he was on the phone with the local weather person at the small airport checking on the weather conditions. In this loud, booming, voice, he asked the weather person, "Are we going to have any PARticipation, today?"

Of course, he meant, "Are we going to have any precipitation?" "Fats" was loved by all the people in his congressional district of Tennessee, which was the Eighth District. Everyone that followed him in that office seemed extremely dull compared to him. He wore one of those Lyndon Johnson Texas-style white hats and suspenders. Interesting individuals such as "Fats" do not come along very often. I wish he was still alive, today. The House of Representatives would certainly be much more interesting place today if "Fats" was a congressman.

Early one evening around dusk, myself and my other three roommates were lounging around in our Congress Park apartment minding our own business. Randy Tyree, our fourth roommate, was not there. However, suddenly, he stormed through the door wearing a white T-shirt, holding his hand over his heart. He was standing there moaning, with what appeared to be lots of blood running down his T-shirt. He stumbled and landed on the floor, as if he were dying. We became alarmed, stating that we were going to phone for an ambulance. As Larry McCain started to dial the number, Randy looked up, and began smiling. SON OF A BITCH, were we angry and scared, but relieved that he was not going to die.

# STRUGGLE TO ZERO

Later, after leaving Washington, Randy earned his law degree from the University of Tennessee. During the 1980s, he became a two-term mayor of Knoxville, Tennessee. He was mayor when the World's Fair was held in Knoxville. In addition, he ran for governor of Tennessee against Lamar Alexander, who defeated him. Randy had a great influence on me as a close friend and roommate. I still have contact with Randy, Bob Gabler, and Max Parr, today. Max Parr became a psychologist, and Bob Gabler earned his bachelor's degree from George Washington University in accounting and retired from the Quaker Oil Company as an auditor. Larry McCain is deceased. I arrived in Washington, DC, on the eighth of June 1958, and in September, I enrolled in two night classes at George Washington University.

I had an unbelievable desire to get a college degree. This desire was overwhelming. I actually did not know how to take class notes or how to study, since I came from a high school located next to a corn field with only eighty students. I would sit in class and watch other students take notes, etc. Prior to leaving for full time college, during May 1962, I did manage to accumulate 12 semester hours. Man, how I struggled to just make it to zero, and then take it from there. I honestly, do not know how I managed to earn two college degrees under the circumstances. I earned a bachelor of science degree from Murray State University in Kentucky and a master of arts degree from George Washington University in Washington, DC. I never had enough money, plus, I was always out there all alone, with no support system. If I screwed up by making a wrong decision, I had no one or nowhere to go or turn to. I never had two choices like most folks. I always had only one choice. The pressure was awful.

Anyway, I continued to search fingerprint cards through the criminal files. The work was extremely tedious, in that, with your naked eye you had to classify these prints and compare the ridges with the prints in the files to determine if they did or did not match. You had to complete an average of six searches an hour. I DID NOT ENJOY THIS WORK! My arms, as I speak, still have rough skin caused by leaning on these damn old cabinets while I searched those fingerprint cards. Also, the Identification Building had no air-conditioning, and believe me, those Washington, DC, summer months were torture. While searching the fingerprint cards, your arms would become so sweaty that they would slip and slide all over the top of the cabinets that held the fingerprint cards.

Needless to say, I was searching for a way out of being a "flipper and picker," another name for a fingerprint clerk. One day while searching fingerprint cards, the word spread that Director Hoover might visit the Identification Division, as he had not done for many years, if ever. Lo and behold, one would be convinced that this would be similar to the second coming of Jesus Christ. Almost immediately, we were advised by our supervisors how to behave, if and when he would arrive. Cleaning crews would come in and clean, paint, and straighten up this old fortress of a building. The Identification Division was not the most desirable place to work in view of its technical nature. It was an assembly line type of setup, due to the fact you had to average searching at least six fingerprint cards per hour, through the criminal files. It was totally unbelievable how the word of Hoover's visit shook up every employee. Guess what! That son of a bitch never came, after all the hard work preparing for his visit. In the minds of many FBI employees, Director Hoover was considered to be on a higher level than GOD. He was literally worshiped and feared.

I recall that in 1958, Director Hoover initiated a weight program for all male FBI employees, nationwide. He allegedly lost thirty pounds of his weight, and therefore, he felt that all male employees should fall within a certain weight category in order to receive their next promotion. Hoover's weight for his five-foot-nine frame should have been 163 pounds. However, he never appeared to weigh 163 pounds. Joe Brabham, our roommate at 407 Seward Square, was 5 pounds overweight the day before he was to "weigh in" for his next promotion. Joe was born with a body frame that made him appear stocky, so he naturally appeared to be overweight. We had to weigh in twice a year. Anyway, Joe had to lose five pounds. Well, he started taking Ex-Lax, drinking water, and running all day long. He did not consume ANY food. He almost passed out. All of us felt sorry for him due to his misery. Actually, he did lose the five pounds by the skin on his teeth. What was good for Hoover was good for every male employee. The female employees were not included in this weight loss program.

I had a streak of good luck one day when I heard about an opportunity to become an FBI Headquarters tour leader. I jumped on this, and thinking that my chances were slim, I did my best during the interviews. However, I was accepted to attend the tour leader class which lasted for three weeks in FBI Headquarters, Ninth and Pennsylvania Avenue. Believe me, I was taught the total and complete history of J. Edgar Hoover, the FBI Laboratory, famous gangsters, and famous cases that the FBI had solved. In other words, I became knowledgeable of the detailed history of the FBI, beginning when J. Edgar Hoover became director on May 10, 1924. He was a twenty-nine-year-old single attorney who had a position in the Department of Justice. He earned his law degree from George Washington University. We were not taught any FBI history prior to May 10, 1924, the date Hoover became director due to the negative image of its four previous directors from 1908 to 1924. The FBI was formed during 1908, with Hoover being the fourth director. Eight Secret Service agents were hired to form the FBI. Three directors prior to Hoover were either fired, or ended up being charged with crimes.

Director Hoover was very strict with the clerical FBI employees, focusing particularly on any involvement between the single male and female employees, such as being in the same apartment overnight, or having another employee report to a superior of any male and female being in the same apartment together, who were not married. Any misconduct of a sexual nature or overtone would get you fired on the spot. You would be escorted to the front entrance after having your FBI badge taken away from you, and left to get yourself back to your residence. I recall that one day, I was working alongside a female employee, and the next day, she did not show up for work. I later determined that another employee had reported her for being with a male friend overnight. Many employees became so paranoid that they could see J. Edgar

Hoover's face on the ceiling of their bedroom, staring down upon them. Director Hoover appeared to be totally against any male/female contact. You would never know which employee would turn you in to your superiors.

A true example of how bad it was occurred during a snowstorm when a male employee was observed on a bus, by a "spy," who turned him in because she knew that he would not take that particular bus to work from his residence. Therefore, she realized that he had stayed overnight with his girlfriend due to the fact that his bus came from the direction of his girlfriend's apartment. He was fired without any recourse. The reason this male employee had remained overnight in his girlfriend's apartment was because he could not get back to his residence due to the snowstorm. The FBI employees had no Civil Service protection, which was totally different from employees in other federal agencies. Therefore, you could be fired without cause, or proof that you had actually broken any rule. I found it ironic that Director Hoover and his extremely close associate director, Clyde Tolson, would travel around the country, together, making certain that they would be close to a horse racing track in order to bet on the horses. They were creatures of habit, being attached to each other like Bennie and Lennie, the Siamese twins.

They always had a standing lunchtime, and table, at the Mayflower Hotel, there in DC. When they came to work, they would get out of their limo at Tenth and Constitution Avenue, a block away from their office, which was located at Ninth and Pennsylvania Avenue. Then, they would walk in lock step down Constitution Avenue to their office. I never figured out what Associate Director Tolson's job description was. As a low paid FBI employee, my attitude was perhaps similar to being a recruit at Parris Island, SC, with no freedom of movement, and observing the officers and drill instructors being able to freely move around. Due to the strict rules as an FBI employee, it was always in the back of your mind of being fired for no reason due to the fact that a co-worker could turn you in regarding some issue that would get you fired. You had no recourse, even though you were innocent.

# STRUGGLE TO ZERO

Another example was when a male clerical employee was on the first floor in the Department of Justice Building waiting on an elevator. When it stopped, Director Hoover stepped off and came in direct contact with the employee, who had a flat top haircut. Well, the next day or two, the employee was advised by his supervisor that he could no longer have a flat top haircut. He must let it grow long enough to have a "part" in it. I got to know this employee, personally, after he became a Secret Service agent.

In addition to being a tour leader, and during the fall of 1961, I coached the FBI Headquarters girls' basketball team. We played in a league consisting of the US State Department and other federal agencies. Sixty female employees tried out to make the team, and I had to choose only fifteen out of the sixty, to be suited out. I made some tough decisions. However, we ended up being the league champions and everyone on the team received a trophy. The championship trophy was very large, and it ended up in Director Hoover's outer office reception area. Our team consisted of some good looking single females, but I never asked anyone for a date due to the fact I did not yield to temptation, even though I wanted to. I have known many people who could resist anything but temptation. Sometimes, as I look back, I regret that I did not yield to temptation more often.

One of my roommates, Randy Tyree, played on the FBI Headquarters intramural football team which competed in a league with other government agencies such as the CIA, Government Printing Office, etc. Randy's team won the league championship, and as a reward the team was going to have a personal meeting with FBI Director J. Edgar Hoover in his office. On the day of their meeting with the director, all the players were lined up in alphabetical order, and due to the fact Randy's last name was Tyree, only one player (Williams) was behind him. Randy bought a new suit and shoes for this meeting.

However, his supervisor who was with the team pointed out to Randy that he forgot to remove the sales tag from one arm of his new suit. Prior to the meeting in January 1960, every player was told exactly how to dress and look their Sunday best. As Randy shuffled along in the line with his new slick shoe soles on a shag-type carpet, inside the director's very revered "Inner Sanctum" office which he occupied for forty-eight years prior to his death in 1972, Randy did not realize that all this time static electricity was building up within his body due to the shag rug. As he reached out to shake the director's hand, the director suddenly jerked his hand back as if he was going to be bitten by a cobra snake. Ms. Gandy, his long-time administrative aide, pulled Randy's trophy back, which convinced him that a director's famous "Letter of Censor" would end up in his personnel file. Later in his life, Randy earned a law degree from the University of Tennessee and was a two-term mayor of Knoxville who was responsible for bringing the last World's Fair to his city. Also, he was a candidate for governor of Tennessee.

As a tour leader, I would go up to Attorney General Robert Kennedy's Office on the fifth floor of the Justice Department Building, to take friends of his on a tour of FBI headquarters. His office was located on the same floor as J. Edgar Hoover's office. I would walk right into his office and be introduced to his friends. He would be there with his shirt sleeves rolled up, doing his job. After completing the FBI tour, I would then take them back to Kennedy's office. Kennedy would drive his light blue Cadillac convertible to work and park it in the Justice Building courtyard. As I would walk by it during my tours, sometimes it appeared that chickens had been walking on it. At that time he had seven children and they probably were the ones that played on the car.

In addition, very often, I would go up to Associate Director Clyde Tolson's office to take individuals who were from Congressman Rooney's office on tours of FBI Headquarters. Congressman Rooney was the chairman of the House Appropriations Committee; therefore, he would be the one to approve the annual FBI budget. So everyone from Congressman Rooney's congressional district who wanted to take a tour of FBI Headquarters was funneled to Associate Director Tolson's office in order to show Congressman Rooney that they were special. As a side note, Director Hoover would not let Associate Director Tolson smoke in his presence. Therefore, Tolson would "bum" cigarettes from various individuals who were smokers, whenever he had an opportunity. Hoover and Tolson were VERY close. They always traveled together wherever they went, such as to horse races and restaurants. Tolson was a very nice gentleman in every way. He was a faithful servant to Director Hoover. He reminded me of someone like President James Buchanan, who was also never married, and was very old "maid-ISH."

Every now and then as I came and went from the offices of Attorney General Kennedy and top FBI officials, I would have a flashback about two years, prior, I was picking cotton in Tennessee, in order to pay for my pair of Levi's pants that I wore to high school. Many tourists, who had been on my FBI tours, wrote nice letters to Director Hoover praising me. His office would then forward a copy of these letters to me.

During the latter part of 1959, a movie was being filmed called *The FBI Story* starring Jimmy Stewart. This was prior to my becoming a tour leader. I searched fingerprint cards every day. Word spread that a segment of the movie was going to be filmed on my floor at the FBI Identification Building. The film crew did come in there one day and shoot a scene, showing all those FBI employees searching fingerprint cards. I was certain that I would be in the movies. I phoned home to tell my family that I would be in the movie, *The FBI Story*. Many people in my hometown community went to see the movie, thinking that they would see me. Hell, the scene showing all those FBI employees searching fingerprint cards was so short that no one could be recognized, certainly, not myself. I began to realize that the sum total of my importance could go through the eye of a small needle. Also, during the period of time that I was a tour leader, I, for whatever reason, purchased a small piece land in a mountain-type area located west of Winchester, VA. An individual could purchase a small lot for a small amount of money as a down payment, and continue to make small, monthly payments. Anyway, I purchased this small lot, which made me eligible to use an unused cabin for a weekend. After making prior arrangements with the developer who was really a nice man, myself, Roy Ronica (another tour leader), Assistant Director Cartha "Deke" DeLoach, another FBI supervisor, plus two of DeLoach's young sons, traveled west of Winchester, Virginia, to one of the furnished cabins for the weekend. We could cook out and stay overnight.

Around dark, a fire was built, and during the course of the night the supervisor wandered off without the rest of us paying any attention. After not returning for a few hours we became concerned and started to search for him. Finally, we came upon him sitting in a path, minding his own business. Actually, we were very concerned, thinking that he could be injured, or perhaps, he could have encountered a bear. However, all was well, and we went back to the cabin and enjoyed the rest of the evening. Assistant Director DeLoach was an extremely nice gentleman. I have nothing but praise and admiration for him. I was glad to learn that he had a long, accomplished, life. During that period of time, I was making approximately $4,000, annually, with no other income, or assets. Therefore, prior to leaving Washington, DC, to attend college, I had to give my plot of land back to the developer in order to go to college. He was a nice person and understood where I was coming from.

My FBI tour leading class, 1960, taken in the courtyard at the US Department of Justice.

Me with my FBI girls basketball team, after we won our league in Washington, DC. The large trophy was placed in the outer office of Director J. Edgar Hoover. I was the coach.

Presenting FBI Agent Ed Armbruster Secret Service award, 1976, on his fiftieth anniversary. Agent Armbruster was oldest working agent at that time, being eighty-four years of age.

I was always pushing the envelope in order to take advantage of every potential opportunity that came along. Here I was, twenty-one years of age, with no more than two thin dimes to rub together, making arrangements for a weekend in the mountains with one of the most powerful individuals in the Federal Bureau of Investigation. DeLoach ended up being the number two man in the FBI, who routinely met with the President of the United States, Lyndon Johnson, for briefings, etc. Also, he maintained an excellent relationship with the US Congress throughout his career. He was Hoover's go to man. He indicated in his book that he was next in line to become the FBI director, but he realized that Hoover would never retire or leave office until he died. He apparently thought he would be too old to be the director if he waited until Hoover left the FBI. He retired and accepted a high-paying position in the private sector. As I previously mentioned, he was the perfect man to represent the FBI. He presented the perfect image to the public. Throughout my career with the Secret Service, I was always aware of how important the physical appearance and personality of our agents was when dealing with the public.

I attempted to personally observe every historical figure that I could, while in DC. One day during 1959, after work at the Identification Division, which was located on Canal Street, I went outside and observed Nikita Khrushchev, premier of the Soviet Union driving by sitting in his convertible limousine in a motorcade on his way to the Blair House from Andrews Air Force Base. I was only a few feet from his vehicle as it passed by. I did not realize that later, when I was a tour leader at FBI Headquarters, one of the displays on the tour that I explained to the public was Khrushchev's "I will bury you" speech, indicating that his objective was for Communism to bury the United States. I explained this exhibit anywhere from two to four times daily for two years to the people on my tours.

On another occasion after work, I walked a long distance to Fourteenth Street, from Second and D Street, in order to see President Eisenhower and Vice President Nixon in their motorcade vehicles as they traveled from Washington National Airport to the White House in their open limousine. Nixon went out to greet Eisenhower, due to all the worldwide press coverage that the falling out between Eisenhower and Khrushchev received. President Eisenhower had just gotten back from a conference in Geneva, Switzerland, with Khrushchev. At this conference, Eisenhower walked out on Khrushchev and came back home, due to the fact he falsely accused the United States of many things. At that time, Air Force One was kept at Washington National Airport. As a young eighteen-year-old, almost directly from the cotton fields of western Tennessee, I, at least, thought in my own mind that gazing upon the president and vice president of the United States was a big deal. I was a legend in my own mind, at least for a few moments.

Every payday, which was always on a Friday, word would spread throughout FBI Headquarters regarding the location of many parties in the area. So the employees, including myself, on numerous occasions would attempt to go to what we thought would be the best parties. Man, some of these parties were rocking and rolling to Fats Domino and Platters music, etc. Sometimes the party location would be so crowded there was standing room only. Always, some beer and soft drinks would be flowing. No hard liquor or drugs ever. Sometimes, these parties would get a little rowdy over a girl and end in a fight or two. I had a friend who worked for the US Senate, who would duke it out with someone every now and then, and leave with a bloody nose. He never had to worry about getting fired from his job because there were no rules against these situations for US Senate employees. I heard about another US Senate employee who stated that he actually had sex with a girl at night on the US Senate floor.

During the years when I first lived in Washington, 1958–1962, the city was one big party town. DC had so many young women living there that it was a young fellow's heaven. Congressmen, senators, cabinet members, and low-level male clerical employees appeared to have nothing on their mind but women, if they were heterosexual. We would constantly be on the go, looking for girls to date. The Rathskeller, a popular hangout located in the basement of a building between Thirteenth and Fourteenth Street, on Pennsylvania Avenue, was a favorite watering hole late at night for a late beer or food. You never knew who you might see hanging out with their buddies, such as the Speaker of the House Carl Albert having a few late night toddies. During this period of time Washington was a jumping city, especially, after Kennedy was elected President. The elected officials had the freedom to do whatever they desired without their voters back home finding out about it.

One evening while I was attending a Kentucky Society dinner, Odessa Stubblefield, wife of US Congressman Frank Albert Stubblefield, from Murray, Kentucky, came to the event after they had attended a Dairy Farmers of America event, plus, an event at the White House. Ms.Stubblefield had been given this bright red half-gallon carton of milk, and she took it to the White House event. As she went through the President and Ms. Kennedy reception line, she gave the carton of milk to the president. She stated that he pretended to be very gracious, grinning as he took it, and naturally, he handed it to an aide. The Stubblefield's were the nicest and most helpful individuals that I met while working in DC.

One evening, Stephanie and I attended a cocktail party and Congressman Stubblefield's residence located in northwest Washington, off Wisconsin Avenue. Naturally, during the course of the party, I had a few "cocktails," and to my surprise, as guests were leaving the party, the Stubblefield's asked Stephanie and I to drop Murray State University President Dino Curris and his spouse off at their hotel in Crystal City, VA, which was on our way to our residence in Springfield, VA. Well, I did not realize that I may have had more "cocktails" that I should have, until I started the drive all the way across Washington, DC. Holy crap! I did make the drive without incident. None of my passengers realized what was going on, because apparently, I did a good job of faking it. Now, during the 1970s it was socially acceptable to drive after consuming alcohol. Thank goodness this has changed. Today, I NEVER drink alcohol and drive.

One Saturday night while residing at 407 Seward Square, which was a short distance from the US Capitol, none of us had a date. We started to dial the phone numbers of females listed in the phone directory, cold turkey, to see if we could get a date. Pat Glover, who worked in Senator Eastland's office, phoned and actually got a date.

However, the rest of us were not so lucky. In addition, on one occasion Pat Glover and I ended up getting fixed up with two girls who were students at the Holden Arms private school, a very exclusive school located on Rock Creek Parkway. Jackie Kennedy attended that school. When we arrived at the school, we were ushered into the waiting area, which had nice fire burning in the fireplace.

As I waited, I thought to myself, man, this is really out of my league. Thankfully, I did not wear white socks, which I did not own any. We went out to a movie and returned to the school, having an uneventful evening. I never had another date with my girl, but Pat went back for a second date. He stated that it was past her curfew, so she came down the fire escape wearing her London Fog coat. I never knew what else happened because I never asked, and he never told me. Again, these young senate and house employees did not worry about losing their job for getting into trouble outside their employment. I always made certain that I never did anything that would cause a problem with the FBI due to the fact my ass would be on the streets or sentenced to hard labor in some feed mill or cotton field in western Tennessee.

While residing at Seward Square in DC, from 1960 to 1962, I had two roommates who worked on Capitol Hill, one being a Capitol police officer. I was always going there for one reason, or the other, due to the fact our residence was a very short distance from the Capitol building. Our two-story townhouse, No. 407, was only three houses from 413 Seward Square, the former home of J. Edgar Hoover. Hoover lived with his mother at this address until she died. I became acquainted with Pete O'Malley, a Capitol police officer who worked on the House side. Pete was from Prince Georges County, Maryland, and he attended Georgetown University Law School at night. Pete was always joking around etc., and one day, while I was talking with him in his Capitol Police uniform, while on duty, he told me that he had met a good looking woman who indicated that she wanted a date. He stated that he could not go out with her that day, but he would get her fixed up with a friend of his. Pete told me that she would serve dinner for me at her residence.

Well, I was game for anything, and told him I would go see her. He gave me her name and address, which was on Connecticut Avenue, in the downtown, area. The next evening I went to her address, which was located above some type of store and knocked on the door. DAMN! This sixty-ish aged woman appears at the door and invites me into her very small apartment. She was extremely unattractive (UGLY), with a bandage on one side of her face, indicating that she had fallen or something. I very slowly went along, until I could get to a point of leaving. For dinner, she opened a quart-sized "Ball" canning jar filled with some type of unidentified meat, which looked awful. I pretended to taste this unknown substance, and finally, I left as soon as I could. Pete O'Malley, the jokester, certainly did play a joke on me, which he was noted for. He was always joking around with his friends and acquaintances. Having dinner with someone such as this lady was a very unusual situation, but later, I had fun with it. Pete ended up being a very successful lawyer and a powerhouse in Maryland politics. He owned a home in Palm Beach, Florida, and shortly, before his death, while Max was visiting me in Vero Beach, Florida, Max talked with Pete on the phone, in order to set up a future meeting with him. Also, at one time he owned the Washington Capitals hockey team. Sadly, he died in Palm Beach, Florida, at age seventy-two, approximately two years ago.

Jose Garcia, a Capitol Police officer from New Mexico, was a very talented artist. He agreed to paint a charcoal portrait of me. I would go to his police officer booth on the Senate side of the US Capitol during 1961 and sit there while he painted the portrait. After several visits he completed the project. He did an excellent job. I have this portrait today and hope to pass it on to our children. Jose died of a heart problem when he was thirty-seven years of age. While visiting him, he would often make the statement, "Jose, Jose, Garcia is a very tired Mexican." He did not feel well as he made these statements. He was truly a nice person. Why do we have to lose nice individuals such as Jose, so soon?

I hated those Washington, DC, Sundays. They were awful, and very lonely. While I resided there, the Blue Laws were in effect. Almost all the restaurants and businesses were closed. There was nothing to do but drive around, or stay in your apartment. As a result of those awful Sunday's, and to this day, one of my favorite songs was sung by Johnny Cash was "ON A SUNDAY MORNING SIDEWALK." How I wish that I was stoned, meaning by beer, not hard drugs. This song brings back horrible memories of those awful Sunday mornings, in DC. I was away from home, not knowing how my life would end up, or whether or not I would ever get the money to attend college, etc. I will never like Sundays as long as I live. My faith is with me all the days of the week, not just on Sundays. Thank GOD for Congressman Frank Albert Stubblefield. He made it happen. He and Ms. Stubblefield had to convince their daughter, Frankie, to come to Washington, and not remain back in Murray, Kentucky. She reluctantly came to DC, and they wanted her to get to know some males in her age group. So the Stubblefield's knew Bob Mason, a next-door friend of mine who resided near Murray, Kentucky, prior to coming to Washington.

Anyway, Bob fixed me up with Frankie. Frankie's friend, Gloria and Bob went with us on a double date to the Warner Theater to see the first cinemascope movie, BEN HUR. During the intermission, Frankie, who was EXTREMELY loud, saw someone she knew, and yelled at the top of her voice to get this girls attention. Being the shy guy that I was, I did not know what to think, since the theater lights were on and everyone could see Frankie and me. Anyway, later, Bob and I switched girls. I began dating Gloria and Bob dated Frankie. Bob eventually ended up marrying her. Bob was a cool dresser who imitated Senator John Sherman Cooper with his appearance and manners. Also, he kept up on the proper etiquette and manners. He reminded me to never use a toothpick in public.

I took his advice, even though I did not use toothpicks, and to this day, I would never use a toothpick after I eat in public. I find it very offensive when I observe others picking their teeth with the potential of food particles flying out of your mouth. I actually observed this happen on more than one occasion. Bob actually had an ice skating date with Linda Bird Johnson, the daughter of President Lyndon Johnson. At that time Lyndon Johnson was the majority leader of the US Senate. I have contact with Bob, today, and

I thank him for his kindness during those years in Washington, DC. He is currently married to a very nice lady, Marty.

Remember, I was still working for the FBI, and the ghost of J. Edgar Hoover was always lurking around, especially in the bedroom. The anti-sentiment regarding any sexual contact in your apartment with a female was so strong within the FBI that many employees would not be able to perform sexually in their apartment. I kid you not, you had to worry about one of your co-workers turning you in to the higher up's if they thought you had been alone in your bedroom or apartment, especially overnight, with a member of the opposite sex. Sex was a word that was feared among FBI employees because it could mean the end of your FBI career.

Mary, who worked in Senator John Sherman Cooper's office, owned a great rustic cabin with a fireplace and land. The cabin was located west of Winchester, Virginia. She knew Bob due to the fact he worked in the Senate Post Office under Senator Cooper's patronage. Mary would let Bob use her cabin almost every time he asked for it. Bob and I, Frankie, Gloria, and others would spend many weekends at Mary's cabin. It was great. Thankfully, J. Edgar's ghost did not show his face sixty miles from Washington, in the mountains. We made the best of any situation, due to the fact that most of us did not have a pot to piss in, as far as extra money. Damn, my life could have been really great if I had just a few extra dollars. Very few people knew that I was always "busted" because I knew how to pick out clothes that looked good for the least amount of money. Being an FBI tour leader certainly helped in this area due to the fact that I had to always be a sharp dresser. I could not have a flat top haircut and had to wear shoes with shoelaces.

Also, suits were required with no colored shirts. Let me be very clear. My experiences as a fingerprint clerk, tour leader, and a security clerk in the Memphis Field Office, gave me unbelievable insight into the FBI that could not be obtained anywhere else. A large number of these agents who came on board from the outside did not really know dip sh-about the overall organization. It appeared to me that they did not have the same degree of insight in the organization that the agents who had held a clerical position prior to becoming an agent. This was just due to the fact that the agents who had prior clerical work experience in non-agent positions had a deeper knowledge of the organization and would more than likely make a career out of the FBI. An example was Associate Director Cartha "Deke" DeLoach, who worked as a fingerprint clerk prior to becoming an FBI agent.

Usually, a large number of agents with law degrees would stay only three years and leave. If they left prior to three years they would not get a good recommendation for other positions. This whole period of time that the FBI required a law degree or an accounting degree was nothing but a publicity stunt by Director Hoover to strengthen the public image of the FBI. The accounting degrees consisted of completing a two year program at one of the accounting schools in DC. Prior to Jack Dawson, a supervisory co-worker in the FBI Identification Division, fighting to get this rule changed, a non-agent employee had to work fifteen years with the FBI, plus, have an accounting degree, in order to become an FBI agent. This system was totally unfair. Get this. Someone from the outside could become an FBI agent with just an accounting degree or law degree with no experience. Public image meant everything to Director J. Edgar Hoover.

Thanks to Congressman and Ms. Frank Albert Stubblefield, during 1961 to 1962, I became a member of the Kentucky Society of Washington, a social organization of well-known Kentuckians, such as honorary members Senator John Sherman Cooper, Senator Thurston B. Morton, and Ms. Alban Barkley, the spouse of Vice President Alban Barkley, who was President Truman's Vice President. I attended many of these social dinners when these members were present. In addition, I was the escort for the 1962 Cherry Blossom Princess, Ms. Barbour Lee Perry, at a reception. During that period of time, many of the large social dinners consisted of a chicken thigh and leg, green peas and mashed potatoes. The chicken thigh and leg always reminded me of a boomerang. Hell, it was free and I was happy. Congressman Stubblefield made all the arrangements for me to attend these functions. I had no influence with anyone in powerful positions. The only influence I had was on me.

I decided that it was time for me to resign from the FBI in order to attend college. I realized that being around all the famous and powerful people in Washington would not, through osmosis or anything else, rub off on me. I had to make my own way in life, and the start was to earn a college degree. My resignation was effective May 10, 1962. Congressman Stubblefield put me on his payroll for one month prior to my leaving Washington, DC, for Murray State University, Murray, KY. I sold my 1961 MG vehicle to Bundy Caldwell, an attorney from Union City, TN, who had just arrived in DC, and needed a car. I bought an old 1951 black Desoto vehicle, which looked like shit. I left Washington, DC, with a total of $1,500, to start my college career. As I look back on those four years working for the FBI, I recall that I never used any of my thirteen-days-a-year sick leave. I would go to work many days sick and feeling awful, but I would never use sick leave. When I resigned during May 1962 to attend college I lost all those sick leave days. Today, I cannot understand how I was able to save any money during my years in DC. I was almost too rigid for my own good in regards to my total commitment to do the right thing and never get into any trouble that would jeopardize my job. I relied on myself, totally, to make the correct decisions that would reward me with a college degree.

While in Washington, DC, from 1958 to 1962, I became friends/acquainted with individuals that would later, during my lifetime, come to my attention for one reason, or the other. US Congressman Robert A. "Fats" Everett, from Union City, TN, US Congressman Frank Albert Stubblefield, from Murray, KY, Pete O'Malley, from Prince Georges County, MD, Larry Forgy, from Russellville, KY, and Gary Whipple, from Louisiana. Congressman Everett, Congressman Stubblefield, and Pete O'Malley, have been mentioned previously. O'Malley was an acquaintance more than a close friend. He was a good friend to my roommate Max Parr. I would run into him on Capitol Hill, very often.

Larry Forgy, a US Capitol Police officer, became friends with my roommate, Max Parr, while we resided at 407 Seward Square. I also became acquainted with Larry. Larry's apartment was located on Capitol Hill, just a couple of blocks from our residence. Many years later, during 1995, Larry ran for Governor of Kentucky, and I was on the same ticket as a candidate for Kentucky State Auditor. We lost, but Larry and I have kept in contact to this day. At that time, the state voter registration was three to one against us. Recently, during a visit with Larry in Lexington, KY, he mentioned that he and Senate Majority Leader Harry Reid were co-workers on the US Capitol Police Department. According to Larry, they have kept in touch over the years. Harry Reid and Larry attended George Washington University Law School at the same time, while on the Capitol Police Department. As young men working in Washington, DC, we did not care about political party affiliations. In fact, during this period of time, with two exceptions, all my political friends were Democrats. Larry was one of the best "stump" political speakers I have witnessed. Also, he was a very good attorney. Today he is very well known throughout the state of Kentucky. I always admired his intelligence because he was able to work while earning a law degree from one of the best law schools in the United States, George Washington University Law School.

One day shortly after hurricane Katrina hit New Orleans and while I was watching TV, General Gary Whipple was speaking about the hurricane, etc. He was a US Capitol police officer that I had met, while in DC, during 1958 to 1962. Later in life he became the General in charge of the state of Louisiana National Guard. It seems that during this period of time I came in touch with numerous individuals who would come to my attention later in life.

# MURRAY STATE UNIVERSITY
# 1962–1965

Thank goodness, Congressman and Ms. Stubblefield let me live in their Murray, Kentucky, home during the summer, 1962, which saved me money that I desperately needed. Prior to my summer school classes beginning, I drove Congressman Stubblefield around his district, campaigning, due to the fact that 1962 was an election year. Here I am, a registered Republican, thanks to his son-in-law, driving a Democrat congressman around in his district. I never thought about being a Democrat or Republican. I only thought about having enough money to attend college. However, due to the fact that he was such a nice and honorable person, this did not matter to him.

## STRUGGLE TO ZERO

**OFFICERS**
Arthur Clarendon Smith, Sr.
  President
John L. Schroeder
  Vice-President & Counselor
H. C. John Russell
  Vice-President
Lester W. Whittington
  Vice-President
Blanche Weaver
  Vice-President
Annette Culler
  Vice-President
Birdye L. Maclin
  Treasurer

**BOARD OF DIRECTORS**
Betty S. Fullilove
George F. Gaul
Maxine Huff
Arthur C. Hyde
Anne T. Kelly
Frank E. Mann
Florence B. Minor
Mrs. Arthur Clarendon Smith, Sr.
Henrietta C. Wright

**ADVISORY BOARD**
Mrs. Hartman Barber
I. E. Lees
Mrs. I. E. Lees
Gertrude Jay Scott
Eva O. Stelmer
Nelle M. Wiggins

### Democratic Club
of the
### District of Columbia
1313 YOU STREET N.W.
WASHINGTON 9, D. C.

NOrth 7-3343

**HONORARY VICE-PRESIDENTS**
Honorable John F. Kennedy
Honorable Lyndon B. Johnson
Honorable Harry S. Truman
Mrs. Harry S. Truman
Senator Clinton P. Anderson
Senator Alan Bible
Senator Robert C. Byrd
Senator John A. Carroll
Senator Frank Church
Senator Thomas J. Dodd
Senator Paul H. Douglas
Senator Ernest Gruening
Senator Hubert H. Humphrey
Senator Estes Kefauver
Senator Oren E. Long
Senator Edmund S. Muskie
Senator Wayne Morse
Senator Eugene J. McCarthy
Senator Gale McGee
Senator William Proxmire
Senator Jennings Randolph
Senator John J. Sparkman
Senator Stuart Symington
Governor J. Lindsay Almond, Jr.
Governor Edmund G. Brown
Governor J. Howard Edmondson
Governor David L. Lawrence
Governor Robert B. Meyner
Governor Stephen L. R. McNichols
Governor J. Millard Tawes
Honorable Wayne Aspinall
Honorable Ken Hechler
Honorable Elizabeth Kee
Honorable John W. McCormack
Honorable Paul M. Butler
Honorable Renah Camalier
Honorable Clarence Cannon
Honorable George Docking
Honorable F. Joseph Donohue
Honorable Harold T. Johnson
Honorable James Kee
Honorable George M. Leader
Honorable John Steelman
Honorable G. Mennen Williams

February 1, 1962

To: Members of the Democratic Club
    of the District of Columbia
              &
    Members of the Kentucky State Society

We are greatly honored by the acceptance of Mrs. Alben W. Barkley to be our guest of honor at our luncheon to be held on Sunday, February 11, 1962, 1:00 p.m., at the Burlington Hotel.

Also, we are inviting the new Democratic members to be our guests - Congressman Morris K. Udall of Arizona, and Congressman Victor Wickersham of Oklahoma, have accepted. The Comptroller of the Treasury, State of Maryland, Mr. Louis Goldstein, has also accepted.

Mr. Ray Smart, President of the Kentucky State Society, has indicated that he will have a well-represented group of the Kentucky State Society to attend this luncheon in honor of Mrs. Barkley.

Of course, you are invited to bring as many guests as you possibly can - Let's make this the Biggest Meeting of the '62 season!

Please get your reservations in before Friday, February 9. Call NO 7-4083.     Tickets $3.00 each.

              Sincerely,

              Arthur Clarendon Smith, Sr., President

              Birdye L. Maclin, Treasurer

His son-in-law convinced me to register as a Republican in the first place. This was my first taste of partisan politics. I would be with him when he would go in and out of these small rural grocery stores, griping and grinning (shaking hands), and making small talk, etc. His son-in-law, Bob, and I went down to the District of Columbia, District Court Building in Washington, DC, during 1960, and registered to vote. Bob had a patronage job under US Senator John Sherman Cooper, the Republican senator from Kentucky, and when we filled out the voter registration cards, due to the fact he worked for a Republican senator, I registered as a Republican. At that time you had to be twenty-one years of age to vote. Bob and I remain friends, today, with frequent contact with each other.

Also, after I started my summer classes at Murray State University, during the summer of 1962, I got a part-time job at the Belk-Settle Department store, selling men's clothing. My tuition for the fall semester at Murray State was $80. I managed to make it through my first year without starving. At the beginning of the fall semester, I rented a room for $20 a month from Hayden Rickman, the supervisor at Belk-Settle Department store. I shared the room with another student. There were a total of six college students renting from Mr. Rickman. All of us, including Mr. and Ms. Rickman, shared ONE bathroom, which meant that we had to be VERY aware of when we could use the bathroom, especially, for doing number two.

During the spring semester of 1963, I joined the Sigma Chi Fraternity, with the dues being $5 a month. Sigma Chi consisted of many good students who were very talented in many areas and serious about their studies. We had the best reputation on campus. Although, as in any organization, there will be one or two who do not follow the rules. No booze was sold in Murray or in the county. The beer had to be imported from another county, or from Tennessee, which was just across the state line. The Cotton Club was the hangout for the college beer drinking crowd. Actually, I was never in the Cotton Club. I never had any extra money to buy beer. Our fraternity had several beer blasts in an old rock quarry, which consisted of kegs of beer and BBQ chicken legs, only. From my viewpoint, after coming off a four year stint in Washington, DC, being in a fraternity was the only way to have a social life at Murray State University. Our Sigma Chi Fraternity would sponsor social events at the college, such as a Bo Diddley dance in the student union building which was open to all students. No alcohol was allowed on campus, but our dates would hide booze in their purses, which were placed under the tables. Throughout the dance, students were constantly bending over and reaching under the tables as if be picking up something that had been dropped on the floor. The fraternity put up $3,000 to have Bo

Diddley play for this particular dance, which was a lot of money at that time.

Frank Rickman, a fellow Sigma Chi, and the son of my landlord, talked me into selling family Bibles, dictionaries, and other religious books during the summer, 1963. I, along with other Sigma Chis, traveled to the Southwestern Book Company, Nashville, Tennessee, for three days of training to sell these books. Rickman told us how much money he had made selling these books the prior summer and he assured us that we would come back with money in our pockets. After the training, I, and my co-worker, Bill, were assigned to Brunswick County, North Carolina, which was our territory for the twelve weeks. We found a place to stay in Shallotte for seven dollars a week at Hilda's rooming house. Hilda was a very nice lady who every now and then would have snuff leaking down the corners of her mouth. I did not give a damn because she certainly knew how to prepare those shrimp to be consumed. Mind you, out of my down payments for the family Bible came my total living expenses.

My vehicle, at that time, was an old 1951 slick backed, black Chevrolet. I learned that Brunswick County was the largest and most sparsely populated county in North Carolina. It is located on the coast, with Southport, being the county seat. I had to hunt for potential customers for my family Bibles. Myself, and Bill split the county in half, as our individual territory. I would drive down these old sandy roads with tall pine trees on each side, looking for human beings. Most of the older women dipped snuff, with the juice running down each corner of their mouth. Also, they went barefooted, which gave them the name "tar heels." One day, as I tooled down this sandy road, I came to the house at the end of the road. On the front porch sat an older female, rocking in her rocking chair, and spitting snuff in her juice can. A large blue tick hound was sitting beside her, and I walked up the steps and sat down beside her in another chair. We talked for a few minutes, and as she continued to spit large amounts of snuff juice into her snuff juice can with the juice seeping down each corner of her toothless mouth, I saw her reach to pick something off the neck of her big blue tick hound. Damn, it was a HUGE tick, full of blood. She popped this tick from the dog, and squeezed it, sending a streak of blood across the porch for several feet. After observing this tick incident, I have never wanted to have anything to do with ticks. They are sickening to me.

As a single college student in Brunswick County, NC, selling family Bibles, I was totally on the lookout for female company. I met only one girl my age, and she sold eggs and chickens. I never had any luck with her, but she was the only show in my half of the county. It was terrible and discouraging as a male in that God-forsaken, no-young-female county. The family Bibles cost $30, and if someone made a down payment of, say, $10, I had to live on that $10 until the end of the summer, when I delivered the actual Bible and collected the rest of the money. The problem that I had with prospective customers was that most of the people did not want me to leave their home.

They wanted me to talk with them all day long. Here I was, a young college student, wanting to sell them a family Bible, and they did not want me to leave. While at one house during lunchtime, the homeowner would NOT let me leave. He had been drinking quart-sized Budweiser beers, and when I started to leave, he stood at the doorway, telling me that I had to have lunch with him and his family before I could leave. I sat down and had lunch with them. Well, at the end of the summer all the Bible salesmen traveled back to Murray, Kentucky, for the beginning of the fall semester. The Southwestern Book Company mailed our checks for the net amount of money that we had made that summer. Mind you, all our living expenses had to be taken from our Bible selling profit. MY TOTAL CHECK AMOUNT WAS $180! Man, was I pissed. I could not pay for my upcoming college expenses on $180. Frank Rickman, who talked me into selling these Bibles, made much more money due to the fact he got a percentage of the sales from all the stupid shits like me, whom he had recruited. Anyway, I did manage to borrow $1,900, as a National Defense Loan, with ten years to pay it back. I also worked part time, to make a few bucks.

No one but me can understand how broke I was. I became an expert at pinching pennies and eating Campbell soup. I was never given one penny, except for the $50 that my parents gave me after graduating from Murray State University, during August 1965. Being broke was totally miserable. Being a member of Sigma Chi Fraternity helped a lot while at Murray State University. At least I had access to a cheap social life. Dues were cheap, $5 per month, plus, the social aspect helped me deal with the lack of finances. I was always able to get dates for Sigma Chi social functions with good looking girls. On the date, that President Kennedy was assassinated, I was standing outside the campus restaurant when the word passed that he had been killed. Another event that I remembered was when Bill Cunningham, Russell Anderson, Danny Kemp, and I travelled to Washington, DC, in Danny's VW Bug. They wanted to see DC, plus, General Douglas McArthur's deceased body was lying in state, in the US Capitol rotunda. I went to the Capitol and lined up with the thousands of other people, in order to view his open casket. Bill, Dan, and Russ went to see a movie. It seems that I was always on the move for one thing, or the other. I had this desire to hurry through life, in order to do everything that I could, before I was too old. I was always playing catch up, due to the fact that I was a twenty two-year-old college freshman.

During my last year at Murray State University, I, along with Bill Cunningham and Russell Anderson rented an old house, which was located a couple of miles outside Murray, on the Mayfield highway. Mind you, this house was not insulated at all. Man, it was cold during the winter. However, Bill was not bothered by the cold, at all. He would walk outside barefooted when it was really cold. We gave him the name "Abe" due to the fact he reminded us of President Abe Lincoln when he lived in Kentucky, prior to moving to Illinois. Bill almost froze us because for whatever reason, he could withstand the cold. I caught pneumonia and became terribly ill, with my nose bleeding, etc. Bill was one of the most genuine, honest, good guy individuals that I have ever met. I cannot recall one negative thing to say about Bill, or Russell Anderson.

During this period of time I had a desire to become an FBI agent. I had made arrangements to travel to Paducah, KY, to take the written exam for this position. However, when I made these arrangements, I had no idea that the exam date would be during the time that I was ill with pneumonia and a nose that was constantly bleeding. I attempted to change the date, but could not. My nose was constantly bleeding throughout the exam. I could not keep my mind on the exam. I stuffed my handkerchief up my nose in an attempt to stop the bleeding, etc. Obviously, I could not keep my mind on the exam in any way, whatsoever. Later, I was advised that I did not pass the exam. I experienced my first taste of how this son of a bitch, inconsiderate FBI agent was. He apparently was afraid that he would get into trouble if he postponed the exam. So he did nothing. Director Hoover's rigid control of the FBI filtered down to every level of the organization. Actually, it was not Hoover's fault that supervisors under him never questioned him about anything. Therefore, over the years, his spineless subordinates would misinterpret his intentions out of fear that they might be fired. Russell Anderson ended up having a career as a school administrator, and Bill is currently a Kentucky State Supreme Court Justice. Dan Kemp became a successful lawyer tobacco war and mayor of Hopkinsville, Ky.

He also wrote books about the Night Riders in the western Kentucky area during the turn of the nineteenth and beginning of the twentieth century.

I earned my bachelor of science degree from Murray State University during August 1965. Now, what do I do? I was twenty-five years of age and broke with no place to live. During the rest of the month, I traveled to Giltedge, Tennessee, and stayed with my sister, Joyce, for several days, and then ended up in Memphis, Tennessee, staying with my brother Garvin, who was renting a room in Ms. Gowling's house.

Ms. Gowling was a heavy smoker, who gurgled when she coughed. However, she was a nice, old lady. Man, I had to have a job. One day while travelling down Jackson Avenue, in Memphis, I passed the Marine Corps Reserve Training Center building. I stopped in and talked with the Bird Colonel about the possibility of joining his Motor Transport Battalion. He was very nice and courteous, telling me that he had an opening, but he wanted to make it very clear that I would end up going to Vietnam without exception. I felt that

I would not have any problem with the physical part of boot camp, so realizing that I was homeless and needed a job and place to live, I signed up. I had no choice. I could not become an officer as a reservist, so I had to go in as a buck private for six months of active duty with a six-year obligation. My reporting date for boot camp at Parris Island, SC, was September 6, 1965, the day of infamy for me. Thank goodness, I had no idea what I got myself into when I signed those documents. Otherwise, I might have backed out of signing them.

# MARINE CORPS RESERVE ACTIVE DUTY SEPTEMBER 1965–MARCH 1966

On September 6, 1965, I boarded a Delta Airlines plane, compliments of the US Marine Corps, in Memphis, Tennessee, destination, Parris Island, SC, via Savannah, GA. I was herded onto a big bus with other young men, with our destination being Parris Island. When the bus came to a stop at Parris Island, a drill instructor came on board, and we were welcomed with yelling and screaming, while being given instructions, etc. After we arrived at our barracks, the screaming and harassment continued throughout the night. Every thirty minutes the drill instructors would roll those huge, empty, metal trash cans down the center of the barracks. Man, did they make a lot of noise! Of course, we never got ANY sleep that night.

After going through the routine of getting measured for our clothing, boots, etc., our heads were shaved. Later, we were informed that boot camp would last for eight weeks, instead of the usual twelve weeks. Therefore, all the training would be compacted into eight weeks in order to send our asses over to Vietnam to get shot as soon as possible. The Marine Corps lost more than their share of young men, due to the stupidity of the political types that were running that war. Many times a week the drill instructors would tell all the reservists that they were being activated and would be sent to Vietnam. So after being told this over and over, it got to where I believed that my butt would end up in Vietnam. At that time, I did not realize that the Marine Corps Reserve motor transport regiment would never be activated. The reason for this was that truck drivers were not needed in the thick jungles of Vietnam.

## STRUGGLE TO ZERO

As the weeks passed at Parris Island, the training got routine. I never had any problems due to the fact I was in good physical shape. Some of those poor rascals had a rough time with the training. If a recruit screwed up during the day, the drill instructors would line him up in front of his bunk that evening, and beat the crap out of him. Every now and then, the recruit would be taken to the base hospital for treatment. One night the drill instructors put a blind fold on one recruit that had goofed up, and made him run around and around behind the metal bunks. Alas, his forehead rammed into the sharp corner of a bunk bed, causing blood to gush everywhere. He was taken to the base infirmary for treatment. Also, the youngest recruit in our barracks was punished for a screw up, and the drill instructors punished him by tying a sheet to the ceiling and making this recruit get into the sheet, staying there all night.

We had only six days to qualify with the M-14 rifle, instead of the usual twelve days. If you failed to qualify on any day, well, that night in the barracks you would be called up the drill instructor's desk and stand in line with everyone else who did not qualify that day. As punishment, you put your index finger down into the firing chamber and the drill instructor would pull the trigger, causing severe pain. As a result of this punishment, your fingernail would come off, completely. This was my punishment for not qualifying one day. However, on qualifying day, I ended up as a Sharpshooter. The only letters I received during boot camp were from my parents. I was painfully lonely. Boot camp was so restrictive that I would have been happier on the battlefield in Vietnam. It would have been a relief. In boot camp, I had no base privileges, such as having the freedom to talk, or to eat candy, etc. It was pretty bad, having to give up small freedoms such as these. I could see through most of the reasons for this type of training, in that, it was designed for these young fellows who had no discipline or had the brain of an amoeba. I believe that beating someone is not the correct approach to instill loyalty or discipline into anyone.

At boot camp graduation, which was a big deal for many recruits, their family members came to the graduation ceremonies. I had no one, but myself. At this point in my life I became somewhat accustomed to being very lonely and without any support from anyone. I was my only support system most of my life. It seemed that throughout my life, when I came to the fork in the road, I seemed to always take the road least traveled, which could be very painful and lonely. Today, sometimes I enjoy my own company more than the company of others. However, in the long run, I seemed to have made the right decisions.

After boot camp, I was sent to Camp Le June, North Carolina, for further training before completing my six months active duty. At Camp Le June, I was assigned to administrative duties in the company first sergeant's office. First Sergeant Blackburn was a good person who had already been to Vietnam. He looked the part—neat dresser with a hairline mustache. Also, as any Marine would know, in any company office, coffee making was an important art to learn due to the fact that if not make correctly, the coffee could be as bitter as green persimmons. Therefore, I was advised to always put a pinch of salt into the coffee grounds, which took away the bitter taste caused by bad coffee or bad tasting water. After my six months were up, I ended up back in Memphis, Tennessee, since my reserve unit was located there. I had to find employment as soon as possible.

# MEMPHIS, TENNESSEE
# 1966–1971

I needed a JOB! My brother Garvin, again, took me in until I could find a job. I responded to a First National Bank ad in a Memphis newspaper. They had an opening in the municipal bond department, at $325 a month. I would compute interest on municipal bonds. I was interviewed by the department manager, Mr. Duncan. During the interview, he kept trying to lower the starting salary. Finally, due to the fact that I had no choice, he wanted me to start at $275 a month. I needed a job so badly that I had no choice but to accept this salary. That son of a bitch! I remain hostile toward him to this day, even after his death, due to the fact that the extra $50 a month would have made a huge difference between being able to buy needed food, and going hungry. However, sometimes there is justice. Fast forward briefly… Shortly after becoming a Secret Service agent, and while down in the US Marshal's Office where all the arrestees were fingerprinted and booked, several of Mr. Duncan's municipal bond salesmen were being booked for fraud, in connection with their municipal bond sales. I got a great amount of satisfaction out of being around them, due to the fact they worked for the "suck the blood out of a turnip" Duncan. Actually, I felt sad for the salesmen, but not their blood sucking boss who forced me to accept $275 a month instead of the advertised monthly salary of $325.

I hated this job in the municipal bond section. In the meantime, I was moved into the management trainee position, until I applied for, and got a security clerk position in the local FBI office. My prior experience with the FBI in Washington, DC was helpful in getting this job. I would be working either the 4:00 PM to midnight shift, or the midnight to 8:00 AM shift. During the 12:00 AM to 8:00 AM shift, I would be working by myself. I began working in the Memphis FBI Field Office during the fall of 1966. I would take phone calls, read messages from the teletype machine, send teletypes, and decode secure messages that came into the office.

During that period of time, I had to deal with receiving information about bomb threats, which came into the office, either from the airlines, police department, or individuals. After receiving the information, I would then advise the duty agent, who would respond and handle the matter. Also, many crank calls came into the office from individuals who were usually harmless. Once, I took a phone call from the spouse of a nationwide, well-known singer, who knew that law enforcement authorities wanted to question a member of his band regarding a minor criminal matter. She gave the location of his band, so that he could be questioned. This was just an example of some of my duties. I believe that I was the only person, except the GSA cleaning crew, who was on duty during the midnight shift in the Memphis federal building. In other words, I had the whole office to myself during these quiet hours, right on the bank of the Mississippi River, with the state of Arkansas on the other side.

One evening during the dinner hour, Stephanie and I were eating at Berrita's Italian restaurant on Airways Blvd. in Memphis. Later, I had to go into work for the midnight shift at the Memphis FBI Office, which was located on the Mississippi River in downtown Memphis. I was hoping to have a quiet night at the office, since I would be the only employee there. As we were eating, these very loud screams came from the kitchen area of the restaurant. Dr. Martin Luther King had been assassinated, causing these screams from the kitchen employees. After I arrived at the FBI Office, around 11:00 PM, there was total pandemonium in the office. My immediate assignment was to prepare and box up Dr. King's bloody clothes that he was wearing when he was shot. The clothes had to be flown to the FBI Laboratory, in Washington, DC, for ballistics tests. The gun that was used by the assassin was also there in the office. I followed the investigation as an FBI employee, until James Earl Ray was captured in London, England. These incidents remain totally vivid in my mind, today. During this period of time, the FBI and the US Army Intelligence worked very closely, together, when demonstrations and civil unrest took place. Needless to say, during the aftermath of the King assassination, this relationship became closer and stronger. I was the last person to touch Dr. King's clothes before they entered the evidence system in Washington, DC.

During the fall, 1966, I met my current spouse, Stephanie Weber. I was "fixed up" by her roommate, Theresa Manning. Both were Stewardesses with Delta Airlines based in Memphis. During this period of time, I was residing with two other males in a house located at Airways Blvd. and Winchester Street, which was very near the Memphis Airport. Doc McCall's Rexall Drug Store was located across the intersection from our residence. In addition, numerous single stewardesses lived across the street in a large apartment complex. Many of them would take their regular walk to the drug store to get their birth control pills, due to the fact old Doc McCall would sell them without a prescription. There were these single, good looking stewardesses everywhere. At that time, Memphis was a hub for Delta Airlines. Stephanie and I were married on July 21, 1967, in the Methodist Church, Ardmore, Pennsylvania, due to the fact that her mother and stepfather resided close by in Haverford. Stephanie's mother was married to a Philadelphia lawyer, James Conwell Welsh.

His father was a US Congressman during the 1920s, and later, President Hoover appointed him to the bench, as a federal judge. He held that position for forty years. We had our wedding reception at Stephanie's mother's residence, on Marple Road, Haverford. Most everyone in Stephanie's family was present, including her father, Harry Frederick Weber, and his nineteen-year-old Vietnamese wife that he brought back from Saigon prior to the time when the Americans were run out at the end of the war. At that time, Harry was fifty-seven years of age and Kim was nineteen. In addition, several of Stephanie's mother's friends who were members of the Merion Golf Club, Ardmore, PA, were present. Everyone was courteous and acted like they had a good time, with the best booze and food being served. My sister, Chris, was the only member of my family present. I did not know what a cheap scape Stephanie's mother and step father were until several months, later. Stephanie's mother hit Harry up for twice the amount of the booze, plus, she charged him double for our wedding photographs. Harry, at that time, was still a CIA agent, in Langley, Virginia. South Vietnam was his last foreign post of duty.

His previous foreign posts of duty were Yemen, during their revolution, Port Said, Egypt, and Kabul, Afghanistan. While assigned to Kabul, Harry would witness public beheadings in the public arena. Since he was a very good photographer, his 35mm photographs were very graphic and clear, as the executioner severed the heads with his sword. If the family of the person being beheaded had enough money, they would bribe the executioner, and the executioner would sever the head with only one whack.

Otherwise, the executioner could take several whacks before the head was completely severed. Harry was in Afghanistan during the late 1950s. Stephanie's mother was also employed by the CIA in their headquarters in Washington, DC. After she divorced Harry, she married the Philadelphia blue blooded lawyer, James Conwell Welsh. Stephanie then left Washington, DC, and resided with her mother in Haverford, Pennsylvania, when she was fifteen years of age.

I had no idea what type of people or family that I was marrying, into. I thought that I was marrying "up," financially, but damn, was I ever fooled. I was not thinking about what happens when divorces come into the picture, with the result being that whatever money one has, it is going to be split up, sometimes many times. Sometimes no money is left due to the selfish family members. I had a positive opinion of the human race, prior to getting married. Harry, was honest and a good person. After Stephanie's mother, Marge, left him for this Philadelphia lawyer and the great "blue blood" upper crust, social life, at the Merion Golf Club, Harry's attitude was "screw it."

At the age of eighty, the Philadelphia lawyer ended up an alcoholic and had to be admitted to a confined area of a private hospital, after he was caught running around in the parking lot at his apartment complex totally naked, keying everyone's car. After Stephanie's mother left Harry for this great life, Harry ended up marrying three other young women—Jean Marie, who was half French and Tunisian; Kim, the Vietnamese; Myia, half French and Vietnamese;

and Promjeet, an Indian from India. Myia was a trapeze artist with a hard body. Harry, who was a very good artist, met her in Barcelona, Spain. He would go the beach and draw portraits of tourists, while they were sunbathing on the beach. We have many of his paintings in our family today. His specialty was nude women. All his wives divorced him. Promjeet was the only dishonest wife. She took him for everything she could prior to his death. Harry never paid any alimony or child support except to Stephanie's mother, since Stephanie was the only child. Harry was confined to his residence for three months in Yemen during that revolution. Little did he know that while his wife, Jean Marie, was residing in Aden, Yemen, she was having an affair with a British naval officer. They would fly back and forth from Aden to Paris, France, while old Harry was confined to his quarters in Yemen. His only form of recreation was watching a praying mantis and a scorpion fight to their death in a glass jar since he absolutely could not leave his residence. His food had to be brought in to him by a young native male. After he got out of Yemen, he determined that Jean Marie had hooked up with a British naval officer. She kept the skyway hot between Aden and Paris while old Harry was on the brink of being killed in Yemen.

However, due to Harry's determination, he located the British naval office that had the hot, sizzling, affair with Jean Marie. Harry "persuaded" him to sign a confession (which we still have) giving the details about the affair. Needless to say, they got divorced. Actually, he remained in contact with all his wives except Promjeet, until he died, at the age of seventy-seven. All his wives were many years younger than him. He always ranted and raved about how older women turned him off. However, Harry's sexual desire for younger women was much greater than his ability to satisfy their physical needs, as is the case with many old men, today. Stephanie and I were present during the time he was on his death bed at Suburban Hospital, Washington, DC. Although he could not speak, the nurses told us that he was grabbing at them until the last minute prior to his death, as they walked around his bed. Regarding women, his eyes were always larger than any other body part, which is a familiar theme among many older men.

Harry owned a condo in the Grosvenor Park Condo complex on Rockville Pike, Rockville, Maryland. While going through his personal belongings at his condo, we found lying on the dresser in his bedroom a receipt from an escort service for over $800, which was dated three days before he was taken to the hospital. Apparently, he was driven around the city for three hours with girls from an escort service. On the day that Harry was found on his bed by his cleaning lady, his foot was lodged between the mattress and the footboard. His foot became lodged during the night as he attempted to get out of bed. Therefore, he could not remove it. He then had a seizure and became unconscious. This incident was the cause of his death. Stephanie and I took the advice of his very nice funeral director who advised us that we could purchase an Urn for his ashes at the local Bloomingdale's department store, which was on Rockville Pike. He stated the cost would be below $50, instead of paying the funeral home $500. So we took his advice and went to Bloomingdale's to buy the Urn.

After locating a salesperson, who was female, Stephanie told her that we were looking for a vase that was going to be used to hold her father's ashes for his burial at Arlington National Cemetery, the next day. Anyway, after being told this, the poor sales girl looked as if she had just seen a ghost. She truly looked frightened. We purchased the Urn and dropped it off at the funeral home on the way back to the condo. Later that night someone from the funeral home came to Harry's condo and left the Earn with us for the burial the next morning. Harry's ashes were still warm when they were given to us by the funeral home employee. Keeping his warm ashes was totally weird and almost macabre. WE HAD NO CHOICE! Due to the fact that Harry was a World War II Naval Intelligence officer and a retired commander in the naval reserve, he was buried in a beautiful location at Arlington National Cemetery. The Lincoln Memorial, Washington Monument, and US Capitol Building, were in plain view. Myia was his only ex-wife who came to his burial, even though all four ex-wives were living at the time of his death.

Getting back to my life in Memphis, Tennessee, from 1966 to 1968, Stephanie continued working as a stewardess (there were no males) with Delta Airlines, and I continued working in the Memphis FBI Field Office. The airlines had recently changed their policy that allowed the stewardesses to marry without losing their job. As a side note, when Stephanie was seventeen years of age she visited her father, Harry, in Port Said, Egypt for the summer. He was assigned there, while a CIA agent. She developed a few male friends, and one day after she and one of her friends got out of their boat at the dock, a photographer requested to take her photograph. However, since Egypt is a Muslim country, she had to put her towel around her exposed shoulders before he would photograph her. She did not think anything about this incident until she saw her photograph on the cover of Egypt's national magazine, which was the equivalent to Life magazine in the United States.

During the fall, 1967, I accidently had a brief conversation with Secret Service Agent Doug Weaver in the federal building coffee shop, in Memphis, TN. He told me about the Secret Service, etc., and after the conversation, I decided to apply to become a Secret Service agent. However, I had to wait fourteen months before being hired due to a national freeze on hiring in the federal government. Due to budget problems, President Johnson would turn the White House lights off at night, as a symbol that he was doing his share of saving money. Thus, he became known as "lightbulb Johnson." The qualifications were having a four-year college degree, passing a general academic four hour test, being in good physical health, getting through personal interviews, and making it through an extensive background investigation. After successfully jumping over all these hurdles, fourteen months later, I was notified that I had been accepted as a Secret Service agent. On the same date, Stephanie advised me that she was pregnant. My reporting date to the Memphis Field Office was December 16, 1968. Their office was located just down the hall from the Memphis FBI Office.

While waiting on the Secret Service agent position, I continued to work in the Memphis FBI Field Office.

On February 23, 1968, at 9:00 AM, I was awakened by the ringing of my telephone, while sleeping in my apartment at 2279 Airways Blvd., Memphis. Sandy, the FBI Office switchboard operator, had forwarded to me a phone call from and individual who was from the Memphis Commercial Appeal Newspaper. I was aware of the fact that no phone calls from the press were to be forwarded to an employee, unless that call had been approved by a supervisor. Needless to say, I took the call, knowing in my mind that the call had been approved for me to accept. The reporter stated that he was doing a human interest story on various members of the military reserve units in Memphis, and since I was a member of the US Marine Corps Motor Transport Battalion, he wanted to talk with me, briefly. He proceeded to ask questions about any family hardships or problems that being in the reserves might cause, since at that time, a large buildup of troops in Vietnam was in the works. I had a short chat with the reporter, without saying anything negative about the military, or my reserve unit.

The next day the reporter's article appeared in the newspaper. My conversation, along with several other Reservists conversations, appeared in the reporter's article. I did not think anything about the conversation. In view of the fact that I realized that the Vietnam War was totally being run in a losing manner by the President and his generals, I did not say anything to indicate this feeling to the reporter. I realized the war was totally wrong and was being run by a bunch of political hacks that had the brain of an amoeba.

However, during the following week, after reporting to work, C. O. Halter, the assistant agent in charge of the Memphis Field Office called me into his office regarding the newspaper article. He appeared to be really pissed off about this article. I explained the whole incident to him, in detail. Trust, me, I became irritated about being questioned as if this incident was my fault, in view of the fact that I was fully aware of the office policy in regards to talking with the press. I made him aware of the fact that this phone call should never have been forwarded to me from the office switchboard. Anyway, the conversation ended, and I went back to work.

To my surprise, on March 8, 1968, I received a PERSONAL letter from J. Edgar Hoover in my office mail box. This letter was signed by Hoover, himself, and not by an autopen, or Ms. Gandy. His true signature was always in blue ink and signed "J. Edgar

Hoover," not "J. E. Hoover," as Ms. Gandy signed his name. The letter read as follows: "Dear Mr. Bell: You exercised very poor judgment in a personal situation which occurred on February 23, 1968. The Bureau has carefully reviewed this matter, and your explanation has been considered. The circumstances clearly indicate that you did not behave in a manner consistent with the high standards expected of FBI employees. It will be incumbent upon you hereafter to conduct yourself in a more responsible manner so there will be no further basis for criticism of a similar nature. Very truly yours, John Edgar Hoover, Director."

This letter was known as a "Letter of Censure" within FBI circles. Hoover was famous for his "Letters of Censure." Actually, I was proud of this letter because it revealed that Halter was a chicken shit. It is the perfect example of how an FBI employee got screwed by the insane mind-set that was in place, throughout the FBI. The Assistant agent in charge of the Memphis FBI Field Office, C. O. Halter, was a squirrelly man who appeared to be scared of his shadow. His physical body would have totally melted if he had to face real danger. Due to the fact his claim to fame was that he had been one of Director Hoover's stenographers, prior to becoming an FBI agent, Memphis was his only field office, after a short stint in his first office as a new agent. To my knowledge, he had no real street experience.

During my 12:00 AM–8:00 AM shifts in the Memphis FBI Office, C. O. Halter's administrative aide would appear at the office door on numerous occasions, at 2:00 AM. I would let her in and she would always go into her office, which was connected to Halter's office, and remain for an hour, or so. I always thought this was VERY strange. In addition, when she would ring the bell for me to let her in, it was a little irritating at 2:00 AM. Years later, I learned that she would come to her office to steal the office cash funds. She got into trouble, as a result of this theft. Apparently, she enjoyed going to casinos which were located there in northern Mississippi. Sometimes GOD will get you. Why in the world would a person come into their office at 2:00 AM, just to sit around for an hour or so? I was the only other person in the office, but she would never discuss or talk about why she was there.

# MEMPHIS, TENNESSEE, SECRET SERVICE FIELD OFFICE 1968–1971

December 16, 1968, was my first day as a new Secret Service agent in the Memphis, Tennessee, Field Office, located in the federal building on Main Street, in Memphis. Maurice Miller, the special agent in Charge, welcomed me, and seemed pleased that I had chosen the Secret Service, instead of continuing with the FBI. I was very happy with myself, in that, after twenty-eight years of my life, I finally, had the start of a real career. I did not realize until later, that the written test to become a Secret Service agent was considered to be somewhat difficult for many individuals with advanced degrees. The only thing that got me though these years was sheer determination only. I had such a poor high school education, such as never being taught how to study correctly, etc. My high school education was less than half the education that a normal high school offered. Lord, it was a good feeling of accomplishment to have conquered so many hurdles, hardships, and near misses, throughout my life, existing on a wing and a prayer, without ANY financial or emotional help, from anyone, except US Congressman Frank Albert Stubblefield, and his spouse, Odessa. I had to be responsible for all my finances, but he gave me the tools to help myself. Man, it was a great feeling to have an extra dollar in my pocket, which did not happen very often. I ate many cans of Campbell's soup while in college. I could never repeat what I went through, again. It was an awful and terrible existence, not knowing where my next dollar was coming from. I never want to be broke again EVER.

Okay, here I am, a big Secret Service agent in my office which was located on the eighth floor, down the hall from the FBI office in the Federal Building, overlooking Main Street and the mighty Mississippi River, with West Memphis, Arkansas, being on the other side. My Secret Service credentials were quite impressive, plus, the fact that I was required to carry a .357 Magnum pistol on my belt, under my suit coat. I, unlike many young agents, was very careful not to "show off" my firearm. Throughout my career, my children did not see my gun a dozen times. After changing clothes after work at home, I took my gun off and placed it out of sight in a secure place. The Memphis Field Office had six agents, plus, the agent in charge.

We covered northern Mississippi and western Tennessee. Every now and then I would head out to small towns in western Tennessee to interview someone. More than once, I would be in the local jail to obtain information on the subject of one of my investigations. Well, if I was in the jail during lunchtime, the jailer would insist that I eat lunch with him. In these areas, the jailer's wife would prepare lunch due to the fact the jailer was responsible for all the inmate meals. The typical lunch would be beans, cornbread, cooked greens, fried bologna, ice tea, and some sort of desert. Man, the vegetables were always extremely salty, really.

We normally investigated the counterfeiting and forgery of the securities and obligations of the US Treasury Department, threats to kill the president of the United States, and others. Later, we investigated credit card fraud, telemarketing fraud, etc. I always preferred the investigations of the federal violations vs. the protection aspect of my job. I felt the investigative aspect was more challenging and interesting. Throughout my career, I ended up with ten years of investigative hours, and ten years of protection hours. It is noted that in order to save money, it was Secret Service policy for agents to share motel/hotel rooms when we were on protective assignments. Can you imagine this? There was nothing worse for me than to be in close quarters in hotel room with another male, sometimes without any clothes on.

To this day, I consider a male's naked body to be the most unattractive thing on earth. So there was one agent who became very well known among agents for his loud snoring. Damn, this agents loud snoring became a legend. It was so bad that other agents could not share a room with him. It was bad enough just to share a room with someone else, let alone sharing a room with an extremely loud snoring agent. Guess what? Thank goodness, this room sharing came to a sudden halt when the Secret Service started hiring female agents during 1972. I am certain that many agents hoped that in order to be equal, their roommate would one of the female agents. That never happened. So our room sharing came to a stop.

Among my first protective assignments, while in the Memphis Field Office, was to assist in President Eisenhower's funeral, at the National Cathedral, Washington, DC. The funeral service was held during April 1969. As the guests arrived at the front door, I was placed at the outside entrance, where all the foreign heads of state arrived, such as Charles DE Galle of France, etc., plus, all his living World War II friends. From a historical viewpoint, it was very interesting to observe all these leaders and hero's, of the Great War. Later, I was placed very high up in the Cathedral tower, which was a good vantage point, for the last part of the service. Good grief, the wind was extremely cold. I soon realized that I did not wear enough clothing.

JOHN EDGAR HOOVER
DIRECTOR

*Federal Bureau of Investigation*
*United States Department of Justice*
*Washington, D. C.*

September 9, 1966

RECEIVED
SEP 10 RECD
FRANK A. STUBBLEFIELD

Honorable Frank A. Stubblefield
House of Representatives
Washington, D. C. 20515

My dear Congressman:

I am indeed pleased to inform you that Mr. Donald Gene Bell of Memphis, Tennessee, about whom you were interviewed in connection with his application, has been tendered an appointment as a Clerk in the Federal Bureau of Investigation.

Sincerely yours,

J. Edgar Hoover

# STRUGGLE TO ZERO

A photo with a friend that I met in Washington, DC, while I was employed with the FBI. The photo was taken in the living room of US Congressman Frank Albert Stubblefield and his spouse Odessa, Murray, KY. I stayed in their home during my first three months while attending Murray State University in 1962.

During August 1969, I was sent to Independence, Missouri, for a protective assignment with former President Harry Truman. He and Ms. Truman resided in a large three-story white frame house located in the middle of downtown independence. They never had air-conditioning. Also, they were very nice individuals, who in their mid-eighties, lived a quiet, non-eventful life, consisting of going to the barber, or hair dresser, plus, shopping at the local K-Mart type store, etc. President Truman was a very humble man. The Secret Service Office was located in the Truman Library, which was a short distance from their residence. Our office had the usual security type equipment, such as closed circuit TV, which could zero in on the Truman residence. One evening, during August 1969, at approximately 5:00 PM, myself, and my co-worker were sitting in the office when the alarm sounded, which indicated that either President or Ms. Truman were in trouble. They had a hand-held alarm button that they could push, which sounded the alarm in our office in the library. According to my co-worker, who had been assigned to the detail for two to three years, this alarm had never been activated. At that time, I did not fully understand the significance of the alarm. When the alarm sounded, my co-worker was in the bathroom. He came running out, pulling up his pants, yelling "let's go," and headed for our vehicle parked outside. We headed for the Truman residence as fast as we could.

When we arrived at the side drive, next to their house, we observed two females, one young, and the other older. We stopped them and asked them what they wanted, etc. During our conversation with them, we determined they were a mother and daughter who had traveled to President Truman's residence in an attempt to request his help in getting the daughter admitted to an Army hospital in order to have her baby. The daughter's husband, who was on active duty, ceased all communication with her for several months, and due to the fact she was pregnant, she could not afford to have her baby in a civilian hospital.

After we determined that they were no threat to the Truman's, they went on their way. Of course, he made arrangements through his contacts and friends, for the young lady to have her baby in a US Army hospital. As one could imagine, all President Truman had to do was to place a phone call to someone in the Army and make a request to help the young lady be admitted to a military facility for the birth of her child. The Truman's were very down to earth type people. My co-worker advised me one evening that the Secret Service special agent in charge of the Truman Detail had the Truman's over to his residence for dinner. After dinner, Ms. Truman jumped up, and headed for the kitchen, where she proceeded to help with the dishes. Also, prior to my leaving to go back to my office, in Memphis,

President Truman autographed his memoirs to Stephanie and I, plus, he autographed one of his photographs to our only child at that time, Rebecca Bell. At that time, she was only three months old. He was a very gracious person with deep humility.

Several years earlier, President Truman attended an annual Al Smith dinner in New York City. This dinner was an annual event that honored Al Smith, the first Catholic to run for president of the United States. He ran against Herbert Hoover in 1928. During the dinner the host began saying great things about President Truman, such as what a great president and human being he was, etc. President Truman turned to the guest seated next to him and stated that he could not understand why he was saying all these great things about him, because he was just the President of the United States. In other words, President Truman was a great historical figure, with deep humility. He did not think that he was better than anyone else.

Back in Memphis, I continued with my routine duties investigating numerous US Treasury Department violations, such as the counterfeiting and forgery of the securities and obligations of the US Government. In addition, we investigated threats to kill the president of the US, and others that we protected, such as foreign heads of state when they visited the US, for pleasure, or to attend the annual United Nations General Assembly meeting, in New York City.

While a new agent in our Memphis, Tennessee, Field Office, I was assigned a threat to kill the president investigation, which entailed that prior to closing every investigation, I had to determine if the person making the threatening statements was, or was not, a danger to the president. There could be no middle ground, such as "maybe." Enough information had to be gathered during the investigation to say "yes" or "no" as to whether this person was a danger or not. In other words, I had to predict dangerous behavior, which under the best of circumstances is difficult.

Anyway, the subject of this investigation had received a medical discharge from the military, after many years as an officer. He was traveling though Memphis in his vehicle, heading to the northeast, and while at his motel, the motel owner became concerned due to his unusual behavior, such as complaining about odors in his room, and remarks that he made concerning the president. Anyway, this subject had several hand written pages mentioning the president, but his writings did not contain a direct threat to kill the president. It was obvious that he had mental issues, plus, he was headed in the general direction of Washington, DC. I conducted a very through, detailed, interview. He denied any intention of harming the president.

Due to the fact that he did not commit any violation of the law, he could not be arrested or held. After the full field background investigation had been conducted, I evaluated this subject as not being dangerous to the president, specifically, although it was possible that he may, or may not, harm other individuals. I had to be concerned about the president only. Once a person is deemed to be dangerous to the president, or others that we protected, this person's whereabouts had to be determined at all times. In addition, this person had to be revaluated with a personal interview every three months. Every agent assigned to conduct these investigations had to work very closely with the mental health community, family, and friends of the person being investigated, in order to be able to reach the correct evaluation prior to closing the case.

Memphis was an active city, crime wise, during the late 1960s and 1970s. Most people associated the US Secret Service with protecting the president of the United States and others. Very few individuals associated the agency with investigating federal violations, such as the counterfeiting of our currency, food stamp fraud, and the forgery/counterfeiting of the securities and obligations of the US Treasury Department. The theft and forgery of US Treasury checks and Savings Bonds kept our office extremely busy. On Social Security check days, which at that time, was the third of each month, the check thieves would follow the mail vehicle around and when the mail man or woman parked their vehicle on the street in order to walk down that street to deliver the mail, the thief would break into the mail truck and steal stacks of Social Security checks with a value of several thousand dollars.

We had to investigate every one of these stolen checks. Back then, the payee of the check had to submit a claim stating that their check had been stolen. Before they could receive a replacement check,

# STRUGGLE TO ZERO

the Secret Service had to submit a preliminary report, verifying that the payee's claim was valid. This process took time, and the payee had to go without their Social Security check until this investigation was completed. Many of these individuals really depended upon those checks on the third of each month. The thieves would steal the checks right out of the mailboxes. In Memphis, the mailbox would be attached to the front entrance to the house, and the checks in their brown envelopes could be seen by the thief from the street. As soon as the check was left in the mailbox by the mailman, the thief would run upon the front porch and take the check.

One hot August day, as I was interviewing an elderly gentleman at his residence, which was a rowhouse, regarding the theft of his Social Security check, he took his pocket knife and went to the closet and opened the door and sliced a piece of ham from a whole hanging ham, which was covered with maggots. He ate two or three pieces as if the maggots did not exist. He chowed down on the ham, paying no attention to the maggots. On Social Security check day, he stated that while he was sitting at the window waiting for the mailman to leave his check in the mailbox, which was located on the porch, he observed the mailman put his check into the mailbox. Before he could get outside to retrieve his check, a thief ran upon the porch and snatched it, then ran away down the street. The very elderly man literally chased the thief for more than a block without catching him, on this extremely hot, Memphis, August day.

One prolific US Government check thief/forger had a system worked out to get his stolen government checks cashed. He worked for a funeral home, and his duties consisted of recruiting dead bodies for the funeral home. Therefore, he was consistently driving over the Memphis streets hoping to talk the family of the deceased into using his funeral home for the burial. As he drove around on Social Security day, he would steal Social Security checks. He stole hundreds of checks prior to being charged. He and his partner in crime, a female, would go inside an Easy Way No. 3 food store at 103 Main Street, to get a Social Security check cashed that belonged to a female, named, say, Mary Smith. He was known around Memphis by numerous people due to his being involved in various civic movements during that period of time. He would stand behind the cashier as his accomplice came through the line with a few groceries.

Since the accomplice was paying for the groceries with the stolen Social Security check in the name of Mary Smith, He would say to the accomplice, "Good afternoon, Ms. Smith, how are you doing, today?" The cashier would assume that he and the accomplice knew each other. Therefore, the cashier would cash the stolen check. Finally, he was arrested and convicted for the theft, forgery, and cashing of numerous checks. During this period of time in Memphis, the US Government check forgers were stealing and cashing the black photo static copies of forged checks that had already been forged and cashed. Many of the store owners in the area trusted the US government checks so much that they would even cash the black photostatic copies, thinking that they had to be good because the US Government name appeared on the copy. So as a young agent, I always had fifty to one hundred criminal investigations assigned to me, plus, constantly being called away for protective assignments. My cases would pile up on my desk until I came back to deal with them. I was recommended for an award by the agent in charge for all my hard work, but headquarters would not approve it due to the fact that I had not been on the job long enough, in their minds. In other words, these awards were apparently for more experienced agents only.

My typical day at the office consisted of dictating reports for every case that was assigned to me, in view of the fact that a status report had to be submitted for each case, with the length of time between reports being determined by the type of case, such as forgery, counterfeiting, threats to kill the president, and others, etc. The threats against the president investigations had top priority, and reports must be forwarded to headquarters extremely frequently, such as immediately, within twenty-four hours, seven days, or two weeks, etc. So in between getting on a plane to go wherever, to assist in a presidential visit, after you came back to your office these criminal investigations had to be continued. Investigative reports involving defendants that had authorization to prosecute were dictated and forwarded to the US Attorney's Office, plus, after an arrest, many hours were spent in federal court, and at trials. Throughout my career, my writing skills were kept up to date. I was in the fast lane every minute of the day in order to stay up to date with my federal violation investigations, plus, assisting in presidential visits throughout the United States and other parts of the world. Memphis was a very busy city, when it came to crime.

Secret Service agents in our field offices which are located in cities throughout the United States and in certain foreign countries had to be very adaptable. Being a Secret Service agent is unlike any other federal law enforcement position. One day, I could be out in a rural area investigating a criminal violation, and literally the next day I would be on a plane headed wherever, to assist in a presidential visit. I had to go from one extreme culture to another, and be able to adapt to that particular situation.

During the summer of 1971, I was transferred to our headquarters in Washington, DC. Well, Stephanie, Becky (two-year-old daughter), and I took off to Washington for our next adventure/assignment. Stephanie was NOT very happy about going to Washington, as she had lived there for many years in the past. At times, our marriage was as shaky as a 9.5 earthquake, but it did survive and has survived fifty years. We did adjust to the Washington life, in view of the fact that we were going full steam ahead with our social and family life, which was NEVER boring. As the saying goes, a bored person is a boring person, and I NEVER wish to be boring.

# SECRET SERVICE HEADQUARTERS
# 1971–1977

During 1971, I was transferred from our Memphis Field Office to Secret Service Headquarters located at 1800 G Street, NW, Washington, DC. I was assigned to the Intelligence Division from 1971 to 1973. Our headquarters was physically located approximately two blocks from the White House. My first assignment in the Intelligence Division was on the duty desk, which consisted of taking threatening and unusual types of phone calls from individuals who had phoned the White House.

These calls were switched over to our phone lines by the White House switchboard operator. The White House switchboard operators would transfer these calls over to the Duty Desk, which were handled by Secret Service agents. These threatening type calls came from individuals located throughout the United States, and every now and then, from foreign countries. Sometimes the White House switchboard operator would mistakenly transfer a legitimate phone call to us, such as one night when I was on duty. My co-worker had a phone call transferred to him from the White House switchboard from an individual who stated he was a friend of President Nixon. This individual phoned the White House and requested to speak with President Nixon, but the operator thought it was a crank call. Therefore, she transferred it to our duty desk. My co-worker thought it was a crank call, and after many minutes into the conversation, this individual became extremely frustrated, and hung up. If the operator knew that this person was known to President Nixon, she probably would have connected his phone call to the proper White House office. Truthfully, the weird type calls would increase if there was a full moon. We knew that during a full moon we would be busier with unusual calls. Every Secret Service agent who would be on duty with me talked about the full moon, and the increase in activity.

Every now and then an individual would come to the White House, for example, from California, and appear at the White House fence located at the Northwest Gate, where uniformed officers were stationed. They would request to see the president, or to present him with a thick stack of handwritten pages regarding a grievance, or problem. An interview office was located at the Northwest Gate, and if the individual insisted upon seeing the president, or if he/she appeared to present a danger to themselves or others, the uniformed officer would phone our duty desk with this information.

Therefore, one of our agents would go to the Northwest Gate and personally interview the individual. Throughout the interview the agent would be making up his/her mind whether or not this individual appeared to present a danger to themselves, or others. If the agent determined that this individual appeared to present a danger to themselves, or others, the Metropolitan Police Department would be advised, and a patty wagon would come and take this individual to Saint Elizabeth's Hospital for a mental health evaluation. The attending psychiatrist would make a determination if this individual did, or did not appear to present a danger to themselves, or others. If not, the individual would be released, but if so, this individual would be confined for further evaluation, usually, for a period of several days. I interviewed an individual who attempted to perform oral sex on his own body. During other interviews individuals would scream, curse, and do unusual things. When I got back to my office, a detailed report of the interview had to be prepared in order to forward the information to the appropriate field office for further investigation.

After every full field investigation the assigned Secret Service agent had to make a determination as to whether the individual was, or was not a danger to the president. There could be no maybes. Enough information had to be obtained in order to make a decision, one way, or the other. While assigned to a field office, I worked very closely with associates, family members, and the mental health community, in order to be better informed prior to making the evaluation. The agent had to predict dangerous behavior in every one of these investigations, which can be very challenging. These threat investigations required a lot of interviewing skills and insight within the interviewing agent. On many occasions during an ongoing visit of the president, or others that we were protecting, I would receive information that a certain person had made a threatening remark directed against the president. I would immediately conduct an interview with this person and sometimes, on the spot, make a determination as to whether or not this person appeared to be a danger to the president. All this was taking place during the visit of the president to that particular city, or location. Obviously, the person making the threatening type statements would be under observation until the president left the area.

# STRUGGLE TO ZERO

| United States Department of Agriculture | Office of Inspector General | Investigations Southeast Region | 1447 Peachtree St., N.E. Room 901 Atlanta, GA 30309 |

August 17, 1988

David Ray
Special Agent-in-Charge
United States Secret Service
601 W. Broadway, Room 439
Louisville, KY 40202

Dear Mr. Ray:

This letter of appreciation is to express the gratitude of the Office of Inspector General - Investigations for the cooperation and expertise of Special Agent Donald G. Bell of your staff.

Special Agent Bell, upon receiving information of violations of the Food Stamp Program by employees of Program Management Systems, a private company which operates a $6,000,000 per month food stamp distribution contract for the State of Kentucky, notified OIG per the written agreement between our agencies.

Special Agent Bell coordinated a joint investigation with the Kentucky Attorney General's Office, OIG, and Secret Service. During the conduct of this joint investigation, Special Agent Bell cultivated sources through numerous contacts and months of investigation which resulted in the indictment of the General Manager and other employees of Program Management Systems.

Special Agent Bell, during the same period, assisted OIG in the investigation of the illegal distribution of USDA-donated commodities in the Louisville area.

This joint investigation has had a significant impact on USDA programs in the State of Kentucky and reflects highly on how well our agencies can work together for a common goal.

We in OIG want to commend Special Agent Bell for his professionalism, enthusiasm, and spirit of cooperation in the completion of the investigations. He is truly a credit to himself and to the United States Secret Service.

*[signature]*
RICHARD F. ALLEN
Regional Inspector General
 for Investigations

Letter of Accommodation from Richard F. Allen, Regional Inspector General for Investigations, US Department of Agriculture, Atlanta, GA.

# DON BELL

UNITED STATES DEPARTMENT OF JUSTICE
FEDERAL BUREAU OF INVESTIGATION

WASHINGTON, D.C. 20535

In Reply, Please Refer to
File No.

March 8, 1968

PERSONAL

Mr. Donald Gene Bell
Federal Bureau of Investigation
Memphis, Tennessee

Dear Mr. Bell:

    You exercised very poor judgment in a personal situation which occurred on February 23, 1968. The Bureau has carefully reviewed this matter, and your explanation has been considered. The circumstances clearly indicate that you did not behave in a manner consistent with the high standards expected of FBI employees.

    It will be incumbent upon you hereafter to conduct yourself in a more responsible manner so there will be no further basis for criticism of a similar nature.

Very truly yours,

John Edgar Hoover
Director

A personal letter from J. Edgar Hoover, Director, Federal Bureau of Investigation, known as one of his letters of censure, widely familiar to FBI employees.
The newspaper article that appeared in the Memphis Commercial Appeal Newspaper.

I always thought that these investigations were the most challenging to me, as an investigator. I thank my lucky stars that I was never wrong with one of my evaluations. Otherwise, I would be in front of a United States Senate committee explaining my decision. Therefore, I preferred the investigative part of my career, versus, the physical protection part. However, the physical protection part appealed to a large number of our agents, which is very understandable, due to the nature of the position, such as being in the public eye and constantly being watched by, and dealing with the news media. I believed that if I could identify threats to the president before the person making the threat had an opportunity to carry out this threat, I was doing my job. One of the unknowns as an agency, we never knew how many assassination attempts were prevented which never came to our attention, due to the excellent work of our agents.

While assigned to our Intelligence Division at US Secret Service Headquarters, one of the duties was to travel as a member of an advance team for presidential visits throughout the United States, and to foreign countries. One such assignment occurred during 1972, as a member of the advance team for President Nixon's visit to Ottawa, Canada. My duties were to work with the Royal Canadian Mounted Police involving any threats or incidents relating to President Nixon. The Vietnam War was beginning to wind down, but thousands of protesters gathered in front of the Parliament building with signs, and yelling at the top of their lungs. The only thing between the protesters and the entrance to the building was a rope and various security personnel, including Secret Service agents. They would lunge forward as if they might break the rope line, but they remained in their designated area.

However, a few months later, after a young man named Arthur Bremer was arrested in Laurel, Maryland, in an assassination attempt on a third party candidate, Governor George Wallace of Alabama, Bremer admitted that he had made an attempt to assassinate President Nixon during his visit to Ottawa, earlier that year. Bremer kept a very detailed handwritten diary, which was in his possession at the time of his arrest in Laurel, Maryland. In his diary, he stated that while in Ottawa, Canada, he tried to get a shot off at

President Nixon, but due to the fact there were so many long, black limo's, he could not determine which one was Nixon's. Therefore, his assassination attempt failed. He was so determined to assassinate a famous politician that he had thoughts of assassinating, for example, Senator George McGovern. He kept Governor George Wallace in his thoughts to assassinate. Well, he was not going to rest until he shot someone.

So down the line he goes. Remember, he was traveling around by himself in his old, I believe, grayish Nash Rambler car. After reading about Governor Wallace's political rally in Laurel, Maryland, he decided to go there and attempt to kill him. So Bremer gets to the rally and places himself along the rope line. After Governor Wallace finished his speech, Bremer began yelling for him to come over to his location, which he did. Wallace was supposed to go directly to his vehicle after his speech, but instead, he veers around and heads in Bremer's direction. As Wallace moved along the rope line and getting directly in front of Bremer, Bremer pulls out his pistol and fires five rounds at the governor. One of the bullets hit Secret Service Agent Nick Zarvos in the throat area, which disabled him. A staff person and an Alabama state trooper were also hit with a bullet. Bremer is subdued and taken to jail. Zarvos and Governor Wallace were taken to the hospital. It is noted that during this period of time I was assigned to our Headquarters Intelligence Division, and my private home was in Bowie, Maryland.

Later, after all the court proceedings, etc., were completed, Bremer's diary ended up in our Intelligence Division. The diary became public record as a result of the court proceedings. Arthur Bremer wanted notoriety and fame, regardless as to how he obtained it. He wanted his name to appear all over the news media, etc. Therefore, he was willing to sacrifice his life just to have this fame. This appears to be a fairly common thread among these assassins. Another common thread among these individuals is that they feel inadequate, when it comes to their sex life and their interaction with women. Bremer would frequent massage parlors and prostitutes in order to help build up his self-esteem when dealing with the opposite sex.

# STRUGGLE TO ZERO

The evening of the Watergate break-in occurred while I was assigned to our Intelligence Division. Two of our agents from the Washington Field Office were dispatched to the Watergate condo complex, due to the fact the burglary occurred in the Democratic National Headquarters, which was located in that complex. Our interest was obvious, since this was an election year and the Secret Service protected both Democrat and Republican candidates for president of the United States. After coming back from this assignment, the agents arrived in our Intelligence Division, explaining that they smelled a rat regarding the burglary. Something was definitely unusual.

During 1973, I, and another agent was assigned as the liaison representatives with the US Department of State. Their headquarters building was located in Foggy Bottom. Our office was physically located on the same floor and down the hall from the national news media offices. President Nixon signed an Executive Order giving the Secret Service the authority to provide protection to Dr. Henry Kissinger during the period of time that he was Secretary of State. Dr. Kissinger did not want any other agency to provide his physical protection. The State Department Security had always provided the physical protection for the Secretary of State.

So one could surmise that having the Secret Service come in and take over the protection duties, did not set well with State Department Security. However, I did everything possible to make things run smoothly, because I knew how I would feel if I were in the same situation. In the end, everything worked out well. After Dr. Kissinger was no longer Secretary of State, State Department Security picked right up and began protecting future Secretaries of State. I have nothing negative to say about Dr. Henry Kissinger. He has been an historical asset to our country. My job was to coordinate with the Secretary of State's staff, and be involved with making advance arrangements for visits of foreign heads of state that would visit the Secretary of State, or attend the many state dinners that were held for visiting heads of state. I recall a visit by Emperor Haile Selassie of Ethiopia. He had a very short and thin physical frame. At that time he was very old and frail looking. He was such an interesting looking character.

Many heads of state visited the State Department for one reason or the other, such as former First Lady Mamie Eisenhower. Dr. Henry Kissinger was the Secretary of State during my time as the liaison representative. One of his aides/assistants was Larry Eagleburger, who was later appointed Secretary of State by President Bush 41. Secretary Kissinger always let his presence be known around his office. He was not shy in expressing his feelings if one of his staffers screwed up. However, he was a very interesting person who was very intelligent, respected, and well-liked by those who knew him. His presence as a public official created more interest in our federal government. He provided many interesting news stories that were welcomed during that period of time, which was the Vietnam War era. He was not a stiff neck or stuffed shirt type. He was down to earth, which could be unusual, in view of the fact that he was so brilliant and well educated. One somewhat amusing antidote that occurred, I believe, during 1973, while on a visit to West Germany. Secretary Kissinger met with the Prime Minister of South Africa in a large resort hotel located about five miles from the Czechoslovakia border. I was sent to assist in his protection for this visit. Early one morning, while at the hotel he came up to the outside casual dining area in his night clothes, which was located on the top floor in a private area near his suite, inquiring about his breakfast. Anyway, he was so typically down to earth. He wanted his breakfast now. When the breakfast arrived, consisting of, I believe, two European style poached eggs (in their shell), he was happy. He knew exactly how to properly tackle those eggs. Many people think that Dr. Kissinger is a national treasure, and wish him well, hoping that he remains with us for many years to come.

While as the State Department liaison representative, the anti-Vietnam war demonstrators would gather next to the Main State Building and demonstrate. I observed Jane Fonda standing on a flatbed truck yelling and screaming against the war in her green fatigues and a green cap. During this period of time anti-war demonstrators were everywhere in the city of Washington. Tent cities would go up, and thousands of disheveled looking individuals with long, greasy hair, were observed everywhere.

I had numerous requests to obtain special tours of the White House for individuals and families while assigned to our Liaison Division. These individuals were mostly members or friends of law enforcement, or someone who was a family member of Secret Service employees. Many were just friends of someone who knew someone that knew about my ability to get them on the special or congressional tour of the White House. I was not happy to receive these requests because frankly, they were a real pain in the ass. I had to be at the East Gate of the White House by 7:00 AM to meet the party. I signed them in on the roster and they were given a tour in a small group, without waiting in the long general public line. This was a BIG favor to the people. On many mornings, I had to travel from my residence in rain, snow and sleet just to do these individuals a favor. I did this out of kindness because I would want someone to do the same for me. I was responsible for hundreds of average people getting a great tour of the White House during the four years I was in the Liaison Division. Guess what? I do not recall ever receiving a true thank you from anyone. I may have received one or two, but I do not recall any. Remember the statement "no good deed goes unpunished." I have been punished so many times in my life by doing good deeds that I could write a book about them. However, this is the real life.

Another one of my duties as the liaison representative to the State Department was to handle and expedite the diplomatic passports that our Secret Service agents needed, prior to their traveling to foreign countries with a protectee, such as the president. All Secret Service agents traveled with a diplomatic passport. I would be responsible for getting visas for each passport, from each respective country. Numerous times I would need to physically take passports to the embassy of the country that would be visited by the protectee. All passports that needed visas had to be coordinated through the US Passport Office, which was headed by Ms. Frances Knight. Ms. Knight was a permanent fixture as director of the US Passport Office.

She and FBI Director J. Edgar Hoover were close friends, possibly due to their many, many, many, many years in office. It was rumored that they would set and talk, and yap with each other at great length about the state of affairs, etc. In other words, they would gossip.

Continuing as the state department liaison representative, I received a phone call from the great granddaughter of James J. Brooks, a former director of the Secret Service, who informed me that during the search of the attic in the old family home in Maryland, she came across many Secret Service documents that belonged to him when he was the director of the Secret Service during the 1870s. These documents included his handwritten daily reports, letters addressed to Edwin Stanton, President Lincoln's Secretary of War, photographs of criminals, plus, other various documents that Director Brooks had stored after he retired. Director Brooks's great granddaughter was currently employed in the main state building. She wanted to give all these documents and materials to the Secret Service. I met with her, and she gave me these materials. I then turned these documents over to Secret Service headquarters, where they are on display as a part of the tour through our headquarters. Today, more than likely, no one would know where these documents came from.

I was a member of the advance team for a visit by President Nixon to Flint, Michigan. His purpose for being there was to dedicate a high school, which bore his name. I was standing on the tarmac, waiting for Air Force One to land, along with members of the White House advance team. As Air Force One was on final approach, one White House advance team member became so uptight and nervous that he pissed in his pants. The weather was very warm, and he was wearing a light tan suit. Therefore, the wet spot had to be covered up, immediately. Luckily, a light raincoat was located and the advance staffer put it on and wore it until the wet spot dried. Working as a White House staff member could obviously be very stressful.

Another incident occurred while I was assigned to assist with visits by foreign heads of state, who attended the United Nations General Assembly, In New York City. Numerous heads of state would converge on New York City, during this period of time. One such visit that I helped out with, was when Nasser Arafat, head of the PL0 (Palestine Liberation Organization) gave a speech before the UN General Assembly, while his pistol was very visible, hanging on his belt. He was not a poplar individual here in the United States. He stayed overnight at the Waldorf-Astoria Hotel, and after his speech, he left the U. immediately. Secret Service agents were the only Americans at the airport for his departure. My only role in this visit was assisting in his arrival at the hotel. Agent Jerry Parr was the agent in charge of his detail. Later in his career, in March 1981, after the assassination attempt, Agent Parr detected that President Reagan had been shot as they raced back to the White House. After detecting blood on the president's body, Parr then directed that President Reagan be taken to the George Washington University Medical Center instead of the White House. Agent Jerry Parr was an extremely nice, competent, and well-respected Secret Service agent.

Another assignment I had was to assist in the protection of the Foreign Minister of Israel during his visit to New York City during the 1970s. He stayed in the Plaza Hotel, one of the best in the city. He brought a few security types with him, consisting of young soldiers in the Israeli army. The reason the Secret Service protected the Foreign Minister of Israel was due to the fact President Nixon signed an Executive Order authorizing this protection. During this period of time, the Arab terrorists were blowing up airplanes, etc., and President Nixon felt that some of the non-heads of state should have Secret Service protection. This protection was not permanent. Anyway, each morning the hotel staff would bring breakfast for the foreign minister and his staff. They put the food in a side room right outside the suite. Bacon was always one of the foods included in the menu. Well, the bacon disappeared first. I learned that bacon was an international food, apparently liked by almost every human being on earth, regardless of their religious beliefs.

Washington, DC, during the 1970s, was a very active city, both politically and historically. Along with everything else that was happening, such as the ending of the Vietnam war, the politicians on Capitol Hill were constantly in the news for the wrong reasons. Congressman Wilbur Mills, of Arkansas, who was chairman of the house Ways and Means Committee, had an ongoing romantic relationship with an exotic strip dancer, Fannie Foxe, a native of

Argentina. One night, at 2:00 AM, on October 9, 1974, while they were driving very close to the Tidal Basin, Mills stopped his car and turned the lights off. Both were tipsy. Upon observing this suspicious driving, a US Park police officer drove up to inquire about their driving behavior. As their car stopped, and after observing the US Park Police car, Fannie Foxe opened her door and ran, jumping into the Tidal Basin.

After being pulled out, the police officer noted that Mills had cuts on his nose and he was determined to be intoxicated. It was later reported that Mills and Foxe had been fighting, and Foxe hit him between the eyes causing the cuts to his nose. Fannie Foxe was well known at the Silver Slipper strip club at 815 Thirteenth Street, NW, as being billed as the "Argentine Firecracker." Her real name was Annabell Ballistella, age thirty-eight. The officer apparently drove Mills home. Mills was known for having too many drinks, far too often. Foxe was lucky that she was rescued from the Tidal Basin. The news media had a field day with this story. At that time many silly jokes were floating around the city, such as "where was Carl Albert," the current Speaker of the House of Representatives, when Fannie Fox landed in the Tidal Basin? The answer was, "in the glove compartment," due to the fact that Speaker Albert was an extremely short man. She was not hurt, just soaking wet. Two months later Congressman Mills resigned from Congress.

Another very powerful US Congressman that became a household name during this period of time 1976, was Wayne Hays, a longtime Congressman from the state of Ohio. He hired a young, good looking female, Elizabeth Ray, to a $14,000-a-year position, just to be his mistress. Later, he resigned from Congress. Again, this story generated an enormous amount of news media publicity. It was common knowledge among the US Capitol police officers that I came in contact with, when I was the US Secret Service liaison representative to Capitol Hill, that Congressman Hays considered certain women to be his private stock. No one should attempt to make time with them. On occasion, I would be having a conversation with the Capitol police officers on the House side entrance, which was located on the ground floor under the main steps. Whenever certain good looking females came through the entrance, an officer would mention, "that one, or that one," was Congressman Hays' private "squeeze," and she would be "off limits." As a result of his scandal he resigned from Congress. Man, was Washington, DC, ever active during the decade of the 1970s. This whole infidelity, sexual thing among members of Congress was definitely a non-partisan thing. The Republican male members of Congress appeared to have a stronger sexual drive than most Democrats.

In addition to being the liaison representative with the US State Department and Capitol Hill, I was the backup Secret Service liaison representative to the Central Intelligence Agency. I would go over to their headquarters from time to time to resolve or handle matters that arose between our agencies. My deceased father-in-law, Harry Frederick Weber retired from the CIA in 1969. Harry is buried in one of the most beautiful gravesites at Arlington National Cemetery, Washington, DC. His gravesite is almost directly in line with the Lincoln Memorial, Washington Monument, and the US Capitol. He was a World War II naval intelligence officer, prior to becoming a CIA agent. His last overseas tour of duty was in Saigon, and in the Vietnam jungles disbursing funds to village chiefs. He was given many Viet Cong ears that had been cut off by his South Vietnamese "troops," as a token of their successes in killing the Viet Kong.

During his career he observed and photographed beheadings in Kabul, Afghanistan, and was confined to his quarters for three months during the revolution in Yemen. Also, he had a tour of duty in Port Said, Egypt. My spouse, Stephanie, currently possesses many color 35mm photos of the Kabul beheadings that her father took in the early 1960s, or late 1950s. The family of the person to be beheaded could pay the executioner a sum of money to sever the head with only one whack, instead of taking several whacks to sever the head from the body. However, if the family was poor, the executioner would normally take several whacks before the head would fall off. Sometimes, heads would be hung in trees to rot if no one claimed the body. Stephanie's dad, Harry, was a "hoot." He earned his master's degree from George Washington University, Washington, DC, during the 1930s.

Also, he was a very good artist. His first spouse, my mother-in-law, was also employed by the CIA. She would attend various CIA-related functions/conferences, in DC, and as a result, she met this true blue blood Philadelphia lawyer who also came to DC, on Department of Justice business. They got hooked up, and when Stephanie was fifteen years of age, in 1958, her mother married the lawyer. His father was a federal judge in the Philadelphia, area, who had been appointed by President Herbert Hoover. Also, he was a US Congressman during the 1920s, and owned five acres of beachfront property in Bermuda. My mother-in-law thought that she had found her type of guy due to the fact he was a member of the Merion Golf Club, in Ardmore, PA. Merion was always rated as being one of the top ten golf clubs in the world. She wanted to climb up the social ladder and he was her ticket. He divorced his spouse, with their four children, and married my mother-in-law. However, they deserved each other. Prior to his death at the age of eighty, he became an alcoholic. The booze screwed up his brain, causing him to do weird things, such as running around the parking lot at his apartment complex, nude, keying cars. After this incident, his oldest daughter checked him into a very upscale, locked, assisted living facility, until he met the Grim Reaper. We took my mother-in-law her back to Kentucky with us. She lived to be ninety years of age. So much for the greener grass on the other side of the fence.

# STRUGGLE TO ZERO

# DON BELL

Donald G. Bell
in recognition of your contribution to the summit meetings preceding President Nixon's visit to the People's Republic of China and the Union of Soviet Socialist Republics

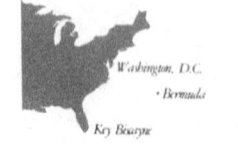

"...We are moving with history and moving history ourselves..."

December 6, 1971 – January 7, 1972

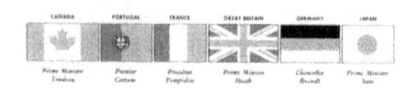

# STRUGGLE TO ZERO

Bell's first presidential assignment was with Harry Truman at his home in Independence.

these powerful men do when outside the public eye. For the Secret Service to do its job there must be that trust between the person being guarded and those responsible for his well-being.

Not to mention, that to Bell's way of thinking it is just plain wrong wallow in gossip.

"Sure you are aware of some personal things about their lives," Bell said from his Abington Woods Circle home in western Indian River County. "I would never speak of them myself. I would just feel like I had violated a trust."

Bell, 71, says he has been lucky in getting this front row seat to history. He is still figuring out what he wants to do with all the memorabilia he has collected. Among those items are two biographies of Harry Truman autographed for Bell and his wife by the 33rd President, an autographed head shot of Vice President Spiro Agnew, a picture from his time with the FBI of then Attorney General Robert Kennedy standing on top of his desk surrounded by Washington D.C. school children and Bell in the background.

These are things Bell never dreamed he would possess growing up with his 10 brothers and sisters traveling rural Kentucky and Tennessee with his mother and Methodist preacher father.

"I never realized I would blunder into all these things," he said. "I was just like a bumper car at the carnival."

Bell started his career in 1958 two weeks after graduating from his rural high school in western Tennessee. He moved alone to Washington, D.C. to take a clerical position at the FBI headquarters.

"My paycheck was $45 a week," he said, noting he stayed at a guest house on 13th and Massachusetts for $60 a month that included two meals a day.

From his clerical position, Bell moved on to providing FBI Tours for tourists and sometimes the friends of Director J. Edgar Hoover and Attorney General Robert Kennedy, who had offices on the same floor at the Department of Justice.

Despite all his other accomplishments, Bell seems most proud of his stint as the 21-year-old head coach of the FBI's girls' basketball team. "We won the league competing against U.S. government agencies," he said with obvious pride.

Despite rubbing shoulders with some of Washington's power brokers, Bell determined he needed a college education if he were to achieve anything in life.

"I realized I could spend the rest of my life being around these famous people," he said. "But it would not make me successful."

So in 1962 he returned to Kentucky and earned a Bachelor of Science degree at Murray State University in Social Science with a minor in English. He would later earn a Master's from George Washington University in Washington, D.C.

After a stint in the Marine Corps Reserves, Bell returned to the FBI in Memphis and took another non-agent position working as a night security clerk. He was on duty the night Martin Luther King was shot in Memphis.

It was Bell who received King's bloody clothes and prepared them to be sent to the FBI headquarters in Washington as part of the investigation.

Bell's next move was down the hall to join the Secret Service field office in Memphis in December of 1968. He has been steeped in the tradition and history of the agency ever since.

"The Secret Service was created on April 14, 1865 by President Lincoln on the morning he was shot at Ford's Theatre," Bell said. "He created the Secret Service at the time because almost half the paper currency circulating in the United States was counterfeit, so the Secret Service was formed to investigate counterfeiting operations."

Bell said he would have as many as a 100 cases involving counterfeiting of U.S. currency, open at any one time. At the same time he would be ordered to participate in the agency's other important function of guarding the President.

His first such assignment was to provide backup help in 1969 for former President Harry Truman at his home in Independence, Mo.

"I was 29 at the time and you can imagine what it was like to be around someone like Harry Truman," Bell said. "He was such a humble man. He lived in a three-story white frame house with no air condition-

He is most proud of coaching the FBI's girls' basketball team to the league championship.

Among the presidents Bell protected were Richard Nixon and Jimmy Carter.

125

However, after my mother-in-law divorced Harry, he decided that to hell with it all. His second spouse was half French and half Tunisian. While Harry was confined to his quarters in Yemen during their revolution for three months, she was residing in Aden, Yemen. She met a British naval officer and did they ever have an affair. After getting out of Yemen, Harry located her lover and convinced him to hand write a confession regarding their affair. A copy of this confession is currently being filed away with his various documents in our home. Obviously, they got divorced. Harry's next wife was Vietnamese. He met her in Saigon while he was stationed there with the CIA. She was only nineteen when they got married. He was able to get her family out of Vietnam prior to the fall of Saigon. She ended up filing for divorce. She actually cared for him more than any of his five wives. Harry could be a son of a bitch to live with. His fourth wife was half French and half Vietnamese. He met her in Spain after he retired from the CIA. They got married and eventually she filed for divorce.

She was also very young trapeze artist. His fifth wife was Indian. She also filed for divorce. Out of his five wives they never bore any children and he never paid any alimony, except to his first, my mother-inlaw. I assume that all of them were happy to get out of the marriage. My spouse was his only child. Three of Harry's wives were younger than their step mother, my spouse. It was somewhat awkward when Harry would visit us with his young wives. They would wear these extremely short mini-skirts, and dress similar to the teens. Harry died during 1989, while residing in Rockville, MD. While in the hospital, he was "grabbing" at the nurses when they came into his hospital room. Also, on his dresser in his condo, a receipt from an escort service for over $800 was found.

Two weeks prior to his death he went out on the town for one evening. I hoped that he enjoyed himself. Since he was cremated, the funeral director advised us to go to Bloomingdale's to purchase an inexpensive vase that could be used as an urn, instead of paying several hundred dollars to them for an "Urn." While at Bloomingdale's, and as we were looking at various vases, the sales lady asked us what we wanted to do with the vase. My spouse, Stephanie, told her calmly that it was to hold her deceased father's ashes. Did the saleslady ever look shocked? Anyway, we dropped the vase off at the funeral home, and later that evening Harry's ashes were delivered to us in the vase at his condo. The ashes were still warm and we had to keep them overnight, since his funeral service was the next morning at Arlington National Cemetery. Having those warm ashes in the condo overnight was somewhat unusual and attention getting, but there was no other choice.

Vice President Spiro T. Agnew resigned on October 10, 1973, and President Nixon resigned on August 9, 1974. Gerald Ford, the Majority Leader of the House of Representatives became Nixon's vice president, replacing Agnew, and after President Nixon resigned, Ford became President, and the former Governor of New York, Nelson Rockefeller, became his vice president. There was a total re-shuffling of the leaders of our country. My co-worker who was the assistant agent in charge of the Secret Service Liaison Division was in charge of keeping the President Nixon White House tapes secure. In addition, he was the agent in charge of the Henry Kissinger Detail during the period of time that Kissinger was involved in all the secret talks in connection with the ending of the Vietnam War. President Nixon signed an Executive Order for Kissinger to have Secret Service protection. Win Lawson, the agent in charge of the Liaison Division was the lead advance Secret Service Agent for President Kennedy's visit to Dallas, Texas. These two agents were very decent individuals. I worked in the same office with both of them for approximately two years. I do not recall Win ever losing his temper or using bad language. He was a true gentleman at all times.

As a result of the Watergate investigation and resignation of President Nixon, Congress passed what is called the Privacy Act of 1974. This gave every employee the right to view their personnel file. Prior to the Privacy Act one could retrieve, or obtain information from someone's medical file, such as that person's psychological profile. An example was when psychological information was obtained from US Senator Thomas Eagleton's medical file, which caused him to withdraw for consideration to be on the ticket with US Senator George McGovern as his vice presidential nominee.

During the years 1975–1977, I was assigned as the Secret Service Headquarters Liaison Representative with the US Department of

Justice, which included all their headquarters offices such as the FBI, US Marshal's Office, and the Drug Enforcement Administration. In addition to these agencies, I was also assigned to several other agencies, commissions, and boards, such as the Federal Aviation Administration. One of the routine situations that I was personally involved with, was during the period of time that the FAA changed the firearms policy, from allowing only Secret Service and FBI agents to carry a firearm aboard an airplane, to allowing other law enforcement types to carry a weapon aboard airplanes. I was the go between, and assisted in relaying information between the Secret Service and the FAA. A copy of all reports regarding FAA violations would be forwarded to my desk for informational purposes. No aircraft was allowed to fly over areas designated by the FAA as restricted areas. Every now and then as the commercial airplanes were on final approach to Reagan National Airport they would veer into the no fly zone, mostly, as a mistake or unintentionally, by the flight crew. Regardless, a report had to be composed by the FAA and forwarded to the Secret Service. I had to review all these reports, as routine duties.

During 1976, while assigned to our headquarters Liaison Division, I was involved in the protection of the President of France, Giscard d'Estaing, during his state visit to the United States during the period of time the US was celebrating our two hundredth birthday. He arrived at Andrews Air Force Base, Maryland, aboard an Air France Concorde aircraft, the first supersonic plane to land in the US. Prior to his visit, this type of aircraft had never landed in the US. I was assigned to President d'Estaing's Secret Service detail during his visit. He attended a Texas style barbecue on a ranch eighty miles outside Houston, and in attendance were many guests in the space industry, including Alan Shepherd, etc. Aboard the Concorde, from Andrews Air Force Base to Houston, Texas, was Senator Lloyd Bensten, who was over six feet tall. The inside of the Concorde was very small, and low. In fact, it reminded me of being inside a toothpaste tube with wings, since Senator Bensten could not stand straight up without his head touching the ceiling. The captain of the Concorde had to fly at a speed below the sound barrier. During climb out, it felt as if the nose of the plane went straight up, as perhaps, being in a rocket.

I was among the first group of Americans to fly on a supersonic jet plane inside the United States. President d' Estaing also made a stop in Jamestown, VA, during his visit. This was just one of those small insignificant firsts that I was involved in during my career.

One of my many duties as the liaison representative at FBI headquarters was to present an award or recognition plaque to certain FBI employees. The one ceremony that I recall, vividly, was presenting a Secret Service Director's award/plaque to FBI Agent Ed Armbruster. Agent Armbruster was, at that time the oldest active FBI agent in the United States. He was eighty-four years of age. The normal mandatory retirement age for FBI agents was fifty-seven years of age. The cut-off age for becoming an agent was thirty-seven years of age. Therefore, in order to get the minimum number of years, which was twenty, the applicant had to be hired prior to the thirty-seventh birthday. Agent Armbruster investigated cases and from time to time he would walk over to Secret Service Headquarters. He worked out of the FBI Washington Field Office, twelfth and Pennsylvania Avenue. He would also walk to the White House on business. He wore a light colored fedora hats and double breasted suits.

Every now and then, I would observe him walking on the street near his office, heading toward the White House, or to our headquarters. FBI Director J. Edgar Hoover convinced Congress and the Executive Branch many years ago, that due to the nature of the FBI responsibilities, it should be exempt from the regular civil service personnel rules and regulations. Therefore, with the stroke of Hoover's pen, he could exempt any FBI agent from the normal mandatory retirement age. However, Hoover exempted himself and that was the only reason that he remained Director past his seventieth birthday. For whatever reason, Hoover exempted Agent Armbruster from the mandatory retirement age. The FBI could fire an employee for any reason deemed necessary due to the fact that no Civil Service rules applied. The fired employee had no recourse, whatsoever. Hoover had such strict opposition to any male employee being in the presence of a female in an apartment or under the same roof, for whatever reason. He was totally against heterosexual males and heterosexual females being together in a situation where they may, or could possibly have any sexual contact.

Heavens to Betsy, if you stayed overnight under the same roof with a female! According to the strict rules, if another FBI employee had knowledge of this happening, this employee had an obligation to report you. If this happened, you WERE fired, without any recourse. This was very weird. Director Hoover had absolute power over FBI employees until the day he died. I am convinced that Hoover's ghost lingered around the hallways of FBI headquarters for some time after his death, and possibly to this day. He was a master at presenting the perfect image of himself and the FBI, to the public. In other words, he was a master at organizational psychology. Many of his subordinates who were in high positions would never question him. Therefore, one can see how things might get out of hand, such as false speculation, etc. Rumors and false impressions ran rampant. One example was given in Cartha D. "Deke" De Loach's book, HOOVER'S FBI, The Inside Story by Hoover's Trusted Lieutenant. Mr. De Loach stated in his book that a memo came across Hoover's desk, and after reading it, he wrote a brief comment on the memo, stating "Watch the borders." The memo was then forwarded to where it was supposed to end up, with this comment. This comment threw everyone into a "tizzy," due to the fact it was interpreted to mean watch the borders of the United States. Everyone was trying to figure out which borders to watch, since the US border is very long. Instead of just asking Hoover what he meant by "watch the borders," everyone was afraid to ask, and the speculation got out of hand. However, Hoover only meant that the person typing the memo should not get the margin too close to the BORDER, on the page. Hoover probably did not realize how his image was portrayed by his own employees, because no one would question him. They were afraid they might lose their job, or be demoted.

Richard Paul Pavlick, a retired US Postal worker from the Boston, MA, area, lined his car with dynamite and parked it across the street from President-elect Kennedy's residence, in Palm Beach, FL. He was waiting for Kennedy to leave his residence for Sunday Mass. Pavlick's plan was to ram his vehicle into Kennedy's vehicle, thus, killing both of them. However, after seeing that Kennedy had his entire family with him, he changed his mind and did not go through with his plan. He wanted to kill Kennedy, only, and not any members of his family. He decided that he would try again, in the future, to kill President-elect Kennedy.

Thomas Murphy, Pavlick's Belmont, New Hampshire, postmaster, became suspicious of the various postmarks on Pavlick's bizarre postcards that he mailed to Murphy. There was a pattern of Pavlick being in the same general area as President-elect Kennedy, dotting the landscape, as Kennedy traveled. Murphy notified the local authorities, who, in turn, notified the United States Secret Service. As a result of the postmaster's information, Pavlick was located and admitted to the bizarre/threatening correspondence, plus, he admitted that he had attempted to kill Kennedy in Palm Beach, Florida. After Pavlick was arrested, seven sticks of dynamite were located inside his vehicle. He was committed to a mental institution on 01/27/1961, and was released on 12/13/1966, being declared legally insane. The charges were dropped, upon his release. Pavlick was born on 02/13/1887, and died in the Veterans Hospital, Manchester, New Hampshire, on 11/11/1975. He was the oldest attempted assassin on record, at that time.

After Pavlick turned eighty years of age, FBI Headquarters notified Secret Service Headquarters that they had automatically purged his criminal file when he had turned eighty years. However, due to the fact that Pavlick was still active with his threatening letters to the President when he turned eighty years of age, Secret Service headquarters had to reconstruct a file on Pavlick for the FBI. After Pavlick died I notified FBI Headquarters of his death, since I was the liaison representative. Thankfully, the FBI could permanently purge Pavick's file. Until his death, Pavlick, a Florida "snowbird," would write threatening letters to the president and travel from his residence in New Hampshire to the Palm Beach, Florida, area, in his old camper pickup truck. Upon arriving in Washington, DC, in his camper, he would drive around and around the White House. The White House police officers would phone over to our Intelligence Division, advising the duty agent that Pavlick was in the area. This became the standard procedure from year to year until he FINALLY died on 11/11/1975. Upon hearing of his death, everyone in the Intelligence Division gave a HUGE sigh of relief due to the fact that Pavlick had been such a headache throughout the years, from 1960 until 1975. The man lived for 88 years. When I was assigned to our Intelligence Division, I recall very well our duty desk receiving the phone call from our White House police officers that "Pavlick is in the area." After driving around the White House several times he would then head south for Florida.

While assigned to our Intelligence Division from 1971 to 1972, I became familiar with one of our Subjects named Samuel Byck, due to the fact the case agent in Philadelphia, PA, had evaluated him as being a danger to the president due to previous threats he had made against the president, who at that time was Richard Nixon. Whenever someone is evaluated as being a danger to our protectees, their whereabouts must be determined at all times. For obvious reasons, these individuals cannot be under twenty-four hour surveillance seven days a week. The Secret Service did not have the personnel to provide this type of surveillance due to the many subjects throughout the United States in this threat category. However, during a visit to the area by a protectee, these subjects are placed under surveillance until the protectee leaves the area. Also, these individuals who are considered to be a danger to the president are personally interviewed by the case agent every three months, for a reevaluation.

On February 22, 1974, unknown to our agents in Philadelphia, Samuel Byck got into his car and drove to the Baltimore-Washington Airport with his tape recorder running, recording in detail his trip to his destination, which was the airport. He mentioned that the US Small Business Administration was corrupt, due to the fact they turned him down for a business loan. He stated further that he was a manic-depressive who was forty-three years of age, and seventy pounds overweight. He stated that the United States was a fascist state and that Nixon should be impeached. Byck stole a .22 cal. Revolver from a friend, plus, he made a bomb out of two jugs of gasoline and an igniter. He stated on the tape that his intention was to skyjack an airplane at the airport, make the pilot fly the plane to

# STRUGGLE TO ZERO

Washington, DC, kill the pilot, and from that point on, he would steer the plane into the White House, killing the President. He said he wanted to create as much havoc and inflict as much damage as possible. He believed that the Watergate scandal did not cleanse the country, but when the skyjacked airplane filled with gasoline hit the White House, the corruption would be cleansed by the fire that would erupt. Byck went on to say that he felt as insignificant as one grain of sand on the Atlantic Ocean and that he had rather be a lion for one day, than a sheep for one hundred years. He stated that after he died, he would miss HIMSELF.

When Byck arrived at the Baltimore-Washington Airport, he saw a Delta Airlines DC-9 airplane parked outside the closest gate, ready to take off. On his way to rushing toward the gate, he shot and killed an airport police officer, then ran aboard the plane and killed the co-pilot. He then wounded the captain after he was told that they could not take off until the wheel blocks were removed. Then, he grabbed a passenger and ordered her to fly the plane, plus, telling a flight attendant to close the door or he would blow up the plane. The Anne Arundel police officers attempted to shoot out the plane tires with their .38 cal. pistols, but the bullets ricocheted off the tires and hit the wings. Eventually, a police officer stormed the plane and fired four shots through the door and two shots went through a window, wounding Byck with a .357 Magnum that the officer retrieved from the deceased airport police officer. Before the police could get to Byck, he had already committed suicide by shooting himself in the head. His last words were, "help me," according to one of the police officers. Byck's briefcase, which was found under his body, contained the gasoline bomb.

I recall an incident that occurred while assigned to assist in protective assignments for various foreign heads of state, during their visit to the United Nations General Assembly, New York City. In between assignments, I would work in our command post located in one of the hotels, waiting for the next assignment. We would sometimes work twelve hour shifts. One evening myself, and three other agents drove down to Little Italy for dinner. As we were on our way back, I was sitting next to the rear passenger side window. While attempting to merge right, in heavy traffic, a vehicle with three or four younger males sped up in an attempt to prevent us from merging. Our vehicles were no more than three feet apart, and as their vehicle merged right next to ours, the driver raised his arm with a pistol in his hand, pointing it directly at us, indicating that he was not going to let us merge. Hell, this got our attention very quickly, and we decided to go ahead and let them merge right in front of our vehicle, which was a Secret Service vehicle with a police radio in it.

We radioed our command post and advised them to give this information the New York City Police Department. When we arrived at the intersection at Houston Street, which was near the UN Building, directly across the intersection, facing our vehicle, we noticed two or three yellow cabs facing us. All of a sudden several plain clothed police types jumped out of the cabs and ran up to the vehicle with the males that we had followed. We had always stayed directly behind their vehicle until we reached the intersection at Houston Street. There was much commotion right in the middle of the intersection, with traffic/buses stopped in all four directions. Upon a search of the car trunk, three or four weapons were found. The males were arrested and taken away. It was, and may be now, customary, for the NYPD to travel around the city in cabs in order not to arouse suspicion.

In addition, while assigned on another foreign head of state protective detail at the Waldorf-Astoria Hotel, New York City, an incident occurred at approximately 2:00 AM. I was on the mid-night shift, and the hotel corridors were very quiet. All of a sudden, very loud screams from a female running down the hallway in the next corridor. Another agent and I walked over there, and observed a female with blood all over her face. A male acquaintance was also there. According to the male acquaintance, he rented a suite at the hotel, paying $33,000, per year. This rental price was the 1970s rate. On this particular evening, he did not have a date, and as he was flipping thought his little black book, he happened to run across this female's phone number. He phoned her and asked her to come over, which she did. As the night progressed, the female began to pressure the male for money, which, according to him, he resisted. The argument turned into a fight, and the male punched the female in her nose, causing blood to gush out.

She then ran out of his suite, and down the hallway screaming. The hotel security and police came and took care of the situation. The reason that we had an interest in this situation was that we wanted to make certain our protectee was not in any type of danger.

I was assigned to our headquarters for approximately six years. Two years in our Intelligence Division and four in our Liaison Division. I finally decided that I needed a change of venue. I had a personal meeting with my assistant director, who asked me what I wanted to do. I could have chosen to remain in DC, to pursue future promotions, but I had grown tired of the Washington scene. I decided to forgo any promotions, and requested to be transferred to our Louisville, KY, field office, for a quieter, relaxing location. Man, was I ever wrong. I soon learned that quieter more relaxing assignments did not existed in the Secret Service. I was totally in the fast lane until I walked out of my office, on the day I retired. However, I had to work three additional hours on my retirement date in order to make certain that I did not leave any unfinished work for anyone in the office. Eventually, the workload was so heavy that I could not return phone calls when they should have been returned.

Prior to relocating to Louisville, KY, I was honored with a luncheon hosted by FBI Associate Director Jim Adams, in the FBI director's new private dining room located in the new FBI headquarters building on Pennsylvania Avenue across the street from the old FBI headquarters building, which is the Department of Justice building. I was the FIRST law enforcement type to be honored in the dining room. The FBI personnel who attended included Associate Director Jim Adams, Ben Cook, Bob Moore and others. Ben Cook was later transferred as the special agent in charge of their Louisville Field Office. Bob Moore was my FBI liaison counterpart. At this time, the Honorable Griffin Bell was the Attorney General. He was appointed by President Carter. While the servers were preparing for the luncheon they stated that they were under the impression the luncheon was for Attorney General Griffin Bell, not Don Bell. I have always gotten a chuckle out of that. Anyway, I thought it was an honor to be the first law enforcement type to be honored in this way by the FBI, and being hosted by the number two person in the FBI.

I received a very nice professional letter of appreciation dated January 28, 1977, from Assistant Attorney General Richard Thornburg (later became governor of Pennsylvania). In his letter, which was addressed to the Director of the Secret Service, Mr. Thornburgh stated, in part, "We wish to take this opportunity to call your attention to the exemplary assistance that Special Agent Donald G. Bell has furnished this Department. During the past two years, Mr. Bell has contributed greatly to our understanding of your Service's functions and problems. He has promptly and efficiently handled our requests for information, thereby, fulfilling an invaluable function in assisting our Department and your Service in defusing situations threatening the welfare of those receiving Secret Service protection. In all his dealings with this Department, Mr. Bell has exhibited a professionalism, integrity, and enthusiasm, which make him a credit to your agency."

The Director of the US Marshals Service, Mr. Wayne B. Colburn, forwarded a letter of appreciation to my director, dated April 1, 1976, which stated, in part, "For the past two years, Special Agent Donald G. Bell, Liaison Division, has represented your Service with this agency, in an exemplary manner. Largely, through his efforts, the relation between our organizations has been greatly enhanced, and the timely exchange of important information with Mr. Bell has significantly enhanced our ability to provide for the security of the federal judiciary, to protect threatened, federal facilities, plus, execute law enforcement operations. Mr. Bell has also extended many courtesies to me and my senior staff, which have greatly facilitated effective relations between our organizations. Mr. Bell's performance of duty exemplifies the highest standards of federal law enforcement, and is appreciated very much by myself and my staff."

The first US Drug Enforcement Administrator, Peter Bensinger, US Department of Justice, presented me with a Certificate of Appreciation, dated March 1977, for "outstanding contributions in the field of drug enforcement."

FBI Director Clarence M. Kelley, in a letter addressed to the director of the US Secret Service, stated, in part, "I would like to mention, at this time, the outstanding cooperation we have received from Special Agent Donald G. Bell, your liaison representative. We will certainly miss our contacts with him, and wish him well in his new assignment." I also had a very good relationship with the US Bureau of Prisons Headquarters. I had a letter written to the director, US Bureau of Prisons, commending my liaison contact, executive assistant to the Director, J. Michael Quinlan. At least, these individuals thought I did a good job in my role as the liaison representative with their respective agencies. I always attempted to present a professional image to the public, and to those that I dealt with as a Secret Service agent. I do not recall, ever, not doing my best to present a positive image to everyone that I dealt with in the public.

I believe this is so important. As a profession of being a Secret Service agent one must dress neatly and make certain that they present a good physical image, plus always act in a professional manner. I believe I did this during my career. For example, during October 1976, while in the town of New City (actual name of the town), New York, I was assigned to assist in a visit by President Ford to that city, during a campaign stop. I had contact with several individuals in the county courthouse, since President Ford used one of the offices in the building as a rest stop, to relax. Well, after the visit was over, and I returned to my office in Washington, DC, I received a copy of a letter that Surrogate John F. Skahen has written to the director of the Secret Service. In this letter, Surrogate Skahen stated, "I am writing to tell you how much I admired the performance of the Secret Service men during a recent visit by President Ford to Rockland County. Although I had previously seen them, in connection with President Eisenhower, I never before had an opportunity close up to watch your men in action. Their appearance, their conduct, their efficiency, politeness, patience, calmness, and ability at protecting the president, were just amazing to all of us here in the courthouse.

It is a great pleasure to see men of such caliber working for government. I was particularly impressed with two of your men whom I met personally, one Mr. Don Bell and the other agent. I am sure you will be pleased to know that everyone here is talking in glowing terms of the work of the Secret Service." I always did my best to present this type of image and conduct to everyone that I met and work with in the general public, because it is so important to always present a professional image, as described in the letter from Surrogate Skahen. I did this for self-satisfaction, because I never expected anything else from my superiors. I honestly believe that I worked too hard for my own good, due to the fact it could be seen as threatening to others. I did make a few mistakes due to the fact that faulty information was given to me, thus, causing some confusion, but this never happened very often.

One of the points that I want to convey is that the Secret Service was formed to investigate federal criminal violations, such as the counterfeiting of our currency, not protecting the President of the United States. Our agents have always been criminal investigators. Today, the Secret Service is responsible for maintaining the integrity of our US monetary system. President Lincoln gave his Secretary of the Treasury the authorization to create the Secret Service on April 14, 1865, the day that he was assassinated. However, the Secret Service was officially created as an official agency, on July 5, 1865. The name came from an intelligence unit in the Union Army.

Throughout the American Revolution the British counterfeited US currency in such large amounts that the Continental currency soon became worthless. "Not worth a Continental" became a popular expression of the era. The counterfeiting of money is one of the oldest crimes in history. During some periods it was considered treasonous, punishable by death. During the Civil War one-third to one-half of the currency in circulation was counterfeit. Approximately 1,600 state banks designed and printed their own bills. Each bill carried a different design, making it difficult to detect counterfeit bills from the seven thousand varieties of real bills. While a national currency was adopted in 1862 to resolve the counterfeiting problem, it was soon counterfeited and circulated so extensively that it became necessary to take enforcement measures. Therefore, the United States Secret Service was created to suppress the widespread counterfeiting of the nation's currency. Counterfeiting is mentioned in Article 1, Section 8, of the US Constitution.

From 1865 to 1908, the Secret Service was the only general investigative arm of the US Government. Eight Secret Service agents were reassigned to form the Bureau of Investigation, which later became the Federal Bureau of Investigation (FBI). However, the Secret Service continued to investigate many federal violations after the FBI was formed. Prior to J. Edgar Hoover becoming Director of the FBI, on May 10, 1924, there were four directors from 1908 to 1924. All four had to either resign, or had various problems. Director William J. Burns ended up in prison. After President McKinley was assassinated during 1901, the Secret Service was granted the authority to provide physical protection to the president and vice president of the United States.

However, unofficially, and without the knowledge of Congress, a few agents would be called upon from time to time to protect, say, the spouse of President Theodore Roosevelt on special occasions. Congress was generally against providing full-time, around the clock, protection of the president of the United States, even after President McKinley's death. They did not see this as a high priority. It took the assassination of President Kennedy for Congress to pass legislation making the killing a president of the United States a federal crime. After becoming FBI Director on May 10, 1924, J. Edgar Hoover truly wanted the FBI to provide physical protection for the President of the United States. The reason was that Hoover believed that he would have an information pipeline directly to the office of the president. Therefore, he would always know what was going on, which he felt would help him be better informed personally, and as an agency. In other words, Hoover would have more control over his agency.

The Secret Service did not begin protecting the president of the United States full time, until 1901, after President McKinley's assassination. President Theodore Roosevelt was the first president to receive full-time Secret Service protection. During my career, I was constantly investigating criminal violations and being involved in the protection of the president, foreign heads of state, major presidential candidates, and others. As a Secret Service agent, I was trained to be an expert witness regarding genuine currency.

If I determined that the bill in question was not genuine, it would obviously be counterfeit. Therefore, I would testify in federal court as an expert witness. I always preferred the challenges of conducting complicated criminal violations versus protection matters. I always resented being called "a guard." Although, protecting the president of the United States is extremely important and necessary, I preferred the criminal investigations because of the challenge, especially, when I became involved in a complex investigation. Secret Service Special agents are required to have a college degree, plus, they received extensive training in the protection of the president and others. Also, when the Secret Service was formed in 1865, our agents were criminal investigators.

Today, a Secret Service agent performs both investigative and protection duties throughout their career. The Uniformed Division of the Secret Service is responsible for the physical protection of the White House and foreign embassies. These officers receive extensive training in this area. Their qualifications are basically the same as the District of Columbia police officers. A typical Secret Service agent who is assigned to one of our field offices may have anywhere from fifty or more criminal investigations assigned to him/her at any given time, plus, the fact they will be called upon to make sudden plans to travel anywhere in the world to assist in a protective assignment. When the agent gets back to the field office, he/she picks up where they left off with their investigative assignments.

Prior to the beginning of World War I, the Secret Service was given the authority to investigate a German sabotage plot against the United States involving the publisher of a pro-German newspaper, The Fatherland, and a Dr. Heinrich Albert. Dr. Albert was being tailed one day by Secret Service Agent Frank Burke on a trolley, in New York City. When the trolley came to a stop, Dr. Albert stepped off the trolley, and a few seconds later he immediately turned around in a panic to get back on the trolley. Seconds later, Agent Burke ran from another exit on the trolley, jumped on Dr. Albert's trolley, grabbed his briefcase and ran down the street. Documents in Dr. Albert's briefcase revealed that he was the chief money man for Germany's spy and sabotage ring in the United States. Dr. Albert's detailed information in his briefcase determined that he had $27 million dollars to finance his spying operation in the United States.

# STRUGGLE TO ZERO

His several plots included longshoreman's strikes, a bombing campaign against munitions plants and certain factories, the purchase of American newspapers, magazines, and book publishing companies. In addition, the spy network planned on purchasing a supply of liquid chlorine to be used for poison gas, purchase an American airplane company, organizing a protectionist labor movement, choking off the supply of cotton imported from Britain, and to work with the American anti-war politicians and unions in order to force an embargo on all munitions from Britain and France. The most alarming information in Dr. Albert's briefcase was a scheme for a German invasion of America. They came up with a plan for the German Navy to land eighty-five thousand troops along the New Jersey coast, and seal off New York City until it surrendered because of starvation. The Secret Service was totally responsible for uncovering this amazing plot against the United States.

During the 1920s and early 1930s, the Secret Service was heavily involved with bootleggers through cases that involved counterfeit liquor labels, prescription slips, and counterfeit revenue stamps. Department of Revenue Form 1403, the form doctors used when they wanted their patients to buy whiskey for medicinal purposes, could not be counterfeited. Therefore, the Secret Service investigated these violations.

Early fraud investigations such as the Tea Pot Dome land scandal (1920–1923), were investigated by the Secret Service. Secretary of the Interior, Albert Fall, persuaded Navy Secretary, Edwin C. Denby, to transfer the Tea Pot Dome oil reserves to the Interior Department. Fall then leased the oil production rights to two oil companies, which was legal. However, Fall, received a $100,000 no-interest loan ($1.29 million today) from one oil company in 1921, plus other gifts. Fall also received other gifts from both the oil company executives, totaling $404,000 ($5.2 million today). The money changing hands was illegal, not the leases. Fall attempted to keep his actions secret, but the sudden improvement in his standard of living prompted speculation. Fall was presumed innocent until a junior US Senator from Montana, Thomas J. Walsh, uncovered a piece of evidence that Fall had forgotten to cover up. It was the $100,000 loan to Fall. Fall was fined $100,000, and sentenced to one year in prison. He was the first and only former US Cabinet official sentenced to prison.

Currently, the primary federal criminal violations investigated by the US Secret Service are THREATS TO KILL THE PESIDENT OF THE UNITED STATES, AND OTHERS, RECEIVING SECRET SERVICE PROTECTION.

## COUNTERFEIT AND FRAUDULENT

HOUSE OF REPRESENTATIVES
WASHINGTON, D.C. 20515

ROMANO L. MAZZOLI
THIRD DISTRICT
KENTUCKY

December 20, 1988

```
Mr. Donald Bell
Street Agent
Secret Service
439 Gene Snyder Courthouse
601 West Broadway
Louisville, Kentucky  40202

Dear Agent Bell:

    I am writing to confirm my planned
meeting with you and AIC Donald Powers

    I understand we are to meet at
2:00 p.m. your office, 601 West
Broadway.

    With all best wishes and regards.

                    Sincerely,


                    ROMANO L. MAZZOLI
                    Member of Congress

RLM:ydm
```

Correspondence from US Congressman
Romano L. Mazzoli, Louisville, KY.

# STRUGGLE TO ZERO

ASSISTANT ATTORNEY GENERAL
CRIMINAL DIVISION

**Department of Justice**
Washington 20530

January 28, 1977

H. Stuart Knight, Director
United States Secret Service
Washington, D. C.

Dear Mr. Knight:

    It is our understanding that Special Agent Donald G. Bell will soon be leaving your Liaison Division for a field office assignment. We wish to take this opportunity before his departure to call to your attention the exemplary assistance he has furnished this Department.

    During the past two years, Mr. Bell has contributed greatly to our understanding of your Service's functions and problems. He has promptly and efficiently handled our requests for information, thereby fulfilling an invaluable function in assisting our Department and your Service in defusing situations threatening the welfare of Secret Service protectees. In all his dealings with this Department, Mr. Bell has exhibited a professionalism, integrity, and enthusiasm which make him a credit to your agency.

    We wish him well in his new assignment.

Sincerely,

RICHARD L. THORNBURGH
Assistant Attorney General
Criminal Division

Letter of accommodation from Richard L. Thornburgh, Assistant Attorney General, Department of Justice.

# DON BELL

February 7, 1977

Honorable H. Stuart Knight
Director
United States Secret Service
Department of the Treasury
Washington, D. C. 20223

Dear Mr. Knight:

    Just a brief note to express the sincere appreciation of both Bob Moore and myself for the photographs which you personally inscribed to each of us. Win Lawson presented them to us several days ago, in the company of Don Bell and George Opfer who we were advised is succeeding Don as our Secret Service liaison man with FBI Headquarters.

    We will miss Don. He is a fine representative of your Service. We look forward, however, to a close, cordial working relationship with George and you can be sure that we will afford him all possible assistance and cooperation.

    Again, thank you very much for the photographs. It was most thoughtful of you.

Sincerely,

H. C. Flemister, Jr.

Letter of Appreciation from FBI Supervisor H. C. Flemister Jr.

# STRUGGLE TO ZERO

830.0

December 14, 1976

Mr. J. Michael Quinlan
Executive Assistant to the Director
U. S. Bureau of Prisons
Washington, D. C. 20534

Dear Mr. Quinlan:

Personally, and on behalf of the United States Secret Service, I wish to thank you for the cooperation that you have extended to our employees since your appointment as Executive Assistant to Director Carlson. Your experience and courteous assistance have been extremely valuable in assisting this Service with its investigative and protective responsibilities.

Special Agent Donald G. Bell of our Liaison Division has advised me of the expeditious and efficient manner in which you have responded to our Liaison requests. Your personal cooperation has been superior and we are grateful to you.

Warm personal regards.

Sincerely,

H. S. Knight
Director

HSK:JWW:KWL:pc

✓ bcc: Liaison Division

cc: Mr. Norman Carlson
Director
U. S. Bureau of Prisons

My letter of appreciation to J. Michael Quinlan, executive Assistant to the director, US Bureau of Prisons, Washington, DC.

DON BELL

**UNITED STATES DEPARTMENT OF JUSTICE**

FEDERAL BUREAU OF INVESTIGATION

WASHINGTON, D.C. 20535

February 28, 1977

Mr. H. Stuart Knight
Director
United States Secret Service
Washington, D. C. 20223

Dear Stu:

    On behalf of Special Agents Frank B. Still, Jr., Karl V. Hetherington, and their entire staffs, I express heartfelt appreciation for your letters of February 11th concerning the assistance furnished your Agency by the Identification Division Front Office Employees and the Name Check Section. We are most grateful for the plaques presented by members of your staff. This was a most thoughtful gesture and we are indeed pleased by these personal presentations.

    Enclosed are copies of the photographs made during the presentations and I am making arrangements for additional copies of these photographs to be provided for each of your employees who were present. They will be made available when they are processed.

    I would also like to mention at this time the outstanding cooperation we have received from Special Agent Donald G. Bell, your liaison representative. We will certainly miss our contacts with him and wish him well in his new assignment in Louisville. We are looking forward to a close working relationship with his successor, Special Agent George Opfer.

Sincerely yours,

Clarence M. Kelley
Director

Enclosures (4)

Letter of appreciation from Clarence M. Kelley,
Director, Federal Bureau of Investigation.

# STRUGGLE TO ZERO

United States Department of Justice

UNITED STATES MARSHALS SERVICE

Washington, D.C. 20530

April 1, 1976

Mr. H. S. Knight
Director
United States Secret Service
Washington, D.C.  20223

Dear Mr. Knight:

    For the past two years, Special Agent Donald G. Bell, Liaison Division, has represented your Service with this agency in an exemplary manner. Largely through his efforts the working relation between our organizations has been greatly enhanced and the timely exchange of important information with Mr. Bell has significantly enhanced our ability to provide for the security of the federal judiciary, to protect threatened federal facilities, and to execute law enforcement operations.

    Mr. Bell has also extended many courtesies to me and my senior staff which have greatly facilitated effective relations between our organization. Additionally, his demeanor and dedication exemplify what we have come to expect from the Secret Service.

    Mr. Bell's performance of duty exemplifies the highest standards of federal law enforcement and is much appreciated by myself and my staff. I would appreciate it if you would pass these remarks on to Mr. Bell.

Sincerely,

WAYNE B. COLBURN
Director

## Letter of accommodation from Wayne B. Colburn, Director, US Marshals Service.

IDENTIFICATION: Someone knowingly, and without lawful authority produces, transfers, or possesses a false identification document to defraud the US Government.

ACCESS DEVICE FRAUD: Crimes involving access devices include debit cards, automated teller machine (ATM) cards, computer passwords, personal identification numbers, long distance access codes, and Subscriber Identify Module (SIM) contained within cellular phones that assign billing.

COMPUTER FRAUD: Violations enforced under this statute include unauthorized access to protected computers, theft of data, such a personal identification used to commit identity theft, denial of service attacks used for extortion, or disruption of e-commerce and malware (malicious software) distribution to include viruses intended for financial gain.

FORGERY: US Government checks and bonds.

MONEY LAUNDERING: It is illegal to launder proceeds of certain criminal offenses, called, "specified unlawful activities."

ELECTRONIC BENEFITS TRANSFER FRAUD: Food Stamp Act of 1977. Possession or use of food stamp coupons, "Authorization to Participate" cards or Electronic Benefit Transfer cards by unauthorized persons compromises the integrity of the Food Stamp Program, and is a criminal violation.

ADVANCE FEE FRAUD: The perpetrators of advance fee fraud, known internationally as "4-19 fraud" (after the section of the Nigerian penal code which addresses these schemes), are often very creative and innovative. A large number of victims are enticed into believing they have been singled out from the masses to share in multi-million dollar windfall profits for no apparent reason... e-mail from someone requesting your assistance in a financial transaction, such as the transfer of a large sum of money into an account, or claiming you are the next of kin to a wealthy person who has died, or the winner of an obscure lottery. DO NOT RESPOND. If you respond, they will continue to harass you.

GREEN GOODS SCAMS: The criminal alters the serial number on a bill, and then places a blank paper in a machine with a false bottom. The criminal tells the victim that his machine can print a genuine bill. The blank paper falls to the false bottom, and the criminal lifts the lid, and lo and behold, a genuine bill is there in the top part of the machine. The victim purchases the machine for a sum of money.

"SHOULDER SURFER": The criminal listens to a person using their phone credit card and gets their card number.

BANK FRAUD: The criminal opens a new account, using fake identification, then writes checks, immediately, before the bank clears them.

DECEASED SOCIAL SECURITY CHECKS: If the Social Security Administration is not notified of the death of the recipient, the checks keep coming. If the checks are cashed, the person cashing the checks is committing a federal crime.

Today, new forms of counterfeiting are on the rise. One reason is the ease and speed with which large quantities of counterfeit currency can be produced using modern photographic, printing, and computer paper.

## EIGHT WAYS TO SPOT COUNTERFEIT BILLS

Detail of the portrait
Detail of the Treasury Seal
Detail of the Border
Serial Numbers
The quality of the Paper

The starch, iodine-based counterfeiting. The pen reacts to the starch in the paper. If the bill is real, the ink turns yellow. If the bill is counterfeit, the ink turns a dark blue or black. If the counterfeiter is good, they will use starch-free paper.

The feel of the paper

THE WATERMARK: One of the easiest ways for the citizen to identify counterfeit bills is to check for the watermark.

# LOUISVILLE FIELD OFFICE
# 1977–1988

A Secret Service agent must be very diverse. One foot was always on the investigative side of the fence, and the other was always on the protection side. You had to be very adaptable. A Secret Service agent is never away from the protection part of the job. In fact, throughout my career I had ten years of protection hours and ten years of investigative hours. They were intertwined and intermingled throughout my career. Every agent was required to submit a daily report, which kept precise tract every hour during the day. A monthly report containing a breakdown of every day during the month had to be submitted.

During the period of time that an agent is assigned full time to protective assignments, that agent only does protection matters. However, when an agent is assigned to any other division, or a field office, he/she will be involved with both protection assignments and criminal investigations. Therefore, one day the agent is investigating a criminal violation and two days later, he/she will be assigned to help in a protective assignment anywhere in the United States, or the world.

During 1978, while in the middle of conducting criminal investigations, I was given an assignment to assist in a Vice President Walter F. Mondale visit to Southeast Asia. My stops were Manila, Philippines, Jakarta, Indonesia, and Wellington, New Zealand. Ferdinand and Imelda Marcos were the dictators in the Philippines during this period of time. Ms. Marcos was very active during this visit. They gave a state dinner for the vice president in their huge white mansion. This was a big event. Hundreds of young, attractive, female singers were part of the program. All wore white dresses and entered the palace in a single line.

During the few days that I was in Manila, all the Secret Service agents stayed in a hotel on Manila Bay. There were Jeepney buses running around everywhere. These buses were old World War II Jeeps, which were converted into buses. Ms. Marcos was very generous to the Secret Service Agents when she gave us various, native, souvenirs. There were several of these items which had no real value. I could not accept a normal gift from a foreign government with any known, monetary value. Most of these items served no purpose in my home and were eventually discarded.

My next stop on this trip was Jakarta, Indonesia. Again, I, and the other agents were put up in a very nice hotel that was recommended by the American embassy. The vice president made various stops around the city. One purpose of the vice president's visit was to assist Indonesia with funds for their rural electrification program. The weather was humid and rainy. During one of the main stops, which took place in big, nice looking building, I heard this "drip," "drip," "drip," and "drip." While the quiet event was taking place, the drips from the ceiling were hitting the floor, making a somewhat loud noise which became distracting. Every morning the hotel would leave a local newspaper outside the door to your room. One morning the newspaper contained a photograph on the front page of an Indonesian man who had been swallowed by a twenty-foot-long boa constrictor snake. This person had attended a local town council meeting, and on his way home that night, he somehow, was swallowed by this snake. The next day a search party located this snake, which had a huge bulge in its midsection. When they cut it open, out pops the man's body with his arms all bent up, etc.

Anyway, from Jakarta I flew on down to Wellington, New Zealand, in advance of the vice president's visit. Naturally, Wellington was a very green, beautiful, city. One of the most horrible, uncomfortable, miserable, airplane flights that I have ever experienced was the twelve-hour flight from Sidney, Australia to Honolulu, on my way from Wellington. This was 1978, and the 747 was totally, full. No empty seats. The seats were very narrow, and to make matters worse, I was sitting next to a female. I did not dare to arm touch, or touch in any way. We had only one arm rest between us, and there was no way to get comfortable or get any sleep during the twelve hour flight. How great would it have been just to have your own arm rest? While in Wellington, we became acquainted with the local police. They were very cooperative. The restaurants closed at 10:00 PM. However, the local police had their own after hours restaurants, and as such, they took us to their restaurants to get something to eat. Usually, it was after 10:00 PM before I/we got off duty, and thank goodness we could go to the police restaurants for a late dinner. These establishments did not close until 4:00 AM.

After getting back to the Louisville Field Office, my stack of criminal cases was waiting for me. I had to pick up where I left off and continue as if I had never been away. The heavy field office casework brought to my attention I could have remained in our headquarters in Washington, DC, and be promoted. However, I chose to be transferred out of the Washington, area, for the sake of my family.

During the early 1980s, I was assigned to King Hussein of Jordan's protective detail while he was visiting the United States, specifically, in a very new hotel in Washington, DC. As I was sitting in the front waiting area of his suite the hotel maintenance crew came rushing in. While the King was taking a shower, the new shower fixture broke and water was all over the bathroom floor. King Hussein was down on the floor with towels attempting to mop up as much water, as possible. You can imagine a King down on the floor fighting the flow of water with his bath towels. King Hussein and his spouse were extremely nice people who were always very kind to the Secret Service agents assigned to his detail.

Another foreign head of state that I was assigned to protect was Prime Minister Henry (Hank) Aaron of Suriname, a small country in the Caribbean that had recently gained its independence. Everyone referred to him as Prime Minister Hank Aaron, the same as the hall of fame baseball player. In many cases these prime ministers, and others, would bring an empty airplane with them in order to purchase items that they did not have access to in their own country. In other words, members of their staff would go on shopping sprees during the prime minister's visit. The plane would leave the United States loaded down with various items for their use in their country. Prime Minister Hank Aaron gave me as a thank you gift a nice booklet of stamps commemorating Suriname's independence. His visit will always be remembered by me due to the fact he has the same name as the Hall of Fame baseball player, Hank Aaron.

On another occasion during the late 1970s, I was assigned to the protective detail of the President of one of the African countries during his visit to the United Nations General Assembly, in New York City. He was staying in a very expensive suite at the Waldorf-Astoria Hotel. As standard procedure, his staff brought with them several of these large dried fish wrapped in big green tree leaves. The staff laid the fish alongside the wall in the hallway, right outside the entrance to the president's suite. I was working the midnight shift, and man, around 2:00 AM these fish developed a sickening, fishy, odor. We had to hold our noses and stand as far away as possible. The president stayed several days in the hotel suite and when his chef needed to prepare fish for dinner he would take a fish wrapped in the tree leaves into the suite kitchen and unwrap them and then lay the unwrapped fish on the carpet floor, thus, leaving a big greasy spot. After the president left to go back to his country, myself, and other agents inspected his suite, which was SOP. In addition to the greasy spots on the carpet, a thick layer of grease was splattered all over the kitchen stove area, plus, all over the wall. The suite had to be totally remodeled, including all new carpeting. The leaders of these countries and their staff brought their culture with them during these visits, which was normal. That was just the way it was, with nothing being unusual. The president and his staff were very courteous and cooperative during his visit. I enjoyed observing firsthand the various cultures of the world.

During a previous visit and while staying in the Plaza Hotel, in New York City, a few members of the president of an African country's staff would stand out on the small balcony to their hotel room and drop $20 bills down to the street prostitutes. At that time, prostitutes were everywhere in the city. Obviously, the hotel management did not approve of the prostitutes congregating next to the hotel picking up $20 bills. The prostitutes were on every street corner. Whenever I left the hotel for a walk to the nearest restaurant I would be approached numerous times along the way.

During my career, I was assigned to protect numerous foreign heads of state when they visited the United States. The prime minister of Israel, Golda Meir, was one of many heads of state whom I was assigned to protect. During her six-day visit, she traveled from New York City to Los Angeles, CA, on El Al Airlines, the official airline that she traveled on. She was a kind, grandmotherly, wrinkled-faced, lady, who was well respected by her peers. She also liked her cigarettes, very much. As a gift, she gave me a solid silver key chain, which I kept among my various memorabilia. She was an amazing person who did not fit the stereotype or resemble someone who was the leader of a country such as Israel. She held a very challenging and tough position. However, she was a tough old bird that everyone respected. In addition to being assigned to protect Prime Minister Golda Meir, others included King Tupu of the Tonga Islands, who at that time was the largest (physically) ruler on earth (four hundred pounds), Prime Minister Mora, Fiji Islands, Prime Minister Hank Aaron, Suriname, Prime Minister of India, Nasser Arafat, head of the PLO, Prime Minister Harold Wilson, Great Britain, Prime Minister of Malaysia, President Mobutu, Zaire, and many others. As a member of Prime Minister Harold Wilson's protective detail, he invited us to stay after we completed our 4:00 PM–12:00 AM shift for coffee in the Blair House kitchen. We sat around and chatted about various subjects prior to going home.

One of my unusual investigations, during either 1978 or 1979, while assigned to the Louisville Field Office, consisted of identifying the forger of numerous US Savings Bonds that were cashed during World War II. I identified the forger as being a retired female postmaster in a rural post office in eastern Kentucky. The son of one of her post office box holders was in the Navy, and each month he would have a $25 US Savings Bond mailed to his parents, who resided in the area. Instead of delivering the savings bonds to the parents, the postmaster would keep them until she was able to cash them. The parents did not know that their son was mailing them the $25 bonds every month. Many years later the son realized that his savings bonds had never reached his parents. Therefore, he filed a claim with the US Bureau of Public Debt, which kept copies of all US Savings Bonds.

After viewing these copies he realized that someone had forged his name to the bonds and cashed them. Therefore, this investigation was forwarded to the US Secret Service, in Louisville, for investigation. I personally interviewed the postmaster regarding the forged savings bonds, plus, I obtained handwriting samples, which appeared to be identical to the handwriting samples of the postmaster. She denied forging the bonds, and due to the fact that the statute of limitations had expired, the US Attorney's Office declined any prosecution in his matter.

In order to show the vast diversity of investigations that I conducted while assigned to our Louisville Field Office, one of my investigations consisted of investigating the counterfeiting of rare, valuable, gold coins. Over in Ashland, Kentucky, during the summer months, there were many flea markets. Certain coin dealers would sell these rare, $20 gold coins, as being genuine coins. This information was brought to our attention by one of the honest coin dealers. Anyway, I had to go over there and seize numerous coins in order to have them examined by the experts to determine if they were, in fact counterfeit. Many were counterfeit. One of the dealers was charged for dealing in counterfeit gold coins, but due to the fact it would be difficult to get a conviction in court and proving beyond a reasonable doubt that the dealer did in fact, know that these coins were truly counterfeit, the charges were dropped, which was the appropriate thing to do. Once a determination was made that these gold coins were counterfeit, they had no value, other than the value of the gold in them.

As I traveled to the eastern part of Kentucky by myself, to interview someone regarding one of my criminal cases, I would catch myself, alone, after dark, conducting an interview in an old home in a hollow that ran between two mountains. As I conducted the interview, I would notice that mice would run across the old warm morning stove and scurry across the floor. I would hope that one did not run up my pants leg, which was a VERY real possibility. I always hoped that my vehicle did not break down or that I would be shot at, because I was 100 percent on my own.

Immediately after President Reagan was elected President of the United States, during November 1980, I was assigned for three weeks to assist in the protection of his 633-acre ranch located north of Santa Barbara, California. The terrain on the ranch was very rugged. The extremely narrow eight mile road up the mountain to the ranch was very intimidating, to say the least. When driving up the road, you had to be very careful. In the event you met a vehicle coming down, both vehicles had to stop and carefully make room to be able to pass without falling hundreds of feet to your demise. I was among the first small group of agents to be assigned specifically to secure the entire ranch. When looking west from the highest point, the Pacific Ocean was in view, which was a beautiful sight. While at the ranch, you felt as if you were totally away from the rest of civilization. I can truly understand why President Reagan chose this location to totally get away from civilization.

At dusk, the wildcats would come out in the field near the ranch house to hunt for their dinner, which was more than likely rabbits or mice. As you drove around on the midnight shift, the darkness was almost overwhelming when all of a sudden the clouds moved through. I could not see my hands in front of me. In addition, the tarantula spiders were everywhere; therefore, care had to be taken to prevent one from latching onto you. A rainfall would come every three months and all of a sudden the brown grass in the fields would turn green. It was like magic. Two or three days after the election president and Ms. Reagan came to the ranch for relaxation, but left after three days. They rode their horses and he would clear brush for exercise. I believe the ranch has been opened to the public for many years for certain tours, etc. The other agents and I, along with one or two of President Reagan's staff, had Thanksgiving dinner at the Double Tree Inn, there in Santa Barbara. Lyn Nofzinger, one of President Reagan's inner circle staff members hosted the Thanksgiving dinner, keeping in mind that we were away from our families. A very pleasant time was had by all, and we appreciated it very much. He was an extremely nice and gracious person, in every way.

During 1982, myself, and two other Secret Service agents were assigned as the advance team for former President Richard Nixon's visit to Bulgaria and Austria. Nixon was scheduled to make three stops in Bulgaria: Sofia, Russa, and Varna. He was scheduled to visit four Soviet bloc countries, Romania, Bulgaria, Czechoslovakia, and Poland, plus, Austria. Our first stop was Bulgaria, which, at that time, was VERY Communist. Secret Service agents had never set foot in Bulgaria. At first, they would not approve our visit to their country.

However, after the US State Department intervened, they finally approved our visit. They had the impression that Secret Service agents were spies. Our final leg of the trip was on Balkan Air, their state run airline that took us to Sofia, their capitol city. I was the first agent to deplane and set foot on Bulgarian soil. This was one of those very "small" firsts, which meant nothing to anyone but me. Our welcoming party consisted of a young fellow from our embassy, plus, a member of the KGB, Col. Yumchef, and a liaison representative, from their foreign ministry. Anyway, all of us were ushered into a very old, 1950s-type black limousine, which took us to our hotel in downtown Sofia. Our driver was an elderly gentleman, who apparently received a very low salary.

On one occasion, I offered him a $10 bill, as a tip for taking me to the airport to fly to Varna to prepare of former President Nixon's visit. He was VERY happy to receive it. The hotel was very old, classy, clean, and nice. That evening, all of us went to dinner in the hotel dining area. We ordered from a very extensive menu consisting of chicken and fish, mainly. The food was very good and we enjoyed the dinner. It is noted that we could not pay for anything, during our visit to their country, due to the fact their government was required to pick up the tab. The Bulgarians were with us wherever we went. I was aware that our hotel room was more than likely bugged. So I naturally, did not say anything that would appear to be offensive to the Bulgarian government. After arriving in Sofia, we went to the American Embassy for a briefing on intelligence matters which included what not to do, such as taking photographs of anything to do with their military, etc.

While in Sofia, I observed many people sitting around on park benches looking bored and subdued. As a Secret Service agent in a totalitarian government such as Bulgaria, there were no security type problems. I have a better feeling for those individuals due to the fact that as a society, they had common suffering, such as the lack of food and other material possessions. This would cause a citizen to share common causes with their neighbors, thus, preventing most from being lonely. Sociological studies have shown that the citizens of the United States are the loneliest people, as a country, in the world. For example, the single Americans who go from their office at the end of the day directly to their cliff-dwelling type apartments without any social interaction. We are known as cliff dwellers in our large cities, which is such a shame, because most Americans desire to have more social interaction. However, due to the fact we are totally strangling ourselves with all the rules and regulations and fear of being harmed by the criminals, many Americans just remain in the safety of their apartment, etc. Continuing, the Bulgarians agreed to any reasonable security request. They were very security conscientious. However, we realized that we were always under some type of surveillance, so I had to be very careful and not do anything stupid.

While traveling to our first stop in Russa, we pulled into a nice looking restaurant located in a wooded area for lunch. Very few buildings in Bulgaria were built with wood. They were built with concrete. However, when we entered the restaurant, the manager pointed us to the right, which had all wood walls. I noticed that the other side was reserved for the "normal" people and tourists. We were the only individuals using the dining area with the nice, wooden walls. It was obvious that the restaurant personnel recognized Col. Yumchef as being with the KGB, making him privy to special treatment. Actually, I felt somewhat guilty with all this special treatment.

Next, our advance team traveled to Varna, a tourist city which is located on the Black Sea, in order to prepare for Nixon's visit to that city. We had two days to prepare for his visit. He was arriving in Bulgaria, from Romania, via motorcade. Varna was located near the

# STRUGGLE TO ZERO

Romanian border, and air travel was not deemed necessary. Varna was a vacation spot for many tourists from various countries. The casino personnel were British, as no Bulgarians were allowed to be employed by them. Our advance team stayed on the grounds of the president of Bulgaria's summer resort home, which was located on the Black Sea beach with trees between our quarters and the actual beach. As I walked down to the beach I passed many uniformed military types with guns, stationed along the pathway. The beach area had very few tourists on it. Parked in plain view and a short distance from shore at a large boat dock, was the president of Bulgaria's huge expensive-looking yacht.

As I walked over the compound, I noticed the grass was high, and it appeared as if it had never been cut with a lawn mower. I asked someone, "What about the snakes"? I was told, "oh no, don't worry, there are no snakes in Bulgaria." I learned that the snakes had been wiped out by Mongoose's many years, prior. There were very few lawn mowers in Bulgaria, due to the fact the sheep are brought in to keep the grass under control, even on their president's summer resort compound. Prior to Nixon's arriving from Romania, and while staying at the compound, my advance team and our Bulgarian counterparts were served to a sit down, table clothed, classy breakfast, lunch, and dinner.

The alcoholic drinks started to flow, at breakfast. However, I could not quite handle this, so I declined to consume their vodka that early in the day. I mean the food and drink flowed three times a day during our stay at the compound. It was unbelievable. One member of our advance team was an organic health food type, and he moaned and groaned every time all this food was put front of him. He was one of these health nuts who considered food to be evil.

On the date of former President Nixon's border crossing from Romania to Bulgaria, I, along with the other two advance team members traveled to the border crossing location to meet his party, which also consisted of his own permanent Secret Service detail traveling with him. The border crossing went smoothly, and we proceeded on to Varna. Later, I was told that approximately twenty thousand, Romanian and Bulgarian military/police types were involved in this border crossing. It sounded unbelievable to me, but then I realized that this was an opportunity for their troops to be involved in an unusual exercise, since they were not fighting any wars, etc. It was busy work for them. These Soviet Bloc countries definitely treated Nixon like royalty. They liked him very much. As I sit here reminiscing, it is difficult for me to believe how history has totally done a 360 since I was there on the Romanian border with Nixon as he entered Bulgaria for a friendly visit. As I sit here, today, I recall so vividly how the horrible Romanian dictator's reign of terror finally ended. Nicholae Ceausescu and his wife, Elena, were shot and killed by a firing squad after a two hour trial, on Christmas day, 1989, which was after the fall of the Berlin Wall. They called their citizens "worms," and practically starved them to death. God, justice was finally served. Hopefully, this great husband and wife power couple are still burning in Hell! They were totally defiant until bullets from the firing squad guns struck their bodies.

On a MUCH lesser scale with no similarities to the Ceausescu's situation and over the years, I have known of several so-called power couples in the political and religious arena who thought that they were above everyone else. I personally knew one such couple (personally met the male) who were in the political arena in Kentucky. They ran for Congress in separate districts with both having the same first and last name, Carol Hubbard and Carroll Hubbard. The wife ran for Congress in a congressional district in another part of the state, which is allowed, and the husband, who at that time was a sitting congressman, ran for re-election in his district. They thought they were hot stuff. However, they were just legends in their own minds, combined with delusions of grandeur. Their plan did not succeed. In other words, they crapped and fell back in it. These "power couples" are very common in Washington, DC. Usually, the male US Senator or Congressman hook up with a rich female in order to become very powerful and richer. They get a rocket up their ass with the delusion that they will "fly to the moon" together. In other words, GREED takes over.

One night while in Varna, Bulgaria, President Nixon and his party went out to dinner at a local popular dining spot that was a favorite place for tourists. The restaurant was actually located outside, under large trees. The setting was very beautiful. A couple of diners sitting at the table behind our table started giving Nixon verbal hell with their anti-Nixon chants, rah, rah, rah, rah, etc. These diners were not Bulgarians because they would have known better. The Communist Bulgarian government would never tolerate loud mouths like these people. They would have been yanked up and taken away if they were from Bulgaria. So help me God, AS these anti-Nixon people at this table continued their chants in the middle of their meal, a good sized bird on a limb directly over their table dropped a shit bomb smack dab on one of the diner's plate. This diner happened to be a female. Their chanting stopped, immediately. What can you say, justice was served. End of case. This incident was very amusing and satisfying to me. I could not hold back the laughter. My experience in Varna was very positive. I definitely developed a feeling of what it was like to live in a Communist country with the government totally controlling every aspect of your life.

I had to depart Varna by myself and fly back to Sofia on Balkan Air in order to make advance arrangements for former President Nixon's visit, after he left Varna. The Bulgarian government made all the flight arrangements. I was told that someone would meet me at the airport, and then transport me back to my hotel. So after arriving at the airport in Sofia, I retrieved my luggage and waited for my contact. I waited and waited, but no contact appeared. Finally, after an hour had passed, this gentleman appeared and said, "Hey," stating he was to take me to my hotel. After getting to my hotel room and unpacking, I went downstairs by myself, to the dining area for dinner. After viewing the menu, I really wanted to order a fish dish, but I was told that no fish was available, just chicken. I obviously had to settle for chicken. I was confused in that when we went to the same dining room with Col. Yumchef on our first evening at the hotel we could order anything on the menu. However, due to the fact that Col. Yumchef was NOT with me, I could not order everything on the menu, such as fish. Just chicken! The meat DID taste like chicken. Sometimes I think that every meat except red meat tastes like CHICKEN, as everyone will tell you. What does it taste like? IT

TASTES LIKE CHICKEN! I thought to myself, hell, the Black Sea is close, and certainly there should never be a shortage of fish, of all things. Then I realized that members of the KGB/Communist Party had certain special privileges such as being able to order fish from the menu. Damn, that would have been a great privilege to have that night! Apparently, there was a shortage of fish.

Well, former President Nixon arrived back in Sofia, which concluded his visit to Bulgaria. The visit went smoothly. Our hosts were very kind. I was given a very nice antique silver bowl, dating back to the thirteenth century, as a gift from the President of Bulgaria. I along with the other two members of our advance team boarded an airplane and headed for Vienna, Austria, to prepare for Nixon's visit to that city in a few days.

While in Vienna, our advance team stayed in a very nice hotel in the downtown area, near a large shopping mall that was within walking distance from the hotel. The next day after Nixon arrived in Vienna, he wanted to walk to the shopping area in order to purchase gifts for his grandchildren. So his staff and our agents escorted him to the store, where he went inside and bought the gifts. As we walked along, on the way to the shopping area, many people began to recognize his face, since he had one of the most recognized faces in the world. As we walked along, more and more people began to follow our party, chanting, "Nixon, Nixon." It reminded me of the multitudes following Jesus Christ, as described in the Bible. Now, I am not saying that Nixon was Jesus Christ.

On the way, we ran into some unusual individuals. One such man, who was completely nude, had a large ad type piece of cardboard hanging down his front, and another piece hanging down his backside. However, his private parts were covered with the two pieces of cardboard, with a rope, holding them up. He came over and requested that Nixon autograph the cardboard hanging from his backside. To our surprise, Nixon was given a pen from a staff member, and he did autograph the cardboard. Everyone got a laugh, or chuckle out of this incident. It did show a human side to Nixon. While in the store a huge crowd had gathered in front of the store waiting for him to come out. After coming out, we walked back to the hotel.

Prior to former President Nixon's arrival in Vienna, myself, and the other two members of the advance team paid a courtesy visit to the Vienna CIA Chief of Station's office, which was standard procedure. During my short conversation with him, I told him that I was from Louisville, KY. At that point he stated that he remembered my Congressman, Mr. Mazzoli, who was a member of a congressional delegation that he visited with in his office, while they were on a tour of certain countries in Europe. As standard procedure, his agency would give each member a sum of cash to purchase gifts, food, or whatever. He said the reason that he remembered Congressman Mazzoli was that he would not accept the cash. He was the only member of the congressional delegation that refused the cash. In other words, the Chief of Station had high praise for Congressman Mazzoli for his very principled character.

After conducting his business in Vienna, former President Nixon, along with his staff and our advance team flew to London, England, on British Airways. Nixon was seated in first class, and I was seated in an aisle seat directly across from his seat, within an arm length from him. He was doing his thing as a former president and I was doing my thing as a Secret Service agent. During the flight Nixon had to go to the bathroom, which was located in the front of the plane, right behind the crew member's door. As he walked to the bathroom, only his backside was showing, but as he made his exit from the bathroom, his face was exposed to all the passengers in first class.

Many Japanese passengers were in first class, and as Nixon started to walk down the aisle they recognized his face. They began to say his name, and the cameras began to click. He was very patient and kind, giving each one a business sized card with his signature and the notation "The Office of President Nixon" on it. Also, he consented to being photographed with those who made the request.

Once we got to London, my mission was complete. Myself, and the other two agents split from Nixon and our agents assigned to his permanent detail. We flew to Shannon, Ireland, staying overnight in order to fly back to New York City the next day. From New York City I then flew on to Louisville, KY. You know, my criminal investigations were there waiting on my return. They looked very lonely and neglected. I picked up where I left off, as if nothing had happened, such as traveling to a Soviet Bloc country and to Vienna, Austria.

President Nixon's July 1978, visit to Hyden, Kentucky, was his FIRST public event since he resigned, due to the Watergate scandal. Hyden, Kentucky, is a small town located in the southeastern part of Kentucky. I assisted in his visit that date, since our Louisville Secret Service Field Office was in charge of this visit, as a former president.

Continuing back in our Louisville Field Office, President Carter visited the residence of one of his political supporters in Henderson, KY, during 1978, for an event. I was assigned as a member of the advance team for this visit to handle any threats, etc., against the president. Therefore, I had to stay in the Henderson area for several days prior to the visit. Also, during this same time period a counterfeit $20 note investigation was being conducted in eastern Kentucky by the remaining agents in our Louisville Field Office. Additional agents were brought in from other offices to assist in this investigation. This $20 note was printed by Paul Kidd, and it was a very good looking counterfeit note which was easily passed all over the United States. Kidd had his printing operation set up in his mobile home residence at the very end of War Creek Hollow, located near Jackson, KY.

For several months, we had attempted numerous tactics, such as airplane surveillance, informants, etc., to get to Kidd's printing operation. An agent who played the part of a mobster from Chicago, driving a big black mob looking vehicle was sent in an attempt to make contact to purchase counterfeit $20 notes. This scene scared the crap out of the contact and he got away from there ASAP. Obviously, this attempt was a failure. Over in the mountains in Eastern Kentucky, these hollows were difficult to penetrate. If a stranger entered the hollow, the individuals residing in the first residence advised the other home owners that a stranger was coming their way. So they had a built in warning system. Therefore, it was impossible for law enforcement to make their way back to Paul Kidd's mobile home without being detected.

Anyway, one day while I was involved as a member of the advance team in connection of an upcoming visit of President Carter to the western part of Kentucky, the other agents in our office were in eastern Kentucky and became involved in a shootout with the counterfeiters. Our agents were detected by the bad guys, and several shots were fired back and forth. I could not believe it. I was very disappointed that I missed out on the action. So this was a perfect example of how diverse we had to be as Secret Service agents. Simultaneously, we had a shootout going on in eastern Kentucky the same time as a Presidential visit in the western part of the state involving agents in our Louisville Field Office. By the way, Paul Kidd, the counterfeiter, went to trial in federal court in Pikeville, KY. He was convicted and received a lengthy sentence in a federal prison.

Kentucky is a large state, consisting of approximately five hundred miles from the eastern boundary to the western boundary, which is the Mississippi River. We did not have enough Secret Service agents in our Louisville Field Office to have the luxury of having another agent with you when conducting investigations. One of the very worst phone calls you could receive in the middle of the night was that a drunk nut was at a bar located one hundred to two hundred miles from your residence making threats to kill the president of The United States. One year I had one hundred of these investigations, and believe me, I had to get out of bed, at say, 2:00 AM, get into my Secret Service vehicle, and hit the road by myself to face some crazy drunk in order to determine if this nut was a danger to the president of the United States, or not.

Usually, our office received the information from the State Police or the local police. They, in turn, had received the information from a bar owner. Many, many, nights, I traveled those lonely dark roads throughout the state of Kentucky, by myself. Sometimes, I traveled as far as Pike County, which is located in the far eastern part of the state, bordering West Virginia. Believe, me, those roads are in a mountainous area. I definitely could not be a weak, faint-hearted, Secret Service agent. These were very dangerous investigations due to the fact that most of the subjects had mental problems, which caused them to be very unpredictable. However, duty calls. If the subject made a direct threat to kill the President, it was a violation of Title 18 USC 871, which carries a maximum penalty of five years. I would phone the duty assistant US attorney and get an authorization to arrest this subject. The local authorities would assist me, and this person would be taken to the local jail to await further court proceedings. In all cases, I would conduct a very detailed and thorough interview with the subject in order to determine if I thought he was a danger to the president or not. A final evaluation would be made at the conclusion of the investigation, in my final report. These investigations made the Secret Service agents job completely different from other criminal investigations. We had to predict dangerous behavior, which is the most difficult thing to predict. I, alone, had to make those decisions and be totally responsible for my decision.

During the early 1980s, while assigned to the Louisville Field Office, one of our subjects who we considered to be a danger to our protectees, moved to Murray, KY, after he had been released from prison in the Detroit, MI, area. He was convicted of entering a bank and creating a hostage taking situation. While inside the bank, he began to shout and make threatening statements against former Vice President Walter Mondale. Upon completing his prison sentence he was released and he moved to Kentucky. The Secret Service case agent in Michigan deemed him to be a threat to the vice president.

Therefore, it was required that I personally interview him every three months for a reevaluation. He was EXTREMELY paranoid. At first, he would not consent to a personal interview, at all. After re-contacting him to set up a date for a personal interview, he consented, but demanded that his psychologist be present during the interview. His psychologist was a professor at Murray State University. In fact, he was enrolled as a student at Murray State. He was so uptight and paranoid that his face turned red, and his neck veins bulged out. After the second, or third, interview with his psychologist present, he finally consented to be interviewed alone by me at his off campus apartment, there in Murray. I scheduled the next personal interview to take place at his apartment. I went to his apartment door, which was on the ground floor, and knocked. No one came to the door, and I continued to knock several times. After it was obvious that he would not come to the door, I left. I re-contacted him and discussed the fact that he did not come to the door for his scheduled interview.

He advised me that he was standing inside the door with a loaded, .45 cal. pistol. He stated the reason that he did not shoot me was because I left just in time. Luckily, for me, I did not linger around.

I was on my way to Hopkinsville, KY, on a nice warm day to conduct a routine investigation in either Hopkinsville, or Ft. Campbell, which is located on the border of Kentucky and Tennessee. As I was traveling down the two lane road near the small community of Fairview, with my mind going a hundred miles per hour, I looked out my car window and saw what I thought was the Washington Monument. Damn, I did a double take as I gazed upon this very tall structure that was identical to the Washington Monument in Washington, DC. I had to check this out, so I drove to this monument. It happened to be a monument to honor Jefferson Davis, the President of the Confederate States. The monument was a state park, with park personnel to take you up the elevator to the top, which was 351 feet. It is the tallest un-reinforced concrete structure in the world. The bottom walls are nine feet thick, and the top walls are two feet thick. It was completed and opened to the public on June 7, 1924. I had no idea that this monument was there in Fairview, KY.

As history tells, Jefferson Davis was born in Fairview, KY, and Abraham Lincoln was born near Hodgenville, KY, on Knob Creek. Kentucky was a neutral state during the Civil War, and it is ironic that both the president of the Confederate States and the president of the Union States, was born in Kentucky. One interesting Jefferson Davis fact that I never heard mentioned is that that he imported camels from Syria to the Southwestern United States. Along with the Camels, a Syrian camel herder came with them to teach the American owners how to handle them. Well, after my Fairview, KY, side trip, I continued on to Hopkinsville and Fort Campbell regarding my Secret Service investigation.

One of the most disturbing and sad assignments I had was that several days after an airplane filled with military personnel from Fort Campbell, Kentucky crashed as it was coming in for an landing in, I believe, Newfoundland, Canada. The charter plane was on its way back from the Middle East with 150–200 passengers, who were coming home on its way to Fort Campbell for the Christmas holidays.

As I recall, the plane was landing to refuel. Anyway, there were no survivors. Several days later, President and Ms. Reagan came to Fort Campbell and met with every family member of the deceased military personnel. The ceremony took place in a large airplane hander. As I stood there watching the president go down the line talking with, and hugging, every family member as they wept, sometimes on his shoulder, I became very emotional. I was thinking to myself, why did this have to happen? This could have been my child or a family member. However, this was one of those sad and awful responsibilities that a president of the United States has, regardless. Here, all those paratroopers and other military personnel were coming home for the holidays, after being away for many months and their life had to be ended under such tragic circumstances. As I recall, the cold, icy weather played a part in bringing down the airplane.

Buster Pate put five bullets into the head of his wife, while standing in their kitchen. He was sentenced to life, serving his time in the La Grange Reformatory, La Grange, KY. He was a large, mean, strong, man. I mean strong and mean, with mental/emotional problems. His thinking was that if the wrote letters threatening to kill the president of the United States, he would be charged federally, and be able to serve time in a federal prison. So Buster continued to write these threatening letters, and due to his violent background, he was determined to be a danger to the president, even though he was in prison. In other words, in the event Pate was not in prison, he would definitely be considered a danger to the president. Therefore, I had no choice but to consider him dangerous. Anyway, I would go to the prison for his three month personal interview. He was brought into a room, sitting across a table from me. One prison guard was standing behind me at the door. As the interview progressed, Pate's face would become red, with his arteries in his neck bulging out. Also, he would attempt to lunge at me, but then he would sit back down. However, he could have jumped across the table and grabbed me, doing severe physical harm, before the guard could have stopped him. Needless to say, I kept a very close eye on his movements during the interview.

On one occasion, which was during the 1980s, our Louisville Field Office received information from headquarters that the Director of the Bureau of Engraving and Printing, plus, one other individual who was traveling with the director, were flying to Louisville, from Washington, DC. The purpose of the trip was to store certain items in the Gold Vault at Fort Knox, KY. On the date of their arrival, myself and another agent met them at the airport and transported them to the Gold Vault. It is noted that the Gold Vault is located in plain view, near a busy highway. The Director of Security at the Vault had been advised that we were coming to his location. Therefore, he expected our arrival. We drove up to the closest gate and got out of our vehicle in order to wait on someone coming to escort us inside the building. There were four of us standing there waiting on the escort. However, we were advised that only the director of the Bureau of Engraving and printing and his companion could enter. I advised the Director of Security that no one would enter unless I and my co-worker also entered.

Our conversations went back and forth for fifteen or twenty minutes. Finally, the Director of Security who was a retired Colonel in the Army, relented, and let us come in. Now, here we were, the four of us standing in plain view in front of the Gold Vault which was built on a slightly elevated area, in a standoff position speaking in sometimes not so friendly loud voices. What a scene! The Gold Vault is in plain view of everyone in the immediate area. It is noted that the US Secret Service had jurisdiction over conducting routine security surveys at the Gold Vaults throughout the United States. As part of my job, I had already been involved in conducting a security survey at the Fort Knox Gold Vault. Therefore, as a Secret Service agent I was allowed to have access to the Vault. Apparently, the Director of Security was not familiar with the current rules and regulations. Everything turned out well and we entered the Gold Vault with or guests, who stored their items. The point I want to make is that the Secret Service has numerous missions other that protection missions.

During the summer of 1984, while assigned to our Louisville Field Office, I received an assignment from headquarters that I was to travel to Riyadh, Saudi Arabia, as part of an advance team in connection with former President Gerald Ford's visit to that city. Several days prior to departing for Saudi Arabia, my wife's pesky cat, Toby, pissed in one of my most expensive shoes. We tried everything to remove this odor, and finally, after trying everything we could think of, we were satisfied that the odor had been removed. So I packed this pair of shoes in my luggage headed for Saudi Arabia. Former President Ford was residing in Palm Springs, CA, at that time. His Secret Service detail also resided in that area, since he had twenty four hour protection, as did all former presidents. All agents traveled on diplomatic US passports, and I had previously forwarded my passport to Palm Springs, in order for them to get a visa for it. Anyway, our plan was for me to meet the other advance agents in the TWA terminal at JFK Airport, in New York City, and then take the nonstop flight to Riyadh.

On the day that I was to hook up with the advance agents, I left Louisville for Washington, DC, for an intelligence briefing at our headquarters. After the briefing, I was to fly to JFK and meet the agents. I departed Washington with two hours to spare. I was very relaxed, knowing that I did not need to rush, etc. However, I almost had a stroke when the Captain advised everyone on the plane that JFK was fogged in, and that we would have to circle the airport until we were given clearance to land. Well, we kept circling, and circling. All the passengers became restless, looking at their watches and appeared to be worried and disturbed. Anyway, we circled for TWO hours before being given the all clear to land. Needless to say, I could not meet up with the advance team at the TWA ticket counter. I realized that they had my passport with them, but due to their clear, great, decision making, they left my passport at the TWA ticket counter.

What a relief! I was told by the ticket agent that a plane was leaving for Rome, Italy, at gate so and so. I started running to that gate, which was not close. As I got to the gate, the door to the plane was being closed. As it was closing, the gate agent let me on. I then headed for Rome, Italy. Just prior to our landing in Rome, we were advised that the baggage handlers were going on strike and that our plane was the last one that they would handle. I had to get another TWA flight for Athens, Greece. After arriving in Athens, I then had to take another TWA flight to Cairo, Egypt. As I was waiting to go through security at the Athens airport, I could not help but notice all the young males who could be potential terrorists. At that time, the PLO was blowing up TWA airplanes and killing certain American passengers. Needless to say, this was not one of the happiest times in my life. Prior to taking off from the Athens airport the Captain advised everyone that the Cairo airport was having a sand storm and no planes were allowed to land. While waiting to get clearance to depart from Athens, everyone stayed on the plane.

    I shot the bull with the TWA captain, and asked him how sand would affect the jet engines. He made me feel a little better when he said that the sand would just blow right on through the engines and come out the other end. Finally, the Captain was given clearance to depart for Cairo. We headed for Cairo, and as we were descending on the airport runway the sky and surroundings were very tan from all the sand. After landing, I met with the TWA representative at the airport for assistance in getting a flight to Riyadh.

    However, no flights were available that day. I had to stay overnight in the Egypt Air hotel located in the airport. This was a hoot. That evening I went down to the terminal area just to get out of my room. A cat was milling around meowing, with ceiling fans slowly going around, and around. An elderly lady was mopping, or moving the sand on the floor from what appeared to be one place to another. The area was very quiet. I did not dare to drink any water from the faucets or fountains in the airport. Also, I did not bathe. I did not want to get sick from having water inside my mouth. Therefore, I consumed no water or liquids for almost twenty-four hours. Throughout the night these loud banging noises occurred, which was caused by their electrical power system. I did not get any sleep. While at the airport and as I would walk around outside, etc., I would go through two or three security gates which had armed military type guards. I had my carry on flight bag with me, which, among other things, had several Secret Service pens and cuff links that were given to me for my counterparts in Saudi Arabia. However, these security guards would take one of these for themselves without my permission.

    Being at that airport at that time made me realize how corrupt and incompetent the government was. How could any American with the brain of an ameba have fun in these countries? Just leave it to the old American tourist. Some would take a trip into the core of this earth knowing they would never come back, if the trip was billed as an adventure/vacation trip. The health/food/water concerns, alone, would make me not want to mingle/dine in the general population. My father-in-law, Harry Weber, ate a steak in a public restaurant during the 1950s while with the CIA in Port Said, which caused him to develop a tape worm the entire length of his intestines. He tried several home remedies for many days to get this darn worm out of his system, but the only remedy that worked was sitting for hours at a time on a pot filled with hot water. Finally, the hot water convinced the tape worm to come out because it apparently could not tell the difference between the temperature inside his asshole, and the outside, due to the hot water. For some strange reason, this thought came to me as I was stranded in the Cairo airport.

The next day the TWA representative at the Cairo Airport finally got me a seat on Saudi Air, which was a jumbo jet plane. Here I am by myself, sitting in this seat thumbing through various magazines, many from the United States, waiting on the plane to depart for Riyadh. The photographs in these magazines showed NO exposed female skin. The exposed skin in the photo's had been removed. The flight attendants were neat and professional. However, just prior to taking off, a voice comes over the PA system. SON OF A BITCH, the voice was saying a prayer in Arabic. This made me feel REALLY good. I believe that I was the only American on this plane. Shortly after takeoff the captain began speaking over the PA system. Guess what? He had a British accent. Damn, did this ever make me feel better?

After landing in Riyadh I finally hooked up with my advance team at our hotel, which was a Marriott. The beautiful hotel pool had NO female bathers, only ugly, hairy, men's bodies, which I absolutely take no pleasure in looking at. In preparing for former President Ford's visit, I, and the two other members of our advance team made our first visit to the American Embassy for a briefing, etc. I was wearing my suit and dress shoes. Yes, I wore the damn shoe which Toby the cat had pissed in, back in Kentucky. During meetings in the ambassador's office for the next two or three days, I constantly thought of the cat piss odor that may be coming from the shoe. I thought that I could smell the odor as I sat there with my legs crossed, talking about Ford's visit. I was hoping that no one else could smell this damn cat piss odor. If they did, no one mentioned it to me. Anyway, former President Ford's visit went very smoothly. There were no security problems. During 1983, the year prior to our trip, there were only four murders in the whole country, and those involved were migrant workers from the Philippines. The punishment for committing a crime was severe. The person who committed a murder was beheaded.

A person convicted of, say, forgery, had their hand cut off. We passed by the public beheading arena each day as we traveled back and forth from our hotel to the American Embassy. Also, after former President Ford departed Riyadh, our advance team was invited to dinner at one of the State Department Security Officer's residence. As we all know, Saudi Arabia follows strict Sharia Law, forbidding any alcohol consumption. However, due to all the foreign construction workers from America and other countries, they would allow the cargo planes to bring beer into the country. No one was allowed by law to be seen outside their home with a beer in their hand. Otherwise, you would go to jail and receive a severe penalty, or be deported. So ALL alcohol consumption had to take place in the confines of your home. Also, we visited one of their malls which consisted, among other items, high-quality gold jewelry. These malls were called Suks. There were thousands of gold jewelry items hanging from the ceilings of each merchant's booth. When prayer time came, five times daily, all the merchants closed their doors for twenty minutes. The three of us were together, but their law prohibited more than two people standing together on the street. Therefore, we had to keep moving.

All of a sudden, this white paddy wagon with old men dressed in white long robes with long sticks, came swooping down the narrow street. They would hit many of the lone merchants who were sitting on the street trying to sell their merchandise if they thought they were in any violation of the prayer time. Many people were thrown in the paddy wagon and taken to jail. The whole situation was somewhat scary. Man, I was happy to get out of there, go to my hotel, and catch my flight out of that country. I have no desire to go back, ever. So I arrived back to my home, and office, in Louisville, KY, thus, continuing with my criminal investigations as if I had not been away. By the way, as soon as I arrived at my residence, I threw those damn shoes that I thought smelled like cat piss into the garbage can. I will never get into a situation like that again. I should have known better!

I had an assignment to assist in the inauguration of President Reagan, which was to take place on January 20, 1985, in Washington, DC. I arrived there a few days in advance for briefings and assignments. However, the weather became so cold that the outside inaugural activities had to be canceled. I was staying in a nice Marriott Hotel located just across the Potomac River, in Arlington, VA. The windows had ice all over them and all the guests came to the lounge area wrapped in blankets and bed coverings. Everything froze in the hotel, including water pipes. The hotel attempted to cover the windows in the lobby area with whatever they could get to make it warmer. No hot food could be served also. The whole experience was totally miserable. It was awful. Due to January 20, falling on a Sunday, President Reagan was privately sworn in at the White House. However, FOR THE FIRST TIME IN HISTORY, the public inauguration address took place in the US Capitol Rotunda due to the freezing weather. The noon temperature was seven degrees. The inaugural parade was re-scheduled for May, at the Epcot Center at Disney World, in Orlando, FL. I did receive an assignment to assist in that parade, which was much warmer than the attempted January, parade and inauguration, in Washington, DC.

During the first part of 1987, my office began receiving information that a credit card scam was operating out of the Hopkins County Detention Center, Madisonville, KY. This investigation was assigned to me. I seemed to always be the lucky one. The suspect was Robert Rector, who, on October 7, 1986, had received a ten-year sentence on felony theft by deception charges. He was being confined in the Hopkins County Detention Center until a cell became open in a state of Kentucky penal institution.

## STRUGGLE TO ZERO

Rector's credit card scheme involved several members of his family, along with one other person who was residing in the Nashville, TN, area. These individuals retrieved the carbon copy of the credit card purchase slips from trash containers, after they had been discarded by the various places of business, such as department stores, and convenience food stores, etc. These carbon copies of the sales slips, which contained the credit card information, were, then, taken to the detention center, and given to Rector. In order to make a purchase over the phone, Rector would place a collect call to his accomplice, in Nashville, since he could make only collect calls from the jail. His accomplice in Nashville had a three-way, or conference call setup, which allowed her to dial the place of business that had an item that Rector wanted to purchase, using the stolen credit card information. Rector would talk directly with someone at the place of business, who in turn would mail/UPS the item to Rector's family residence, in Nortonville, KY, a rural area in the same county as the detention center. Sometimes, Rector would have the illegally purchased merchandise sent to the jail, using the jail street address.

On Wednesday, March 5, 1987, with the assistance of local and state law enforcement officers, a search warrant was obtained to conduct a raid/search of the Hopkins County Detention Center. I, along with riot-geared, shotgun wielding officers, entered the jail through a district court room and began herding prisoners into the hallways in order to search their cells. Almost three hours later, we carried from the detention center almost ten gallons of jail brewed alcohol, crude jail-made weapons, knives, razor blades, a sledge hammer, screwdrivers, pliers, scissors, pills, marijuana, bludgeons, assorted cigarette lighters, and jail made water heating devices. A screwdriver was removed from the wall of the maximum security section of the jail, where a prisoner had been digging away the mortar around a concrete block. The electrical locking system was disabled, thus, making it impossible to lock this section down. According to the jailer, the lockdown system had been inoperative for at least three years.

During the search, the maximum security cells were so cluttered that it was difficult to search them. Some of these cells were fitted with cable TV service, radios, and a police scanner. The floors were littered with "sex" magazines, books, newspapers, clothing, shoes, food containers, and many other items. The jailer blamed the horrible conditions to overcrowding. However, if you were a prisoner, you would consider the conditions to be GREAT. As prisoners, they had it made. What prisoner would NOT want to be confined in this jail? During the raid the prisoners were chanting, "You guys are too late. We have been cleaning house for two days. Take what you want. We'll have it all back in two days."

Following the jail raid/search, a search warrant was obtained to search of Daisy Rector's residence (Robert Rector's mother), near Nortonville. We found diamond rings, watches, gold bracelets, video, cassette recorders, huge quantity of new tools, a sewing machine, typewriter, set of tires, battery, baby crib, and numerous credit card slips. Rector's family members would take illegally obtained merchandise to the jail, put it on the ground floor elevator, and send it to the second floor where it was picked up and delivered to Rector without any jail employee inspecting it. No one would accompany the merchandise after it was left by the family members. It was estimated that between $100,000 to $200,000, worth of illegally obtained merchandise was ordered by Robert Rector during his relatively short stay as a prisoner in the Hopkins County Detention Center. The UPS delivery trucks were keeping the road to Rector's family home red hot. It was unbelievable. He was supplying gifts to all his friends, inmates, jail officials, and family members. It was Christmas every day!

Two deputy Jailers, plus, members of Rector's family were charged along with others, for theft, receiving stolen property, and credit card fraud. Some received prison time, others received probation, and others received no time, at all, due to their cooperation. As a result of this investigation, the county got a new Jailer and a new detention center. The people in the county were grateful that this horrible jail situation was brought to light. I was the only Secret Service agent involved in this investigation, which was a monumental task. With the help of many local and state law enforcement officers, we did our job without any formal recognition. I never received even an "atta-boy." Throughout my career, I just did my job because it was my duty and I never expected anything other than self-satisfaction. I have nothing but disgust for these "brownnosers," whose noses become like heat seeking missiles. Believe me, my agency had its share of these heat seeking noses. These heat seeking noses are very common in all federal agencies. With very few exceptions, all my supervisors in the Secret Service were very decent people.

Overall, I feel very lucky that I had a career with the Secret Service instead of another federal law enforcement agency. One benefit was that my retirement pay was substantially more than my counterparts in other federal law enforcement agencies due to the retirement system that was available only to Secret Service agents at that time. The main benefit for me was that the Secret Service was very unique due to being involved in both protection and criminal investigations. As I have previously stated, I always preferred the investigative part involving complicated investigations due to the challenge in solving these crimes. However, I must admit that the protection part sometimes provided a relief from the criminal investigations.

On Sunday, May 28, 1989, *Louisville Courier-Journal Newspaper* staff writer, Deborah Yetter's article appeared in the newspaper. Her article was titled, "Stung into Action," State plans to change the way it handles food stamps. The article stated that when B & B Foods opened its doors in 1987, as a small "survivalist" food store in a Shively home, customers promptly appeared, due to the fact the proprietors had put out the word that their real business was the illegal trade in food stamps. B & B Foods was a front for a government sting. The main target was Program Management Systems, Inc., a company under contract by the State of Kentucky to distribute over the counter food stamps for the state. The undercover operation revealed a thriving food stamp black market. Over the next several months, we bought and sold food stamps for cash, guns, drugs, used furniture, and were even offered a stolen tractor-trailer loaded with cameras.

As a result of this investigation, twelve individuals were charged and convicted. The person who ran Program Management Systems Inc., received a prison sentence for falsifying federal documents. One of his office managers and her boyfriend, plead guilty to illegal trafficking in food stamps, and another employee also plead guilty. Seven others plead guilty to various charges, such as food stamp fraud, and one for embezzling government commodities. This individual, a self-proclaimed Reverend Earl Thomas Dowell, died before he could be prosecuted. He had an accomplice who worked at the US Department of Agriculture, Louisville Commodities Supplemental Feeding Center. Dowell operated the Beacon Hope Ministry Mission. He had a store, wherein, he would give away US Government cheese, old doughnuts, and other old pastries to the disadvantaged street people, and others. He placed these old food items in plain view on a shelf, where they could easily be seen as you walked by the store front. Roaches, ants, and other creatures would run all over these items. He had several dogs upstairs, and they were never taken outside to do their business. The floor was totally covered with dog waste. The smell was horrific.

Dowell had already been convicted and received a ten-year sentence for selling the sexual services of a ten-year-old child, for $6,000, in food stamps. I interviewed Dowell in his store, and throughout the interview he told me about the arrangement that he had with families of young boys in Eastern Kentucky, wherein, they would bring their children to him and leave them over weekends in order that he satisfy his horrible sexual desires. He was very despicable, and for me, as an investigator, I almost vomited throughout this horrible and uncomfortable interview. I thought to myself, *GOD, why am I here talking to this despicable man!* My answer was always the same. There was no one else to do it. The whole interview was on tape. In addition, during the course of our investigation an informant received information that a woman was so desperate that she was willing to sell her small child for $3,000, in food stamps. We were never able to make contact with this female, although we tried. Food stamps, as a street currency, were used to purchase almost anything. For example, in Albuquerque, NM, during 1988, undercover policemen were offered two surface-to air stinger missiles for food stamps. Unbelievable!

I ran the entire investigation for the Secret Service. I was assisted by one investigator from the US Department of Agriculture, and one

# STRUGGLE TO ZERO

from the State of Kentucky Attorney General's Office. Only three investigators were involved to investigate this very stressful, complicated, and very successful investigation. My headquarters was very helpful with the electronic setup, which included a gun room with a two-way mirror right next to the desk where all transactions took place. We offered eighty cents to the dollar for the stolen food stamps, which was a little higher than the normal street price. We told the prospective customers that we (B & B Foods) were authorized to redeem the stamps, due to the fact we had federal authorization to accept them. Our first customers were Michael and Irma Sloan. Irma was the manager of the Program Management's office, on Rockford Lane, Louisville, Ky. We knew in advance when Sloan, the office manager would steal the stamps, and during the same evening her husband would bring the stolen stamps to B & B Foods.

Many food stamp recipients failed to come to the food stamp office and pick up their stamps for that month. So at the end of each month, Office Manager Sloan would forge their name to their IBM computer card, indicating that the recipient had, in fact, picked up their food stamps for that month. The unsigned computer cards and leftover food stamps had to be returned to the state. Sloan would then take all the food stamps that were not picked up for each month. Then she would give them to her husband, who in turn, would bring the stamps to our undercover business, B & B Foods, where we would buy the stolen food stamps from him. We paid him eighty cents to the dollar, which was a good price due to the fact it was all profit for him. Anywhere, from $5,000, and up worth of food stamps were not claimed by the recipients each month for whatever reasons. We almost knew in advance when the office manager would steal the stamps. On the date of the theft her husband would show up in our office with the stolen food stamps and we would purchase them.

The legitimate food stamp office in Louisville was located next door to the Broadway Meat Company. The food stamp recipients who had just picked up their monthly allotment from the food stamp office, walked next door to the Broadway Meat Company, and sold their stamps, anywhere, from fifty to eighty cents to the dollar.

Broadway Meat Company would then take the stamps to the bank and redeem them for cash. They were making a good profit. Another defendant who cooperated with this investigation introduced me to Steve Martin, the head of the Kentucky Program Management Office. He was the big boss. Due to the fact that Martin was a good golfer who really enjoyed the game, arrangements were made to set up a golf game with him at Valhalla Golf Club, the most expensive and prestigious golf club in the Louisville, area. I, and one of my co-workers, played eighteen holes of golf with Martin. I was just a weekend hacker golf player and Martin was a very good golfer.

Man, was I under a lot of pressure. I was using an assumed name, but on one hole I missed a putt and without thinking, I blurted out my real name. Thank goodness, Martin did not catch this. One slip of the tongue, or one mistake could blow the whole undercover investigation. I had this pressure three to four months, straight. The paperwork was the biggest pain in the ass. Every phone conversation that was recorded had to be approved through our headquarters and the Department of Justice. The Secret Service was very strict in regards to the Title III Statute. Sometimes it seemed as if I did not have time to do anything but handle the paper work. The end result with Steve Martin was that he went to trial, and was convicted. He was originally sentenced to two years in prison, but the federal judge suspended all but ninety days, and placed Martin on probation for the remaining time, and ordered him to pay a $10,000, fine.

On another occasion, a huge man wearing a very loose hanging shirt showed up at our sting operation office, wanting to sell a tractor-trailer load of cheap cameras for $20,000, in food stamps. Our informant had directed him to our office. I advised him that we did not have that many stamps on hand, but I would check and see what could be done. He and his accomplice had parked the trailer part of his rig, and they were driving around in the tractor part. The informant and the accomplice met, without the big man, in front a convenience store in west Louisville. Man, was it a hot August evening. As the informant and accomplice were sitting in the truck, the accomplice reached underneath his seat and pulled out a shoe box. He opened it and pulled out a snake. He proceeded to put the snake's head in his mouth, and would you believe, he bit the head off. Blood was squirting everywhere, and finally, he spit the head out on the pavement and threw the rest of the snake down alongside the head.

As customers passed by the truck they noticed the squirming, headless snake. As a result of the commotion, the store manager came out and requested that the snake be removed, along with its head. The next day, the informant took me to the convenience store and showed me the dried blood from the headless snake. Apparently, the accomplice just wanted to show the informant how tough he was, and that he was someone to fear. However, I had to advise these individuals that I could not come up with $20,000, in food stamps. I then told them that they might make a deal in Indianapolis, IN, since I knew that their police department had a sting operation set up.

On another occasion during this sting operation my informant and I were driving slowly down the street in west Louisville. He knew the area extremely well, since over the years he had dealt with numerous criminals in this area. He said he wanted me to meet this one guy. As we slowed down and stopped in front of his house, he came to our vehicle and started talking with the informant, since they knew each other. The informant proceeded to ask him how his business was doing, and he indicated that business was good. During rabbit season this guy would round up as many cats as he could and keep them in his back yard. I could see a few cats walking around in his yard as we were speaking. He would kill and skin them, put them on ice, and sell each one for $5, as rabbits. He had a set number of customers who thought they were buying rabbits. Also, during squirrel season he would go down to the Ohio River and round up big river rats and sell them as squirrels, also for $5, each. This guy was very casual as he described his business, as if there was nothing unusual about it.

During the course of this undercover operation we ran into many "side bar," unexpected situations, such as having a gun turned over to me that had been used in a drive-by murder in Los Angeles. I took possession of the gun and turned it over to the local police department in order that they forward it to the Los Angeles Police Department. During this period of time the Los Angeles Police

Department could not keep up with all the drive-by murders in their city. The same person who gave us the gun, also, knew individuals in Los Angeles who were dealing in counterfeit money. So in conjunction with our Los Angeles Field Office, I sent him out there to make contact with these individuals. He drove straight to Los Angeles, from Louisville, KY, in twenty-two hours without any sleep, or anything. I relied on our Los Angeles office to handle the situation. The point being is that during these undercover operations you come into contact with all types of crimes and criminals, as an off-shoot, during the operation. SURPRISES every day. My first day as a Secret Service agent was December 16, 1968. At that time, I had no idea that my career would entail such a variety of EXTREMELY unusual investigations and situations.

On December 30, 1989, which was one year after I retired from the Secret Service, one of the *60 Minutes* TV Program producers was sitting in the Los Angeles, CA, airport, waiting to depart for New York City. The producer was reading the Sunday, *Los Angeles Times* newspaper, and on the front page was an article by Eric Harrison, a staff writer, titled, "Trading in Fraud and Despair: Food stamps have become the currency of the street, fueling vast illegal market in drugs, guns, and cash." Within this article the writer mentioned my food stamp sting operation, in Louisville, KY.

The *Louisville Courier-Journal Newspaper* had printed a story on my food stamp fraud investigation, dated May 28, 1989. This story then appeared in many newspapers in many large cities throughout the United States. As the *60 Minutes* producer read the *Los Angeles Times* article, apparently, she got the idea to do a *60 Minutes* segment on food stamp fraud. During the first week in February 1990, I received a phone call from *60 Minutes* TV program, wanting to come to my residence and interview me, in Buckner, KY, for a segment on food stamp fraud. I consented, and several days later the *60 Minutes* filming crew showed up at my doorstep. Arrangements were made for me to be interviewed in our living room. I was not briefed on the questions, due to the fact *60 Minutes* is a news program, and the questions could not be revealed in advance. Anyway, the next day Harry Reasoner flew in from Hungary, to do this segment. So when the interview started, here I am, sitting directly across from Mr. Reasoner, who, at that time was extremely well known throughout America. I was sitting there hoping that I would not make a fool out of myself by answering his questions in a knowledgeable way. You know, I did make it through the complete interview okay. Appearing on *60 Minutes* back in 1990 was a much-larger deal than today. Today, the TV cameras are everywhere, due to the fact there are so many twenty four hour news TV programs to watch.

After my interview, Mr. Reasoner wanted to take a trip around Louisville in a van with the TV cameras inside, in order to film and reveal what could be purchased with food stamps. My informant, who knew many street people, was also inside the van out of sight, in order to give directions, etc. Mr. Reasoner really wanted to approach a street prostitute to see if she would accept food stamps for her services. The informant knew where to go in order make contact with a prostitute. The van, with Mr. Reasoner in the passenger seat, slowly pulled up beside a prostitute, who was walking on the sidewalk. He asked her if she would accept food stamps for her services. She stated that the cost would be $100 worth of food stamps. Mr. Reasoner made some excuse to keep going, and the van left the area. This incident was part of the segment on TV. I must say, Harry Reasoner was very kind and gentle. He was a gentleman at all times. Approximately three years later he fell down the stairs in his home in Connecticut, and died as the result of this accident.

While in Louisville, KY, earlier this year, which is 2015, Randy Ream, the Assistant US Attorney that prosecuted this case advised me that recently, he was in contact with the Regional Director for the US Agriculture Department in Atlanta, GA, and during their conversation, the regional director mentioned that this food stamp investigation is remembered in their office and that it continues to have an impact on their operations after thirty-seven years. So it appears that some lasting good came out of this food stamp investigation. The procedure for issuing over the counter food stamps throughout the state of Kentucky was changed. Randy Ream was, and is, today, one of the nicest and most competent prosecutors in the business.

During January 1988, my assignment was to go to New Hampshire for three weeks to assist in protecting the presidential candidates, in both the Democrat and Republican primary. My duties included being the lead advance agent and other duties, as needed. I stayed at the Holiday Inn, in Manchester, which was our headquarters during the primary season. There were numerous candidates traveling back and forth, campaigning in almost every city of any size, with a deep snow on the ground. Luckily, the roads were kept clear of the snow. We had no extra agents at all, due to the many candidates that we had to protect. On any given day, I could be protecting a Democrat, such as Governor Dukakis, in the morning hours, and later that evening, I would be protecting Vice President George H. W. Bush at one of his political functions. During my career with the Secret Service, I was TOTALLY non-partisan. I never discussed or was involved with partisan politics. As a Secret Service agent you had privileged information regarding candidates in both political parties. The fastest way to get fired would be to discuss any privileged information with the opposite political party. Brother, you would be fired and immediately sent home. That was the way it should have been.

One of my assignments that I recall extremely well was to be the lead advance agent for presidential candidate Congressman Richard Gephardt. After the Iowa caucus he flew during the middle of the night to Concord, NH, in order to then travel by vehicle to the University of New Hampshire, which was forty miles from Concord. He had to be there for an early morning debate with all the other Democrat candidates. I was the ONLY Secret Service agent available for this trip. I had to set up all the vehicles to be used in the motorcade, plus, make all the other arrangements with the Concord Airport manager. I had no other Secret Service agents, OR local and state law enforcement personnel available to help me. The Secret Service agents traveling with Congressman Gephardt had to be assigned to drive the vehicles in his motorcade. Along with the Secret Service agents assigned to Gephardt's detail, we had sufficient security for this trip. His plane was scheduled to arrive at the airport at approximately twelve midnight.

I thought that I had everything ready for the arrival. As the time came close to twelve midnight, I noticed that there were no runway lights turned on. This was not good. I then phoned the airport manager at home, due to the fact the Concord airport closed down at night. He advised me the procedure that was used by the airline captains to turn the runway lights on as they approached the airport. However, while making the advance arrangements with the airport manager the day before, HE FAILED TO TELL ME THAT IN ORDER TO TURN ON THE AIRPORT RUNWAY LIGHTS, THE AIRPLANE CAPTAIN HAD A CLICKER IN THE COCKPIT, WHICH WAS USED TO LIGHT UP THE RUNWAY, WHILE ON FINAL APPROACH.

All he had to do was to click two or three times, and the runway lights would come on. Man, was I relieved when those runway lights came on. Anyway, the plane landed and away we went, on our way to the University of New Hampshire. I was the only person in the lead vehicle and it was totally up to me to get the motorcade to the University. That forty-mile two-lane road in the dark middle of the night was mighty lonely. I knew the route to the University on this road, but I realized that if I made a wrong turn, I would never be able to find my way to our destination. I could end up in Canada. I realized that I COULD NOT make a wrong turn, and you know what, I managed to get us to our destination without any problems. After that successful mission, I had a more positive attitude about myself. Again, as in so many other situations, after my mission was completed I hopped on an airplane and returned to my residence, as if nothing had happened. Throughout my three weeks in New Hampshire, I really missed my two very young sons. Well, I also missed my spouse. My daughter was in college.

My criminal cases kept piling up while I was away, and life continued. I had to be very adaptable, as did all successful agents. The paperwork was very tedious. Everything that I did as an investigator had to be put in a report. My writing skills, including my grammar, certainly improved as the years went by. I would challenge myself by always trying to write perfect sentences, realizing that many of these reports would end up in our headquarters and other

US government agencies, such as the US Department of Justice, in Washington, DC.

Probably the closest I came to getting shot while on duty occurred during the middle of 1988, in Louisville, KY. I was assigned as part of the advance team for Vice President George H. W. Bush, during his visit to Louisville. While standing outside in front of the Brown Hotel gift shop, alongside Detective John Kirkwood, a shot rang out. There was TOTAL silence. Our agents and the Louisville Police officers who were assigned to the motorcade were milling around, waiting on the vice president to come down, so that we could depart for his next stop. Immediately after hearing the gun fire, everyone froze, and looked around to see if anyone had been hit. However, we observed that a bullet had gone through the gift shop window and landed inside. To my surprise, the bullet entered the glass window, no more than a foot above my head and my counterpart's head. The gunfire was extra loud due to the fact it echoed as a result of buildings being very close across from each other in an alley type location. One of the officer's with the trunk lid raised was showing a fellow officer his new handgun. During this process of showing off his new handgun, the gun accidently fired, and the bullet went directly over my head. The officer who accidently fired the handgun got into hot water with the police department.

Also, during 1988, in Louisville, KY, another incident occurred due to one individual making a threat to kill presidential candidate, Rev. Jesse Jackson. The threat was so obvious that the US attorney authorized prosecution of this person. I obtained an arrest warrant and I and Agent Bill Cravens went to this person's residence to arrest him. After he was advised why we were there, he turned around and headed back inside his house. The only thing I could think of at that time was that he would go inside and retrieve a weapon, and a possible hostage situation might occur. I then pulled out my handgun and yelled to him to turn around and come back, which he did. This person went through the federal legal system, receiving an appropriate sentence. Congress had passed a law that made it a federal violation to threaten to kill presidential candidates who had Secret Service protection. A panel consisting of members from both the Executive

# STRUGGLE TO ZERO

Branch and US Congress would determine which presidential candidate was considered to be a major candidate. The major candidates would then receive Secret Service protection. This law came about as a result of the assassination of US Senator Robert Kennedy when he was a candidate for president, in 1972.

During October 1988, two anonymous handwritten letters addressed to President Reagan, containing threats to kill Vice President George Bush were received at the White House, in Washington, DC. One letter stated, "Obviously, you have chosen to ignore my warning, which tells me that you are a very foolish man. I've given you enough time to tell Bush to drop out of the race. If he wins, he will be executed, and his blood will be on your hands. Remember that." The second anonymous letter which was postmarked September 29, 1988, stated, "Either Bush drops out of the race or I will kill him. I didn't use my pistol this time. I will next time." This letter was accompanied by photographs showing that the letter writer was within fifty yards of Vice President Bush during his political rally stage on a large riverboat on the Ohio River, at English Park, Owensboro, KY. He stated in the letter that during the rally, he possessed a .45 caliber pistol, and that he could have pulled the pistol out and killed him.

Needless to say, my headquarters wanted this person identified as soon as possible, especially, due to the fact that President Reagan was scheduled to visit Bowling Green, Kentucky, in three weeks, which is a short distance from Owensboro. So I had no more than three weeks to locate this person who mailed the letters threatening to kill Vice President Bush. I used every investigative technique possible to identify this person, such as reviewing photographs and video tapes taken by the news media from thousands of people who attended the rally. All the news media agencies, including the national media that attended the vice president's rally, that date, were contacted. Photographs of the crowd, which was in an amphitheater setting, were reviewed, hoping to view the people who were sitting in the area of the camera angle, used by the person who made the threats. I compared this person's camera angle at the rally in order to determine approximately where the person was sitting that mailed the photograph of the rally with the threatening letter.

Also, employees at all the Owensboro businesses that developed film were interviewed. Anyway, within two weeks I identified the anonymous letter writer through extremely hard work, beating the bushes, and using imaginative and effective investigative techniques. The local police department was also very helpful. David Allen Russell, a twenty-one-year-old depressed, loner, was the author of the threatening letters. He had recently inherited several thousand dollars after his father died, and was financially able to purchase at least six handguns, recently. He admitted that he had an interest in Charles Manson and assassinations, and that he had carried a pistol to rallies for Senator Albert Gore, and the governor of Kentucky.

David Allen Russell was arrested and charged with violation of 18 USC 871, threatening to kill the President, and others, plus, US Postal Violations. He was sent to the Federal Medical Center, Springfield, Missouri, for a psychological evaluation prior to spending two years in federal custody. Eventually, he was released on probation and returned to Owensboro, Kentucky. Later, he walked into his US Probation Officer's office in the federal building with a gun and attempted to kill his probation officer. The only thing that saved his life was that the probation officer pushed his panic button and the building guard ran into his office just as Russell was about to pull the trigger. The guard was able to push his arm and the bullet hit the ceiling. Again, Russell received prison time for this incident. As a result of solving this case very quickly, I did receive a glowing letter of appreciation from Secret Service Headquarters, thanking me profusely. Myself, and our headquarters did not want President Reagan to visit Bowling Green, Kentucky, which is a short distance from Owensboro, without the anonymous letter writer being identified. I fully understood that I had to solve this matter, quickly, and I did.

I decided to retire from the Secret Service on December 31, 1988. By that time, I had worked for the US Government over twenty-six years, twenty years as a Secret Service agent and six-plus years, in a non-agent position with the FBI. I was comfortable within my own skin with my Bachelor's Degree from Murray State University, and my master's degree from George Washington University, Washington, DC. Besides, I was just tired. The travel, extremely heavy workload, and lack of personnel, became tiring. It seemed that I was usually the only one left standing, when the difficult work surfaced. However, one other agent, Bill Cravens, was a hard worker, which helped. Throughout my career I was always commended by those outside the Secret Service, but with two exceptions, I never received any recognition from my own headquarters or my supervisors. Again, I never expected anything. I did my duty.

On December 20, 1988, US Congressman Romano Mazzoli, Louisville, came to meet with me at my office before I retired. He had previously made the appointment for that date. Anyway, the purpose for the personal meeting was for him to thank me, and congratulate me on my retirement. I advised him of my meeting with the CIA Chief of Station, in Vienna, Austria, during 1982, in connection with a former President Nixon visit. In addition, I told him that the Chief of Station had remembered him for being the only member in that congressional delegation that refused to accept the cash money that was handed out to the other members to spend on gifts or other personal items. I also advised him that the Chief of Station had nothing but respect and praise for him, by not accepting the money. Congressman Mazzoli was very pleased, and thanked me very much for relaying this information to him. Thank goodness, certain good and honest people, such as Congressman Mazzoli, are remembered by other good and honest people.

Again, I received plaques and letters of appreciation from the Louisville FBI Field Office, US Attorney's Office, and the Louisville Police Department. The Louisville Police Department gave me an Honorary Chief of Police Award. So it appeared that all the agencies that I worked with in Louisville thought I did my job, well. I never sought recognition or praise. I just did my job out of loyalty and duty. As a Secret Service agent, I was always tuned in to the Fourth Amendment to our Constitution, which is the Search and Seizure amendment that allowed law enforcement to search a person's home. I was never eager to enter someone's home even with a warrant due to the fact I truly respected a person's privacy in their home, although out of my duty and responsibilities as an agent, I did carry out searches and seizures in homes. However, I never did get any pleasure in searching a home. I have great respect for our Fourth Amendment.

At 5:00 PM, my career with the United States Secret Service came to a close. However, the final curtain did not come down for another three hours. As I have previously stated, my workload was so heavy that out of duty, I could not leave until I had gotten all my investigative work in order for the next agent who would inherit these cases. I was thinking to myself, *THIS IS NOT SUPPOSED TO HAPPEN!* No one else in their right mind would do this. I knew that none of my office staff and co-workers would give a big crap one way, or the other. They would understand if everything was not in perfect order. But out of dignity and respect, I had to make certain that everything was in proper order. So the curtain came down and I entered into a new, completely different life. I wanted to do so many other things, and have many other experiences in life other than having been a Secret Service agent before I passed over the River of Jordan. I realized that a person has eternity to rest, and I wanted to go out tired as hell. After leaving my office, I went home to my family and continued on as if nothing had happened for the past twenty years. Throughout my Secret Service career, I was in control of my destiny due to the fact that I was comfortable in my own skin. I requested to leave our headquarters in Washington, DC, knowing that I would forfeit any further promotions. However, this did not matter to me.

My Secret Service career was just one of several chapters in my life as I sit here, today. I looked forward to having total freedom of speech as a former Secret Service agent. The one thing that I would never do would be to criticize the individuals that I protected throughout my career. That would be disgusting to me. However, as a private citizen, I could have opinions regarding public policy that may conflict with those who hold political office. Therefore, I could be a partisan candidate for political office, as a former agent. I firmly believe that whenever possible, all citizens should be involved in our political system, such as a candidate for office.

## STRUGGLE TO ZERO

Believe me, my involvement was an eye opener, plus, it broadened my knowledge as to how our governments on all levels actually work. I would take nothing for this experience. I did this mainly for the experience, knowing that I would lose. Remember, I never lost a primary race.

# POST–SECRET SERVICE CAREER

Shortly after retiring from the Secret Service, I became self-employed as an investigator who conducted investigations for law firms and corporations in the Louisville, area. I worked out of my office in La Grange, KY, and eventually relocated to a very nice office in downtown Louisville. I became so busy that I wanted a rest. One example of an investigation involved two huge corporations located in Louisville. These corporations had been taking trash to a huge dump in the adjoining county for many years. The dump became such an environmental problem for the surrounding area that the US Environmental Protection Agency (EPA) had to determine how much trash each corporation had taken to the dump in order to determine who would pay for the cleanup.

I was hired by one of the corporations to find out exactly how much trash the other corporation had taken to the dump since the 1940s. This corporation ran dump trucks twenty four hours a day for approximately fifty years. I had a monumental task. However, due to my vast experience as an investigator in conducting interviews, I located every dump truck driver, except those who were deceased. I interviewed all those still living, and they volunteered the detailed information that I needed. This investigation lasted approximately two years. However, during the course of this investigation, I was told that a long time theft ring had been operated by employees at the corporation and the owner of the huge dump. As an example, if the owner of the dump needed various items, or whatever, he would advise one of the dump truck drivers, who in turn would tell the employee who worked on the loading dock. The items would then be loaded on a dump truck with all the other trash and taken to the dump. This theft ring went on for many years, without detection.

My client was able to determine, in detail, approximately how much trash the other corporation had taken to this dump over the past fifty years. I could not believe that I was able to locate all these dump truck drivers and accomplish such a large undertaking. This was just one example.

During 1996, I began doing contract work for several United States government agencies that were headquartered in Washington, DC. This employment was much easier, plus, it paid well. I was in control of the number of hours that I wanted to work. In other words, I had my independence. However, my writing skills were always put to test, since all my reports were reviewed by many individuals in the DC, area.

During 1999, I discontinued the investigations that I conducted on behalf of law firms and corporations. My only self-employment consisted of only the contract employment for these several US Government agencies. I also discontinued the contract employment due to the fact I have many other things to do before meeting the grim reaper.

# ENTERING INTO THE TOTALLY NEW WORLD OF POLITICS

During my twenty years as a Secret Service agent, I saw every angle of the federal political system, especially, during the presidential campaign seasons. The Secret Service was mandated to provide physical protection to the major presidential and vice presidential candidates, due to the Senator Robert F. Kennedy assassination in 1972, while he was running for president. One of the facts that I learned was that the world and our existence is controlled, one way or the other by politics, whether we like it or not. Many of my friends and neighbors throughout the years would say, "All politics are dirty, including the politicians" or "I hate politics," etc. Well, politics and many politicians since the beginning of time have been liars, cheaters, and scoundrels. This is the nature of this business. Nothing has changed during the past thousands of years, and I believe that nothing will change in the realm of politics for the next thousand years.

If Americans would learn about our history, since George Washington was elected president, they would know that the political arena can be a dangerous, hateful, stinking, awful, arena due to the sheer nature of its being, which is power and control over other people. From the most lowly, local political races, to electing the president of the United States, these races can get extremely dirty and unethical. They are not for the faint hearted. Take running for President, as an example. The candidate will be put in situations where he/she lose their dignity, be shamed, mocked, make enemies, and made to look like a total idiot. Many candidates will make themselves look like fools, just for a vote. Look at the recent presidential races, plus, the races and campaigns of John Adams-

Thomas Jefferson, Andrew Jackson-John Quincey Adams, Abraham Lincoln-Stephen Douglas debates, and others.

Photos of me at Reagan Ranch, 1980.

# DON BELL

**DEPARTMENT OF THE TREASURY**
UNITED STATES SECRET SERVICE

WASHINGTON, D.C. 20223

OFFICE OF THE DIRECTOR

November 7, 1988

Special Agent Donald G. Bell
United States Secret Service
U.S. Courthouse, Room 439
601 West Broadway
Louisville, Kentucky  40202

Dear Don:

I wish to extend my appreciation for the recent intelligence investigation you completed regarding a suspect who threatened the life of the Vice President. I have been informed that the investigation used imaginative and effective investigative techniques resulting in the identification and apprehension of the suspect.

Your efforts represent the finest tradition of those men and women who serve in our field offices and resident agencies. Your diligence and devotion to duty reflect favorably on your office and most certainly on the Secret Service.

I thank you for your dedication and wish you continued success.

Garry M. Jenkins
Assistant Director
Office of Investigations

*Letter of accommodation from Assistant Director of Secret Service Garry Jenkins.*

# STRUGGLE TO ZERO

United States Department of Agriculture

## Certificate of Appreciation

*awarded to*

DONALD G. BELL

For recognition of outstanding services rendered by Donald G. Bell to the United States Department of Agriculture in the food stamp and donated commodities programs. These services had a significant impact on the elimination of fraud in the Commonwealth of Kentucky and resulted in the indictments of numerous individuals and in substantial savings to the United States government.

August 17, 1988
*date*

RICHARD F. ALLEN
Regional Inspector General
for Investigations

Certificate of Appreciation from the US Department of Agriculture.

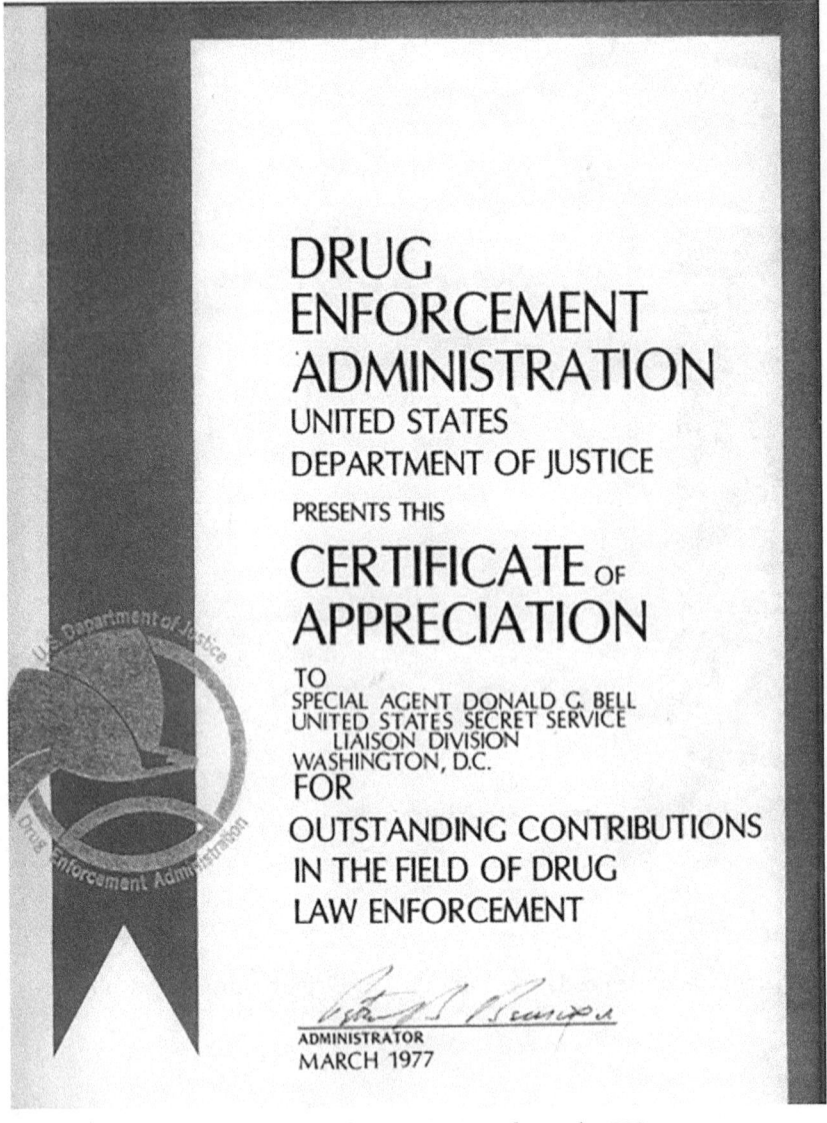

DON BELL

# DRUG ENFORCEMENT ADMINISTRATION
UNITED STATES
DEPARTMENT OF JUSTICE

PRESENTS THIS

# CERTIFICATE OF APPRECIATION

TO
SPECIAL AGENT DONALD G. BELL
UNITED STATES SECRET SERVICE
LIAISON DIVISION
WASHINGTON, D.C.

FOR

**OUTSTANDING CONTRIBUTIONS IN THE FIELD OF DRUG LAW ENFORCEMENT**

ADMINISTRATOR
MARCH 1977

A certificate of Appreciation from the US Drug Enforcement Administration.

# STRUGGLE TO ZERO

United States District Court
FOR THE
Western District of Kentucky
247 U. S. Courthouse
Louisville, Kentucky  40202
March 6, 1991

Chambers of
Thomas A. Ballantine, Jr.
Chief Judge

Mr. Don Bell
1802 Fairway Drive
La Grange, Kentucky  40031

Dear Mr. Bell:

As you may know, the Court has now selected Cleveland Gambill to serve as Magistrate Judge for the next eight years.

On behalf of all the judges of this Court, I want to thank you for your dedication and your service in screening the applicants. The five names which were finally submitted to the judges prompted considerable discussion and, as you might imagine, the choice was a difficult one to make since all of the applicants were felt to be highly qualified.

Under the regulations adopted by the Judicial Conference, you are entitled to reimbursement for any expenses which you may have incurred. I know that some of you drove a considerable distance to attend meetings and that some of you drove a considerable distance to interview applicants outside Jefferson County. If you incurred any expense, you should notify Mr. Grider, the Clerk of the Court, and I will see to it that you are reimbursed.

Thank you again for your services on the Merit Selection Panel, and congratulations on a job well done.

Yours very truly,

Thomas A. Ballantine, Jr.
Chief Judge

TAB/lk

Letter from US District Judge Thomas A. Ballantine Jr. thanking me for being a member of the Magistrate Judge selection panel which selected a new US Magistrate Judge.

DON BELL

# U.S. Department of Justice
Office of the U.S. Attorney
for the Western District of Kentucky

## CERTIFICATE OF APPRECIATION

presented to

*Donald G. Bell*

for meritorious service to the citizens of the Western District of Kentucky and adherence to the highest standards of professional law enforcement in the pursuit of justice in the United States of America.

United States Attorney          Date 1/12/89

Certificate of Appreciation from the US Attorney's Office for the Western District of Kentucky, Louisville, KY.

# STRUGGLE TO ZERO

Myself and Stephanie with former President George H. W. Bush.

I am part of the greeting party at Vice President Dan Quayle's airplane upon his arrival in London, KY, 1991.

Best wishes to Don Bell – Jimmy Carter

Me and presidential candidate George W. Bush, taken during one of his campaign stops in the Covington, KY, area, 2000.

# STRUGGLE TO ZERO

**U.S. Department of Justice**

United States Attorney

Western District of Kentucky

~~JMW:RR:bah~~

July 25, 1989

Tenth Floor, Bank of Louisville Building    502 / 582-5911
510 West Broadway    FTS / 352-5911
Louisville, Kentucky 40202

Donald G. Bell
1802 Fairway Drive
LaGrange, Kentucky 40031

Dear Don:

Enclosed is a copy of the <u>Courier-Journal</u> story indicating that the twelfth (12th) and last defendant has been sentenced in the food stamp investigation involving this office and the United States Secret Service over much of the past two (2) years. I wish to take this opportunity to thank you for all of your assistance and tireless efforts from beginning to the end of these cases and particularly your assistance at trial in February of 1989 which resulted in the conviction of Steven D. Martin, the Executive Director of Program Management Systems, who was previously in charge of the food stamp program in Kentucky's four largest counties.

Your tireless efforts in proving our case against Martin paid off. No one present at trial will soon forget the impact on the jury of the conversation between yourself in an undercover capacity as Don Penn and Mr. Martin in which he agreed to sell you food stamps. This, combined with the search which you conducted of his private Citizens Fidelity Bank lock box were instrumental in his conviction and is something in which you can justifiably take immense pride.

Although I recognize that you have now retired after twenty (20) plus years with the Secret Service you still deserve the thanks and appreciation of this office.

Good Luck and Best Wishes in all endeavors.

Very truly yours,

JOSEPH M. WHITTLE
UNITED STATES ATTORNEY

Randy Ream
Assistant U.S. Attorney

cc: SAC David Ray

203

# Sentence set for 12th person convicted in food-stamp case

The last of 12 people charged and convicted following an undercover investigation into food stamp fraud in the Louisville area was sentenced yesterday in U.S. District Court.

Lorraine Gilmore, formerly of Louisville and now living in Ohio, pleaded guilty to a misdemeanor charge that she illegally trafficked in food stamps. U.S. District Judge Ronald Meredith sentenced Gilmore to 30 days in jail, placed her on probation for two years and ordered her to pay $42 in restitution, the amount lost to the government in stolen food stamps.

Assistant U.S. Attorney Randy Ream said Gilmore stole the food stamps from the office where she worked and sold them to an informant.

Gilmore was one of three people charged in the case who worked for Program Management Services Inc., a company that distributes food stamps in Jefferson, Fayette, Kenton and Campbell counties for state government.

Steven D. Martin, the company's vice president and general manager, was convicted on two counts of falsifying federal documents involving $40,000 worth of food stamps. Office manager Erma Lee Owens pleaded guilty last year to trafficking in food stamps. Federal authorities said Owens also stole food stamps from the office and sold them to an informant.

Program Management's contract expired June 30, and the state is seeking bids on a new contract for food-stamp distribution. The deadline for proposals is Tuesday.

Meanwhile, Program Management is distributing about $6 million per month in food stamps from storefront offices in the four counties under a temporary contract extension.

To All to Whom These Presents Shall Come, Greeting: Know ye that

### DON BELL

is hereby commissioned an

# Honorary Chief of Police

With thanks and appreciation for your contribution of services to the Louisville Police Department

Done in the City of Louisville Commonwealth of Kentucky this the __12th__ day of __January__, 19 89

Colonel Richard L. Dotson

# DON BELL

**DEPARTMENT OF THE TREASURY**
UNITED STATES SECRET SERVICE
WASHINGTON, D.C. 20223

DIRECTOR

December 31, 1988

Mr. Donald G. Bell
Special Agent
U.S. Secret Service
Louisville Field Office
Louisville, Kentucky

Dear Donald:

I take great pride in extending my heartiest congratulations upon the close of your distinguished 20-year career with the U.S. Secret Service.

Your contributions to this Service as a whole, and particularly the Louisville Field Office, have been substantial. Our activities would not have been as successful without the loyalty and dedication of special agents such as yourself. I am sure that as you leave, you will take with you a great sense of pride in your many accomplishments.

Please accept my personal thanks for a job well done. Your many friends and colleagues join me in wishing you the best of luck in your retirement.

Sincerely,

John R. Simpson

# STRUGGLE TO ZERO

UNITED STATES GOVERNMENT
## memorandum

DATE: August 10, 1982

REPLY TO ATTN OF: AD - Protective Operations    U. S. Secret Service    205.0

SUBJECT: Commendation for Advance Personnel

TO: SAIC - Paris
SAIC - Newark
SAIC - New York
SAIC - Louisville

Reference is made to the attached memorandum of SAIC ▓▓▓▓▓ dated July 21, 1982.

Please add my personal thanks to SA's ▓▓▓▓▓ and Donald Bell for their assistance to the Nixon Protective Division during Former President Nixon's foreign trip.

Edward J. Pollard

Attachment a/s

cc: AD - Investigations

Another memo of appreciation regarding President Nixon's visit to Communist countries and Europe.

# DON BELL

**CHAMBERS OF THE SURROGATE**
**County of Rockland**
NEW CITY, N.Y.
10956

JOHN F. SKAHEN
SURROGATE

October 18, 1976

Mr. Stuart Knight
Director of Secret Service
1800 G Street NW
Washington, D. C. 20223

Dear Mr. Knight:

    I am writing just to tell you how much I admired the performance of the Secret Service men during the recent visit of President Ford to Rockland County. Although I had previously seen them in connection with President Eisenhower, I never before had an opportunity close up to watch your men in action. Their appearance, their conduct, their efficiency, politeness, patience, calmness and ability at protecting the President were just amazing to all of us here in the Court House. It is a great pleasure to see men of such caliber working for government.

    I was particularly impressed with two of your men whom I met personally, one Mr. Don Bell and Mr. Dennis Kinnelly (not sure of the spelling).

    I am sure you will be pleased to know that everyone here is talking in glowing terms of the work of the Secret Service. I congratulate you and hope that we will continue to have such a fine organization as an arm of our government.

Sincerely yours,

John F. Skahen
Surrogate

JFS/ed

Letter of Appreciation from John F. Skahen, Surrogate, Chambers of The Surrogate, New City, NY.

STRUGGLE TO ZERO

UNITED STATES GOVERNMENT

## memorandum

DATE: MAR 14 1978

REPLY TO
ATTN OF: Robert O. Goff
Legal Counsel

SUBJECT: House Select Committee on Assassinations

TO: SA Donald Bell
THRU: SAIC - Louisville

  In connection with its investigation into the circumstances surrounding the death of Martin Luther King, Jr., the House Select Committee on Assassinations has requested that you be made available for interview by Committee Staff counsel.

  In accordance with an agreement between the Secret Service and the Committee, a representative of the Secret Service is available to answer any questions you may have relative to these interviews at the time such interviews are being conducted. However, a representative of the Secret Service is not authorized to be present during the interview itself.

  Several of our present and former agents who are residing in the metropolitan Washington, D.C. area have already been interviewed. If you have not already been contacted by a member of the Committee Staff, you probably will be contacted very shortly. In the event that you should have any further questions regarding this matter, please contact this office. My telephone number is 634-5770.

Robert O. Goff
Legal Counsel

MAR 17 8 40 AM '78
LOUISVILLE, KY.
RECEIVED
U.S. SECRET SERVICE

Buy U.S. Savings Bonds Regularly on the Payroll Savings Plan

OPTIONAL FORM NO. 10
(REV. 7-76)
GSA FPMR (41 CFR) 101-11.6
5010-112

Memo from US Secret Service Legal Counsel regarding the House Select Committee on Assassinations, Reverend Martin Luther King.

## DON BELL

UNITED STATES GOVERNMENT

# memorandum

U.S. Secret Service

DATE: July 21, 1982

REPLY TO ATTN OF: SAIC - Nixon Protective Division

SUBJECT: Commendation for Advance Personnel   143-205.0

TO: AD - Protective Operations

Former President Nixon recently completed a seven country foreign trip, including a visit to two communist block countries where a Protectee of this Service never visited. This division furnished lead advance personnel for all stops, however, they were assisted by the following field agents:

▇▇▇▇▇▇▇▇▇▇▇▇▇▇▇ - Paris, France
▇▇▇▇▇▇▇▇▇▇▇▇▇▇▇ - Romania; Hungary & London, England
▇▇▇▇▇▇▇▇▇▇▇▇▇▇▇ - Bucharest and Budapest
▇▇▇▇▇▇▇▇▇▇▇▇▇▇▇ - Paris; Prague; Czechoslovakia and London, England
SA Donald Bell (Louisville FO) - Bulgaria and Austria

I would like to express my appreciation for the effective and low key performance of these agents which set a very good precedent in the countries that were not familiar with this Service.

Would you pass my appreciation to the respective agents and their supervisors.

Michael A. Endicott
Special Agent in Charge

Memo of Commendation regarding President Nixon's visit to Austria, England, France, and various Communist countries.

Queen Elizabeth exiting church, Versailles, KY.
I am located in the lower left corner.

DON BELL

*The Inaugural Committee
requests the honor of your presence
to attend and participate in the Inauguration of
Richard Milhous Nixon
as President of the United States of America
and
Spiro Theodore Agnew
as Vice President of the United States of America
on Saturday the twentieth of January
one thousand nine hundred and seventy-three
in the City of Washington*

# STRUGGLE TO ZERO

Me along with advance team during former President Nixon's visit to Bulgaria.

DON BELL

The Inaugural Committee
requests the honor of your presence
to attend and participate in the Inauguration of
**John Fitzgerald Kennedy**
as President of the United States of America
and
**Lyndon Baines Johnson**
as Vice President of the United States of America
on Friday the twentieth of January
one thousand nine hundred and sixty one
in the City of Washington

Edward H. Foley
Chairman

Attorney General Robert F. Kennedy standing on his desk in his office holding a photograph of his seven children (he had a total of nine children). I am in the left center background.

## STRUGGLE TO ZERO

With CBS *60 Minutes* host Harry Reasoner in my living room in Buckner, KY, 2/1990.

My family with CBS *60 Minutes* host Harry Reasoner, in my home, Buckner, KY, 1990.

For example, after Thomas Jefferson arrived in France in 1785 to replace Ben Franklin as Minister to France, he had an affair with the beautiful wife of a Londoner and artist, Maria Casway. She was a worldly, fun-loving lady, which caused Jefferson to become very fascinated with her. One day, while Jefferson was inside her home, the husband arrived unexpectedly. In his haste to escape, Jefferson jumped out of the window, breaking his wrist. He was never able to play the violin again. Jefferson told his friends that he broke his wrist as he was trying to jump over a fence. Although he was never President of the United States, Ben Franklin fathered a child out of wedlock, named William. William became the thirteenth Colonial Governor of New Jersey. After leaving that office, he became a loyalist and returned to England, never returning to America.

In the presidential race of 1800, between Thomas Jefferson and John Adams, the Adams supporters suggested that if Jefferson became President, everyone would see our wives and daughters become victims of legal prostitution. The Jefferson supporters counteracted by having articles written in newspapers that Adams was a rageful, lying, warmonger fellow. Also, he was a repulsive, pedant, and gross hypocrite, who behaved neither like a man nor a woman, but instead possessed a hideous hermaphroditical character. Adams was labeled a fool, a criminal, and a tyrant. The Adams supporters called Jefferson a mean-spirited, low-lived fellow, who was the son of a half-breed Indian squaw, sired by a Virginia mulatto father, and was well known in the neighborhood where he was raised, wholly on hoecake (made with coarse ground southern corn), bacon, and hominy, with an occasional change of fricasseed (cut up) bullfrog, for which abominable reptiles he had acquired a taste during his residence among the French. Jefferson was branded a weakling, an atheist, a libertine, and a coward. Even Martha Washington became involved by telling a clergyman that Jefferson was one of the most detestable of mankind. This was the first time that the race card was used in a presidential campaign.

President Jefferson greeted Ambassadors at the White House while in his pajamas, and spoke publicly against slavery, while owning many slaves. At the time of his death, he was $107,000 in debt.

# STRUGGLE TO ZERO

After freeing his chef, James Hemings, the poor guy did not know what to do. He became an alcoholic and ended up committing suicide. President Jefferson had affairs with wives of his friends. Another affair was with Betsy Walker, the wife of a friend who worked in his cabinet. President Jefferson sent her husband to negotiate a treaty in New York City, and the husband asked him to keep an eye on Betsy while he was away. President Jefferson's watchful eye on Betsy soon turned into romance. Jefferson believed that sex was perfectly right and normal for lovers, even those cheating on their husbands. Sally Hemings, a mulatto, and President Jefferson's favorite slave, was the half-sister of Jefferson's wife, Martha. Their romance began when she (Sally Hemings) was seventeen years of age, and Jefferson was forty-eight years of age. The romance continued until his death at age eighty-three. Jefferson expressed outrage at interracial relationships and he never gave Hemings her freedom. Does the late US Senator Strom Thurmond come to mind? What a disgusting hypocrite he was! For sixty years, President Jefferson soaked his feet every morning in cold water. Also, he had severe migraine headaches. On his tombstone he failed to mention as an accomplishment that he had been president of the United States.

During the 1964 presidential race between President Lyndon Johnson and US Senator Barry Goldwater, Johnson ran the "Daisy" TV ad, which said that electing Goldwater would bring on nuclear destruction, killing all our children. Of course, the ad was false, but that did not matter to the Johnson supporters. During 1940, while serving in the US Naval Reserve in Australia, while a US Congressman, Johnson reported that his plane had been attacked. His report was not confirmed as being true, but General Douglas McArthur awarded him a Silver Star, anyway. Johnson wore the Silver Star ribbon on his coat the rest of his political career. Later in his career, when Lyndon Johnson ran for the US Senate, according to a *60 Minutes* TV Program that aired many years ago, Johnson's good friend, and Duval County, Texas, County Executive, who was known as the "Duke of Duval," withheld turning in the final voting tally until all other counties in Texas had turned their votes in to the county clerk.

Johnson needed a few hundred votes to win, and Duval County just happened to turn in a few more votes for Johnson than were needed for him to win this race. Actually, I viewed this *60 Minutes* Program. I believe that President Lyndon Johnson was one of the most political minded individuals that ever walked on this earth. He became bogged down in dealing with the Vietnam War, knowing not what to do to end it, due to the fact he could not separate politics from reality. He is a classic study of why an individual seeking the office of President needs experience in the real world outside of politics. When you know nothing but politics, your world becomes nothing but politics, thus, warping your mind to where you cannot make a proper decision on anything. Your political mind-set is morphed into your god given mind which leads to nothing but confusion, when it comes to making the correct decisions for our country.

It is noted that during the Abraham Lincoln, Stephen Douglas debates, Douglas accused Lincoln of being a drunk, stating that he could ruin more liquor than all the boys in town together. Lincoln's opponents during the 1860 campaign also called him a "Buffoon," "Ignoramus Abe," and "well-meaning baboon." In turn, Lincoln said of Douglas, "His argument is as thin as the homeopathic soup that was made by boiling the shadow of a pigeon that has been starved to death." Apparently the idea that Lincoln was uneducated, bordering on illiterate, stayed with him as president.

During Grover Cleveland's campaign for president in 1884, his opponent, James G. Blaine, leaked information that he had fathered a child out of wedlock with a friend of his from Buffalo, NY, Maria Halprin, a department store clerk. Cleveland went ahead and supported the child, anyway. He told the public the truth and they came to respect him for his courage. Cleveland's supporters countered that Blaine's first born, who, as a toddler, had died thirty years before, had been conceived before Blaine and his wife were married. In an attempt to make it seem as if Blaine was hiding something, vandals chiseled the date of birth from the child's grave stone. On July 1, 1893, President Cleveland had a cancer removed from his upper palate, and in order to totally remove the cancer, a deep hole was cut in the palate. He was anesthetized with laughing gas. The hole was filled with a rubber prosthetic.

In order for this operation to remain a secret from the public, it was done on a yacht moored on Long Island Sound. Three weeks later he addressed Congress with no one noticing a change in his speech delivery. His surgeon was W. W. Keen, of Philadelphia. This surgery was not released to the public until twenty-four years later. While he was the sheriff of Erie County, NY, from 1871 to 1874, President Cleveland personally threw the noose around the necks of two convicted criminals. He is the only president to have killed anyone, personally. President Cleveland's daughter Ruth had the candy bar Baby Ruth named after her by the Nestle candy company due to her extreme popularity among the American people. Cleveland became the legal guardian of his wife and mother of his children, Frances Folsom, when she was eleven years old. He married her only ten years later. He is the only president who was married in the White House (*Secret Lives of the US Presidents* by Cormac O'Brien).

One former president that had unusual interests was Woodrow Wilson. Colonel Frank House, his closest advisor once said, "He is the biggest bigot I have ever known." President Wilson segregated the military barracks and restroom accommodations in the District of Columbia. He would tell "darkie" stories about "rastus," or "Moses," in shuffling dialect to amuse his guests at the White House. President Wilson was also fascinated with D. W. Griffith's movie, Birth of a Nation, which glorified the Klu Klux Klan. D. W. Griffith invented motion pictures. He was born in La Grange, KY, my residence for many years. The reason I mention President Wilson is that most people would never associate him with anything like this. He is remembered as a "progressive" president.

During the presidential election of 1824 between Andrew Jackson and John Quincy Adams, Jackson won the popular vote, but Adams won the electoral vote. Jackson and his supporters thought they should have been declared the winner in this race. Therefore, bad blood existed between Jackson and Adams due to the outcome of this race. So during their second matchup in the 1828 election the Adams supporters called General Jackson's wife, Rachel, a slut due to the fact that when Jackson married Rachel in 1791, they believed she was divorced. However, the marriage had not been finalized. Jackson and Rachel had to remarry once the legal marriage papers were complete. The Adams campaign really jumped on this, calling Jackson an adulteress who ought to be convicted, and that he should not be President. Jackson was further attacked as a slave trader who court martialed his troops, executed deserters, and massacred Indians. He was also accused of pimping, bigamy, and dueling. It was estimated that he had approximately one hundred duels in his lifetime. However, all these duels did not involve actually firing a pistol at his opponent. Jackson's supporters accused Adams, while he was Minister to Russia of surrendering an American servant girl to the sexual desires of the Czar. Adams was also accused of using public funds to buy gambling devices for the White House, which actually turned out to be a chess set and pool table.

Throughout President John Quincy Adams' presidency, during the summer months, he and his aide would go to the Potomac River for a swim early each morning. President Adams would take off his clothes and lay them at the edge of the riverbank, then swim out halfway across the river, with his aide in the canoe, as he swam along. One day, Anne Royal, a reporter for a Washington newspaper got wind of the President's swimming habit, so she came to the river bank where his clothes were lying and refused to leave until he consented to an interview. Adams finally gave in, and Anne Royal became the first female reporter to interview a President of the United States. Regarding President John Quincy Adams, he was the first President of the United States to be photographed. He had already left office and was photographed during 1848.

Jackson won the 1928 election. At his inauguration ladies fainted, men had bloody noses, and there was total confusion. The White House Ball honoring his victory had poor people with muddy boots standing on chairs, plus, dishes and decorative pieces were broken. The crowd was so large and wild that the White House attendants poured punch in tubs and placed them on the White House lawn, in order to lure the people outside. His wife Rachel died before inauguration day and he blamed his opponents for her death. He stated that he could never forgive them. He was the first president to take the oath of office on the East Portico of the US Capitol. President Jackson died on June 8, 1845, of tuberculosis, dropsy, and heart failure. Dropsy is an accumulation of fluid (swelling) under the skin and cavities in the body, which is a form of lymphedema.

One side note that further indicates how vulgar and vicious the political atmosphere can get in the political campaign after the revolutionary war was a theory by John Adams as to why Alexander Hamilton cheated on his wife. Adams stated that Hamilton had "a superabundance of secretions, which he couldn't find enough whores to absorb."

President John Adams once stated, "That George Washington is not a scholar is certain. That he is too illiterate, unlearned, unread for his station is equally beyond dispute."

Theodore Roosevelt, who at that time was an Assistant Secretary of the Navy, said that President William McKinley, who was serving his first presidential term, had no more backbone that a chocolate éclair.

# KENTUCKY STATE SENATE CAMPAIGN 1990

During my twenty years as Secret Service agent, I was fortunate enough to observe the campaigns for president of the United States from every angle. I always had an interest in our history and the political system. As I have previously stated, as a Secret Service agent, I was NEVER involved in partisan politics. I have friends in both parties, plus, I respect both parties. After retirement, I was residing in La Grange, KY, which is in Oldham County, KY. I became involved in the local political party, and soon thereafter, I decided to become a candidate for the Kentucky State Senate seat, which consisted of eight counties.

Up to this point, I was the first person in my party to run for this seat, EVER, since Kentucky became a state. After completing all the necessary paper work to become an official candidate, it was announced in the local newspapers that I was running for this office. One of the local party activists, Mary Glen McMurray, came on board as my unofficial campaign manager. A few months prior to the filing deadline she helped me with my campaign by going with me here, and there, etc. However, a short time before the deadline, damn, she filed her papers to run against me in the primary. Well, the flood gates opened up. Two other individuals became candidates. Alas, there were four candidates, including myself, that were running for this office. Get this, until I filed to run for this seat, all the Republicans for the past two hundred years were too chicken shit to run.

Then, all these "me to" individuals decided to run. They came out of the woodwork like termites. I do not like "me to" people. The voter registration in this senate district was ten to one Democrat.

Therefore, the odds were against me winning, ten to one. I became a candidate, realizing that I would more than likely lose. I did it for the challenge and desire to gain knowledge about our political system. Larry Forgy, a long-time friend that I first met in Washington, DC, during 1960, and who ran for Kentucky Governor, in 1995, got the biggest kick and laugh out of the fact that my campaign manager, Mary Glen McMurray, turned around and ran against me for the state senate position. To this day, for whatever reasons, he still laughs about this. One day, while I was campaigning in Carrollton, KY, I introduced myself to a lady coming out of the grocery store.

After asking her for her vote, she then asked me if I was a Democrat or a Republican. When I told her that I was a Republican, she gave a loud sneer, made an awful face, yelling that she had never met a Republican, before. I was treated like I had just landed in my spaceship from Mars. The campaign was grueling. It was extremely hard work and I worked hard. I attended more county fairs and damn truck/tractor pulls than you could shake a stick at. To this day, I groan and shiver when I think about them. These campaigns definitely cut down on my social life. None of the political events served booze due to the fact many voters thought that consuming alcohol was a sure way to end up in hell.

Actually, one of my issues was creating health insurance savings accounts. This was 1990, and this issue was way ahead of its time. Besides, none of the voters gave a crap about issues. As I learned in a hurry, and generally speaking, the best way to win an election is to be able to look the voters in the eye and lie to them, if need be. Personal morality usually means nothing. In certain areas of Kentucky, the voters want someone who is a no good son of a bitch, because it makes them feel that you are just one of them. They can relate to that. A majority of voters vote for you based upon your personality, combined with your ability to have a strong media campaign, NOT issues.

In most cases, it is not possible to campaign door to door, due to the size of the voting district. Therefore, you must rely on the media to get your message out. Otherwise, you are just pissing in the wind, or develop delusions of grandeur. I won my primary race with huge margins, but lost the general election by a small margin. My total vote was 11,298, and my opponent's total was 14,045. I did better than all the experts expected, in view of the fact that the voter registration was ten Democrats to just one Republican. One of the "tricks" that the controlling political party can use to bring out the voters is to put "certain" amendments on the ballot. One such amendment that hurt my chance to win was the "church amendment," which made the voters believe that churches would be taxed.

In view of the fact there were ten registered Democrat voters for every one Republican voter a low voter turnout would help me. These church people turned out in droves and most of them were Democrats. I chose not to run for this office, again, and as you would expect, another Republican saw how close I came to winning this seat. He ran for it the next time, winning it. I laid the groundwork and after working my butt off, and then, again, the "me to" syndrome set in. He did thank me for being responsible for his winning the race, which was very kind. At that time, US Congressman Jim Bunning, who later became a US Senator, supported me in this race. He donated $1,000, to my campaign. He was one politician and human being that keeps his word, and told it like it is. I have great respect for him.

I received a letter dated January 7, 1991, from my friend, the late US District Judge Ron Meredith, Louisville, KY, regarding my State Senate race. Judge Meredith stated in part, in his letter, "Like a lot of folks who know you well, I was sincerely, disappointed, that you did not prevail. I hope that you will stay involved in public affairs. The Commonwealth desperately needs good people like you, concerned with its future. If you are down this way, I hope you will take the time to stop by and see me." Judge Meredith was one of the finest persons that I ever met. He was a great judge who never let partisan politics enter in any of his decisions. His decisions were always fair, regardless of anyone's political leanings. In his fairness, he would go against a member of his own family if that was the right thing to do. Politics NEVER entered into any of his decisions.

Also, I received a letter dated November 15, 1990, from US Congressman Larry Hopkins, Lexington, KY. He stated that he wanted me to know of my sincere appreciation for my willingness to endure the sometimes harsh demands of our political system. He stated further that through my efforts and those of all who joined me in my effort, I have made a positive contribution to stronger representative government for our state, and in that sense, there is no loser among those who have dared to be in the arena. He stated that he hoped that I would always feel free to contact him whenever I need any assistance. I received numerous additional letters from office holders, regarding this race. Of course, the only thing that matters in political races is to win. Most voters do not care how you win, just win.

On February 11, 1991, I received a request from Thomas:

> A. Ballantine Jr., Chief Judge, US District Court, Louisville, KY, to serve on the Merit Selection Panel to review applicants for the position of United States Magistrate Judge for the Western District of Kentucky. I was honored to receive the request, and I accepted. The panel consisted of several professional individuals, such as the most well-known defense attorney's in Kentucky, plus, two other attorneys, the US Attorney, and others. One attorney was the uncle of movie star Tom Cruise. We, as the panel, had to consider all applications with regard to academic record, legal ability, professional reputation, character and judgment, and commitment to equal justice under the law. The process was actually very difficult, in that, we had to make our selection from thirteen applicants. Anyway, we did our job as requested, and one applicant ended up being the new Magistrate Judge.

# KENTUCKY STATE TREASURER CAMPAIGN 1991

I traveled to the state of Kentucky Republican headquarters, located in Frankfort, KY, on the filing deadline, which was in January 1991. The actual primary voting date was in May, of the same year. All candidates for all the Kentucky constitutional offices had to file their documents by 4:00 PM, in order to get their name on the ballot. My intention was to determine if anyone had filed for the office of Kentucky Secretary of State. I talked with various individuals, including my longtime friend, Larry Forgy, whom I met in Washington, DC, during 1960, when he was a US Capitol police officer and a George Washington University Law School student. Larry and the state chairman of the state Republican Party, Bob Gable, stated that someone had already filed for the Secretary of State office, but that no one had filed for the State Treasurer's office. They convinced me to become a candidate for this office, since it appeared that no one would file for this office.

  Chairman Gable did not want this office to go unchallenged. However, five minutes before the filing deadline at 4:00 PM, in comes a candidate with his filing papers just in the nick of time. After going through a primary race, I found it totally disgusting and I certainly did not care to go through another. However, I had already filed my papers and could not reverse my decision to run at that point. DAMN! Here we go, again. The gentleman that became my opponent was a very nice person, and I felt bad about having to run against him. I did not enjoy this primary race due to the fact that I had to run against a nice, decent, person. I wished that he had become a candidate before I filed my documents. I would not have run for this office if anyone else had filed for this position. Anyway, I won this race by a margin of two to one.

So here I am in the general election for Kentucky State Treasurer, which requires that I campaign in all 120 counties in a state that is over five hundred miles from the eastern boundary to the western boundary. In the primary race, I also had to travel throughout the state. In other words, the state of Kentucky runs from West Virginia to the Mississippi River. My opponent was Frances Jones Mills. Frances was a legend in her own time in the state capitol. Beverly Bartlett, in her May 29, 1991, Lexington Herald Leader newspaper article stated that Mills won her primary race because of her name recognition. Bartlett stated, "Francis Jones Mills is a name large enough to embody either the good or bad of Kentucky politics, depending on who utters it, and powerful enough to propel a woman some considered a political has-been."

Mills held an elected state office continuously from 1972 to 1987, serving twice as treasurer, once as Secretary of State, and once as Clerk of the Court of Appeals. She had been virtually absent from Kentucky politics since 1987, when she was defeated in the Democratic primary. That was a year after she was acquitted of illegally using state employees and funds in her campaign. At her trial, she testified that there was a "meshing" of her office and her campaign, and there was no way you can distinguish between the two. One of Mills' opponents in her primary race was so distraught by her victory that he stated he may never vote, again. He stated that for the life of him, he could not imagine her winning the race.

One incident that occurred during my primary race took place in Somerset, KY, at a big Republican Party gathering. Among the Republicans, there was a vicious split between the Larry Forgy forces and the US Congressman Larry Hopkins forces. Due to my mere association with Forgy, the Hopkins forces were suspicious of me. Anyway, at this gathering in Somerset, due to this fact, I was not allowed to be recognized as a candidate by the president of the state senate. This was quite unusual and it truly pissed me off. I am a get even type of guy if I am convinced that I am right, and several days later at another rally, I definitely told that he was a no good SOB and that he could go to hell. I am my worst critic. Approximately two years later when he ran for the US Senate, I co-hosted a fundraiser for him in my county. I did this because I thought it was the right thing to do.

As you can see, this political thing is similar to being in a barrel of snakes. You can become entangled, and sooner or later, many candidates cannot tell the truth from a lie. Winning is everything if you have the mind-set of not having any morals. I saw a dark side of politics that I never knew existed in humankind. This doesn't mean that 100 percent of everyone involved in the political process is dishonest. There ARE those who want to do the right thing and become involved for the right reasons (the 10 percent). The political process will definitely expose the dark side of anyone, if there is a dark side inside that person.

Another incident that took place during my race for state treasurer occurred in London, KY, at a fundraiser for our candidate for governor, US Congressman Larry Hopkins. The setting for this event was at a private residence located on a hill in plain view of everyone down the hill. Vice president of the United States Dan Quayle was the guest speaker. Almost all of the candidates for the other offices came to this event, thinking that they would be invited into the residence. We approached the front door and assumed that we could enter. However, we were told that we could not enter. So here we are, pushing at the door. Mind you, I, along with the candidate for Attorney General, Secretary of State, Auditor, and Agriculture Commissioner were standing there at the front door of the "house on the hill" like a group of rejects. What a scene?

There were hostile words exchanged back and forth. Finally, we decided to surrender and leave. The group of Republicans that attended this event were Mitch McConnell type Republicans. They were the liberals, or RINOs. As for myself, I got along with all wings of the Republican Party. Around 1986 or 1987 evangelist Pat Robertson's Christian Coalition came into existence within the Republican Party. Prior to his followers spreading themselves across the country, the party did not emphasize social issues. Boy, this movement spread like wildfire, and as a result many voters with extremist views surfaced. During my race for state senate, and when I campaigned door to door, I was constantly pressured to answer specific questions about abortion. I was a pro-life candidate, but being just pro-life was not enough to satisfy the views of extremist voters. In fact, I realized that I could NEVER completely satisfy the hard core pro-life types.

When I was growing up in our household abortion was never discussed as an alternative. My father was a strong believer in the Bible, plus, being a hell fire and damnation old time (1920s–1960s) Methodist preacher he expressed his beliefs to us, stating basically that if it was fun or enjoyable it had to be a sin. I thought that I might get past St. Peter at the Golden Gate but after listening to my parents and these radicals, they would make a weak minded person believe that they would die and go straight to hell. I remain perplexed as to why so many men are so consumed with the inside of a woman's womb. I do not enjoy listening to these old men in robes, suits, and otherwise, get up there and blow hot air about their own selfish viewpoint on abortion. I prefer to listen to women speak on this subject, not men. We should follow the moral compass of our faith and religion, not politicians. The subject of abortion disgusts me, and I am not in favor of abortion, but keep your own religious view points and issues to yourself. The snake handler's warped interpretation of the Bible is just as valid as many of the other so-called religious groups.

At least they get their viewpoint from verses in the Bible, such as transforming a staff into a snake in the Temple. I firmly believe that religious fanatics who justify every evil in the name of GOD will be responsible for the downfall of western civilization. I am almost certain that our greatest worldwide enemy, today, is the radical Islamist terrorist. As you know, they justify all evil in the name of God. They are really scary, as are certain other warped minded religious fanatics who can have evil religious beliefs.

My inner faith kept me going as I swam through the great white sharks in life. I believed there had to be a higher being because so many so-called human beings should never be called human beings. These horrible so-called humans do not deserve to be put in the same category as humans. Another category should be added and be called "OTHER." So we would have humans, animal species, and "OTHER," as categories for living species. Enough of this, I must continue with the issues at hand. Have you ever thought about how many TRUE believers there would be in our country if church donations were not tax deductible? Just food for thought.

My long-time acquaintance/friend Larry Forgy lost his primary race for governor to US Congressman Larry Hopkins, in May 1991. Therefore, due to the fact that Hopkins won his race, I was on the Hopkins ticket, running for State Treasurer in the general election. As the general election campaign progressed, I was running all over the state attending various events such as parades, fundraisers, etc. One thing is for certain, if the top of the ticket does not win, it is almost impossible for a lower office to win. I had to run a very, very, frugal budget campaign, due to the fact that it was extremely hard to raise money for these constitutional offices. However, I lead the Republican ticket in total votes, 311,000, which was eighteen thousand more than the head of the ticket, Congressman Larry Hopkins. Here I was, running on the least amount of money, but getting more votes than anyone else on the ticket.

At least, that was somewhat satisfying due to the fact that I knew I would not win my race. My motivation was to help bring a two party system back into the Kentucky political system. Kentucky state government had always been controlled by one party, the Democrat party. Almost all the state government employees got out in force in order to help defeat any Republican candidate for governor and other constitutional offices. My main motivation for getting involved in partisan Kentucky politics was to help break up the one party system that existed in the state government for fifty-plus years. George H. W. Bush, president of the United States, gave a speech in Louisville, KY, during my campaign for Kentucky State Treasurer in 1991. As a matter of courtesy to all our Republican candidates for state wide offices, I was invited to set on the same stage with President Bush. He had Secret Service protection and during this whole program I felt somewhat out of place, due to the fact that I had always been on the other side of these presidential visits. I knew many of the Secret Service agents and this was a very unusual situation for me to be in.

Here I was, on the same stage as the president, as a political candidate. I was involved in his protection on numerous occasions while he was the vice president.

Throughout this campaign, I attended NUMEROUS parades, festivals, rallies, and radio/TV appearances, but ended up losing the race. Kentucky has 120 counties and over five hundred miles from east to west. Most counties had some type of festival, parade, or event every year, so I was always very busy as a candidate for office. Therefore, campaigning in a state-wide race in Kentucky was a monumental task.

# MY MOST DISGUSTING POLITICAL RACE

The Ancient Greek aphorism "know thyself" is one of the Delphic maxims and inscribed in the pronaos (forecourt) of the Temple of Apollo at Delphi, according the Greek writer Pausanias.

This race was the most sickening, down in the gutter, disturbing race that I was ever involved in, including those that I read about throughout the United States. If one political race could turn the Devil against politics, this was the race. I was exposed to the deepest, darkest side of politics in existence. I will not identify this race or my opponent due to the fact he and his family remain alive, today. This race made me ashamed to be identified with the local Republican Party. Therefore, I ran as an Independent and beat my opponent, the Republican candidate. However, the Democrat did win this race.

This campaign was bizarre due to the fact that as it progressed, a genuine KKK robe surfaced, which came from a family member of one of my opponents. What in the devil do you do with a genuine KKK robe in a political campaign? Well, I was stunned, and felt dirty by being in the presence of this item. I turned it over to someone who was assisting me in my campaign. This person got rid of the robe. I had no idea who took the robe. I never wanted to know anything else about this disgusting item. However, one of my elderly supporters told me that a Republican supporter of my opponent came to her home and threatened her if she ever mentioned anything about the KKK robe. I never mentioned the KKK robe in my campaign due to the fact the whole thing was too disgusting to me. This race was so repulsive to me that I realized there are far too many Republicans doing bad things. Out of all my races in Kentucky, I never had a problem with Democrats, maybe because the Democrats were very confident they would always win anyway.

## STRUGGLE TO ZERO

One day, I received a phone call from the Kentucky state Democrat chairman, Grady Stumbo, asking me to switch over and become a Democrat. Sometimes, I wonder if I should have taken him up on his offer. I try not to think about this disgusting race. Deep differences between me and my Republican opponent prevented me from running as a Republican. I had nothing but total disgust for anyone who would have associated themselves with the KKK. To this day, I have a clear conscience, and I am very satisfied with myself as a human being. I had this sickening feeling throughout this campaign whenever I was in the presence of this person. Guess what, I was never hurt in my other campaigns, due to the fact that I ran as an Independent. I believe that the most perfect political party platform would be taking the best issues of both the Democrat and Republican parties, and combining them into one party platform.

# KENTUCKY STATE AUDITOR'S RACE 1995

Prior to the filing deadline, which was January 31, 1995, I filed my documents to run for Kentucky State Auditor. Again, it appeared that I would not have any opposition in the primary race, since no one else had expressed any desire to run for this office. However, during the last hour before the deadline to file, state senator Tom Buford filed to run for this office. He was a well-known senator throughout the state, since he had been in office for several years. Obviously, he felt that he would win without a problem, since he was a senator. I have nothing negative to say about Tom. He was a gentleman, in that he gave me a campaign contribution immediately after I won the primary race. Throughout the primary race, which lasted until May 1995, I again traveled throughout the state, going here and there, attending parades, truck pulls, and any gathering of a group of people.

I became very familiar with every highway in the state. I was able to hire Rex Elsass, a nice political consultant from Ohio, who later became known in national political circles. Well, as it turned out, I beat Senator Buford by four thousand votes. Therefore, I was on the ticket as the Kentucky State Auditor candidate in the general election. My long-time friend and acquaintance, Larry Forgy won his primary race as the Republican Party nominee for governor, and Will T. Scott became the party nominee for Attorney General. Also, Steve Crabtree won his primary race, thus, becoming the party nominee for Secretary of State. I should also mention Jimmy Lambert, who won his primary race for Kentucky State Treasurer.

I mention these individuals due to the fact they supplied numerous entertainment through the campaign as it progressed toward the general election, in November. Jimmy Lambert was a unique fellow, small in stature, and who would always show up late at the campaign events. Therefore, he would always speak last. He definitely had a very strong Kentucky accent, topped off with a twang. His brother was the Chief Justice of the Kentucky Supreme Court, plus, his family was very well known in the southeastern section of the state. He is a very nice fellow who is enjoyable to be around. He and his spouse, Brenda, visited us here in Florida while we had a house in The Villages. I truly enjoyed being around Jimmy and his spouse. He was a very nice person. Jimmy is currently a sitting judge on the state of Kentucky Court of Appeals.

Next, Steve Crabtree, the candidate for Secretary of State was a local television personality, in Bowling Green, KY. He was able to get up there and speak forever, without missing a beat. He would convince his audience that he was almost Jesus Christ. He would go on, and on, with his pro-life statements. He was usually the first speaker on the ticket, and his speeches were so long that he took up all the time for the other candidate speeches. We would set there on the stage in front of the crowd, rolling our eyes, hoping to GOD that he would shut up, and sit down. After the election in November, his life went downhill, fast. He was a total fake with his religious beliefs. He left Kentucky, and to this day, I do not know where he is residing. Did he ever deceive the voters?

One unusual incident that Crabtree was involved with occurred during the annual Fancy Farm, Kentucky, picnic, which was always held in August. The picnic was an annual event hosted by the Catholic Church, and over the years it became more and more popular. Thousands of people would attend the picnic. During election years, all the state-wide candidates, plus, federal candidates for office were invited to attend and give a speech from a stage that was erected specifically, for the candidates. Okay, here I am sitting on the stage with US Senator Mitch McConnell, US Senator Jim Bunning, the Governor of Kentucky, and several other office seekers, waiting on our turn to go the podium and speak. Steve Crabtree's Democrat opponent was John Y. Brown II, the son of former Governor John Y. Brown. His father, the former Governor, purchased Kentucky Fried Chicken from Colonel Harlan Sanders, the original owner, for $2 million dollars, and three years later, sold it for over $30 million dollars.

Col. Sanders felt that he had been ripped off, and until his death he remained an arch enemy of Brown. Getting back to the matter at hand, during Crabtree's speech, he really lambasted his opponent, John Y. Brown II. Crabtree used every negative word in the dictionary to describe him. He was very nasty. Well, while Crabtree was still speaking, Brown jumped from his chair and headed directly toward him. However, two or three of us jumped up and grabbed Brown before he could get to the podium. Mind you, this incident occurred in plain view of the people, in the presence of all the well-known office holders and candidates, who were sitting on the stage. What a day! I wondered what in the hell could happen next on the campaign trail.

One interesting/amusing story told by very reliable sources was the one about a former extremely high state political office holder that had a sex organ implant in his later years.

I knew this person very well, and he was always nice and friendly to me. In other words I have nothing but nice things to say about him. He always had younger good looking females around him. On one occasion he has a serious health issue and had to be transported to the emergency room. When the EMS arrived, they had to deal with the fact that his tallywhaker was very noticeable under the sheet that covered his body. Well, they decided the best thing to do was to tape it to his leg to hide it. This is what they did and the problem was solved as they pushed his gurney down the hospital hallway to his room at the hospital.

Will T. Scott, the attorney-general candidate on the ticket, and his wife, Tracy, were my friends on the campaign trail. Their home was in Pikeville, KY, and during Pioneer Days in Pikeville, I stayed overnight at their residence. Will T. had been a Circuit Judge there in Pike County, but he chose not to run again, he then set up his private law practice. He was also an airborne, Vietnam veteran. He would jump out of airplanes as part of his campaign events. He was an excellent speaker who knew the issues. I had a closer relationship along the campaign trail with him and Tracy than the other candidates. I truly appreciated their kindness. As the campaign progressed, Steve Nunn, a state representative from Glasgow, KY, would show up at our campaign events more often, as time passed. After the campaign was over, Steve and Tracy got married. Steve was the son of former Kentucky Governor, Louie Nunn. It appeared that Steve may have been thinking about running for governor later in his future.

In 2003, I made the horrible mistake of running for Lt. Governor with State Senator Virgil Moore. Steve Nunn was a candidate for governor but he lost his primary race to Ernie Fletcher, who went on to win his race, thus, becoming the first Republican governor of Kentucky, since 1967. Steve's father, the former Governor, died, and after his death Steve's life became very mixed up. His mother had died several years prior and his father was his anchor. After the 1995 state wide races, Nunn married Tracy Scott, the ex-spouse of Will T. Scott, the 1995 candidate for Kentucky Attorney General. Steve and Tracy's marriage ended in divorce a few years later. Everyone that knew Steve could never have ever predicted the next chain of events in his life. Steve Nunn was the son of Louie Nunn, a former governor of Kentucky.

After his father died, Steve's life continued to be in a free fall after he was beaten by a weak candidate for his State Representative seat. However, he met another female companion, who lived in Lexington, KY. She had a good job in state government, in Frankfort, KY. According to the 20/20 national news program, Steve and his new female companion dated hot, and heavy. Steve became a Democrat and supported the current Governor of Kentucky, Steve Breshear. Breshear then appointed him to a high paying position in the state Cabinet for Human Resources. After Steve's relationship with his finance went south, she took out a restraining order which caused Steve to lose his good job. He apparently thought she was responsible for his job loss. In order to get revenge, he shot and killed her in 2009, at her exclusive townhouse in downtown Lexington, KY. He was located by the authorities at the cemetery where his family is buried. He ended up pleading guilty and received a life sentence. Today, he continues to serve his time in a state prison located in La Grange, KY.

During my campaign for State Auditor, plus, when Steve Nunn ran for governor in 2003, I was with him on numerous occasions. I got to know him quite well. He is a good example how someone can get entangled in the political web and let it ruin their life. Politics can be an evil and dangerous game, especially for the individual with a weak character and no strong moral points of reference in their brain. One must be well grounded, in order to survive this game with any sanity, left. Today, the 20/20 TV program continues to show the Steve Nunn murder case. Steve's father, the former governor, always supported me in my political races. He was very kind to me. He is turning over in his grave as we speak, as a result of his son's actions.

As time has progressed, I believe that when it comes to love, marriage, and sex-drive, the Democrats have more personal morality than Republicans. I base this opinion on my extensive experience in the political arena (ten races, which including primary and general elections), and observing political races on the national level as a former Secret Service agent. I believe that I have earned the title of an expert in this area.

Will T. Scott, our Attorney General candidate hired Steve Schmidt as his campaign manager to run his state Attorney General race in 1995. All candidates were provided an office space in the same area of the building. My office space was next to Schmidt's office. With my very limited campaign funds, I did hire a young fellow from New Jersey to help me for a short period of time. Therefore, I rented an apartment for him, which was located near our campaign office, in Lexington, KY. Prior to the apartment lease expiring, Schmidt moved in and remained there until the election date. He then left for his next consulting job. When I and Robin Walter, my assistant, opened the apartment door for an inspection, I could not believe my eyes. Unwashed dishes were stacked in the sink, and paper plates with food in them were scattered over the floor. The dishes had never been washed. The apartment was in shambles. I could not believe that any decent person would live in this filth. We had to clean this mess up in order to get our deposit back. We carried several large bags full of garbage out of the apartment. Man, was I ever pissed, because we had to work like hell to clean up the total mess left by Schmidt. He needed to attend a how to keep your house clean seminar.

The point I want to make regarding this situation is that STEVE SCHMIDT was Senator John McCain's top campaign advisor when he ran for president in 2008. Also, today, Schmidt is a political analyst, and routinely appears on the *Joe Scarborough*, MSNBC TV program. Schmidt definitely owes me one! I was a guest on the *Joe Scarborough* MSNBC program during 2004 in reference to a person in the crowd with a gun at a President George W. Bush event in the country of Georgia, a former member state of the Soviet Union. Schmidt was also a top campaign advisor in the George W. Bush reelection campaign for president. So Schmidt was very successful as McCain's top political advisor, AS WE CAN ALL SEE, but he definitely appeared to enjoy living in filth.

While a candidate for Kentucky State Auditor, 1995, while attending a breakfast of supporters, I found myself sitting directly across from the indvidual (a huge, not fat man), who had done some "physical damage" to the face of a very high state political office holder. This office holder had to take a two week vacation in order for his face to heal. What happened was this: The office holder was running around with his wife, who also was an office holder. The husband got wind of this and one night he located them at a motel. He proceeds to enter their room and then worked him over quite severely in the face. As a result, the husband switched political parties. Damn, here I am sitting directly across from the poor victim husband, at this breakfast. Many other "things" happened during this episode, such as divorce, etc. In addition, the media had knowledge of this situation, but never mentioned it. No candidate on our ticket used this incident as an issue, although, it could have been very interesting in a political campaign, mainly, for the head of the ticket. I mention this incident due to the fact I had personal contact with ALL the players, and was aware of all the details.

Continuing on, everyone on the 1995 state of Kentucky Republican ticket lost their races, including mine. Vote buying ran rampant on Election Day. Our candidate for Governor, Larry Forgy, refused to go along with this criminal activity. However, in this case, in Louisville, KY, the Democrats and unions bought votes by the thousands. I am not implying that Republicans did not buy votes in certain areas of southeast Kentucky. However, the Republican Party is more "legalistic" than the Democratic Party and this attitude may prevent Republicans from committing as many crimes as Democrats in many elections. In this case, the Democrats were just more successful.

Forgy lost the race by only fifteen thousand votes, state-wide. Most of these bought votes came from one section of Louisville, the west end. Two individuals were convicted of these illegal activities. I was never approached to get involved in vote buying. It was probably due to the fact that I retired from federal law enforcement. My career worked against me in certain sections of the state, due to the fact that many voters thought that I was too honest. As I have previously stated, if the voter is a son of a bitch, that voter will vote for a candidate that is a son-of-a-bitch. Crooks want crooks elected. Someone just like them!

# US CONGRESS RACE 2000

I was contacted during the summer months of 1999 by United States Senator Mitch McConnell's northern Kentucky representative in regards to the possibility of me being a candidate for US Congress, in the Fourth Congressional District of Kentucky. He came to visit with me and my spouse Stephanie, in La Grange, KY, to discuss this matter. As I look back, today, how I wished that I had not been approached to run for this office. Even today, I wish to be left alone regarding many requests for this or that. However, I guess that I am the type of guy that must be in the battle instead of standing on the sidelines watching the world go by. The visit took place in the local Holiday Inn Express, in La Grange, due to the hardwood floors in our residence being resurfaced.

Therefore, we had to leave the residence for two days. I told Senator McConnell's representative that if no one else surfaced to run for this office, I would do it. The filing deadline was in January 2000, several months away. Well, guess what, on the filing deadline a young Republican fellow, from Washington, DC, who worked in a congressman's office, swooped in and listed a relative's address as his Kentucky residence. Kentucky had motor voter registration, so he obtained his driver's license and filed for this office. Everything occurred the same day. The rules for filing to run for a federal office are different than those for state offices. A US congressional and US Senate candidate can file as a candidate anywhere in the United States. All they need to do is to become a legal resident of a state, which can be done in one day, as in this case.

I was not surprised that someone would run against me, in view of the strong Christian Coalition/Oral Roberts type groups in the district. Many of these individuals were extremists in their views on social issues, such as abortion, etc. This young fellow was a graduate of Oral Roberts University, in Oklahoma, which I understand is a good school. I always listed myself as being pro-life, but these extremists were not satisfied with someone just being against abortion, you had to come up with many more reasons you were against abortion than just being pro-life. You had to be seriously, extremely, no wiggle room, against abortion. I truly believe that all our churches and religious leaders should be more vocal on these moral social issues such as abortion, etc., and get these politicians to rely on their religious leaders for guidance. Speaking of evangelist Oral Roberts, I would watch his tent revival services on TV, or in news clips during the 1950s. He would heal members of his congregation under these tents. He would put his hand on their head and direct God to heal them. The person would fall backward as if to pass out, and one of his assistants would catch this person before they hit the ground. This would make one almost believe that we might not need any doctors or medical professionals, because ORAL ROBERTS COULD HEAL EVERYONE THAT HE CAME IN CONTACT WITH!

I was talked into selling family Bibles, religious books, and a nice Webster's dictionary's during the summer of 1963, while in college. One of my fraternity brothers stated that I could make a lot of money doing this. Bullshit, I came back at the end of the summer, netting only $180! That SOB made a lot of money because he got a percentage of my total sales, plus, the total sales of everyone that he recruited to sell these books. I met many people who were Oral Roberts believers while I was in Brunswick County, NC. Mostly, senior citizens would mail him a $10 donation and in return, he would mail them a white cloth, which was actually a standard sized handkerchief. Roberts called this cloth a "PRAYER" cloth. He instructed the person to lay this cloth on their head before they started to pray in order to have their prayers answered by God. Many years later, Oral Roberts needed $8 million dollars to complete a building on his college campus. He did raise this amount by staying in his prayer tower which was located on campus, until his believers raised the money. So this deceiving man and his spouse "cloned" a son to carry on this deception. Other evangelists have "cloned" their children to carry on their work because it is an easy way to become rich.

Since Jim and Tammy Faye Bakker, the current trend is for evangelists to hook up as a husband and wife team, thus, becoming a "power couple" for Jesus. Many of these power couples are on TV wearing extremely expensive clothes and appearing to look like movie stars. Hey! They do this for the money! Take away the huge amount of money and the tax exemptions, then, see how many TV evangelists would be on TV. Some TV evangelists are decent individuals who are there for the right reason. They do serve a good purpose. Honest ones are needed to help the people who cannot physically attend a church. Anyway, I got off track. My opponent was truly a cocky, smart-assed young fellow. The only reason I mention Oral Roberts was because I came in personal contact with individuals who had their lives directly affected/deceived by this man. I do not like deceptive people.

Continuing with my race for US Congress, US Senator Mitch McConnell did not do, or say anything to help my campaign, in view of the fact that his office approached me to run for this office. He never even mentioned my name. This is standard procedure for McConnell. The Republican Party may never reach its potential in the U.

S. Senate as long as McConnell is the Majority Leader. My opponent, Ken Lucas, who was the sitting Congressman labeled himself as being a "blue dog" Democrat, meaning that he becomes a fake conservative in order to get Republican votes. He tried to have the best of both worlds, deceiving the voters into believing that he was a Republican. His campaign spent $700,000 to defeat me, in comparison to my being able to raise only $60,000. He got 124,000 votes to my getting 101,000 votes. The voter registration in this district was eight to one, Democrat. My opponent's campaign conducted their own poll in September and October, just prior to the election. I was even in one poll, and one point ahead in the other. I had a good chance of winning this race, but could not get any help from the NRCC (National Republican Congressional Campaign Committee). US Senator Jim Bunning donated a $1,000 to my campaign and co-hosted a fundraiser for me, but Senator McConnell's office, who approached me to run for this office, did not donate a dime. I later found out that Senator McConnell did not want me to win this race due to the fact that he wanted one of his "butt" boys to run for this office the next time because my opponent, Democrat Ken Lucas, promised that he wanted only six years in Congress. Their retirement checks will arrive after serving five years.

During my campaign for US Congress I was included on the platform at a huge political rally for presidential candidate, and Governor of Texas, George W. Bush at Devou Park, in Covington, KY, which is directly across the Ohio River from Cincinnati, Ohio. In a Cincinnati newspaper article, headlined "Bell on Stage with Bush," it stated that the battle for the Fourth Congressional District is a "George Bush and Don Bell vs. Ken Lucas and Al Gore" race. I spoke to the crowd prior to Governor Bush speaking. I was introduced by Bill Cunningham, a radio/TV personality. Today, he has a national syndicated TV program. Cunningham gave me a great introduction, which made me feel good. I was thinking to myself, what do you talk about when you speak to thousands of people who came to hear our presidential candidate, only? I realized that everyone came to hear the presidential candidate.

Well, I just came out on that stage, which was out in the open and ad-libbed, relying on my standard stump speech. Thankfully, I did not screw, up, because I knew I HAD to do a good job. I had no other choice, realizing that no one truly gave a shit what I said. After my talk, I was photographed with Governor Bush, and as a campaign handout, I had thirty thousand baseball cards with our photo on the front and issues on the back, very similar to real baseball cards. I did not realize how fast people grabbed these things up, along the campaign trail. I never had anyone refuse to take one. Would you believe that I ended up with only one of these darn cards? I believe the person who was helping me in my campaign kept many of the cards. President George W. Bush is a good person, as is all members of his family. My biggest political disagreement with him was when he entered Iraq, in 2003, instead of going all out in Afghanistan. We had Saddam Hussein under control with the fly overs, etc.

Plus, one can deal with someone who is a secularist and likes females. There is no way that you can deal with these extremist, radical, racist, religious fanatics who treat women as slaves. How can anyone with the brain of an amoeba believe this garbage? There are extremists in many religions who justify everything, including murder, in the name of GOD. There was another factor that could have played a part in the final decision to overthrow Saddam Hussain. Hussain had put out a contract on the life of President George H. W. Bush, and being a loyal son, this could have been the straw that broke the camel's back, in his final decision to overthrow Hussain. This is my opinion.

One of my campaign workers, Mike Moreland, from Union County, KY, was a second amendment nut. He probably slept with a gun beside him in his bed, between him and his spouse. He wanted me to attend every gun event in the congressional district, which was huge. Moreland was able to locate these gun events like an A-Wax plane, and as a result, he was pushing me to spend far too much time on this one issue, which did not translate into more votes. I was spinning my wheels. These one issue voters can become a pain in the ass. Moreland was a go getter regarding the Second Amendment during the campaign. However, when I needed him most to help with my bus tour at the end of the campaign, this gimlet ass fizzled out. I did manage to have a successful bus tour, anyway. This happens often during these campaigns. Therefore, the candidate must screen volunteers thoroughly prior to bringing them on as a volunteer. They will leave you hanging.

As a candidate representing your political party in a congressional race you are in the big leagues inside the political arena. I had live TV and radio debates with my opponent. One such live TV debate was broadcast from Huntington, West Virginia, which covered a huge area of my district in eastern Kentucky. My opponent had a TV hookup from the House of Representatives TV studio, in Washington, DC. We were interviewed by reporters in the TV studio, in Huntington. The only negative issue that the reporters questioned me about was a prior statement on abortion from a ten-year-old newspaper article, which appeared to not be strong enough against abortion. I am a member of the Methodist Church, and I agreed with my church's position on abortion, which may not be as strong as the radical pro-life position. My opponent was trying to make my position a pro-choice position, which was not the case. A large part of our Fourth District in northern Kentucky consists of these extreme radical pro-life voters, and he wanted them to believe that I was pro-choice.

US Senator Jim Bunning co-hosted a fundraiser for me in a private residence, in Kenton County, KY. He was a true, reliable supporter. His spouse, Mary Bunning, was a very gracious person. Also, former Kentucky Governor Louie Nunn was one of my supporters who came along on my bus tour near the end of the campaign. When a candidate gets to this point, he/she can become more uptight and stressed. Throughout all my campaigns, I was responsible for the financial reports, including the reports for this campaign, which had to go to the Federal Election Committee, in Washington, DC. I never had a problem with any of my financial reports, which were carefully examined in every case. I could have won this race if I had received twelve thousand more votes.

As the saying goes, if the hunting dog had not stopped to shit, he would have caught the rabbit. The losing letdown is tremendous, even though I realized from the start that I would not win this race due to the one sided voter registration. After a loss, it is very easy to blame others, instead of yourself. The next day after the election, I received a phone call from Geoff Davis, who stated that he was going to run for this congressional seat the next time. I could not believe that this SOB bothered me before my body had grown cold. This really pissed me off, and I told him to go to hell. Here he is, realizing that I did very well, getting 101,000 votes with no money. Due to my hard work, I had laid the groundwork for the next candidate and he realized that he would have a good chance of becoming the new US Congressman. I told this SOB that he never supported me and did nothing to help, and that he wanted me to lose so that his chances of winning were better due to my hard work. I had been aware of this guy because at one time he lived in my neighborhood. He appeared to have some type of problem. He did not act right. He was an odd fellow. He did run for this seat and won.

However, three terms later, he resigned for some strange reason. It should be noted that he will receive a retirement check from the House of Representatives after serving five years. The purpose of that phone call was to let me know that he was going to run, in order to intimidate me into not becoming a candidate the second time. My chances of winning would be better if I chose to run again, due to my name recognition and the fact I did so well with no money. I had no interest in running for this office the second time.

So here we are today, in 2018, with a new president. When I hear a voter talking about how dirty the campaign has gotten, I think to myself, man, this voter should learn more about our own history in regards to presidential campaigns in the past, as I have outlined. The candidates, today, are mild compared to the ones in the past.

# KENTUCKY LIEUTENANT GOVERNOR RACE 2003

I made the mother of all political mistakes when I agreed to become the lieutenant governor running mate with Kentucky State Senator Virgil Moore. Senator Moore filed to run for governor, and he wanted me to be his running mate. Man, did I ever have a lack of judgement when I agreed to this setup. Moore had run for Kentucky State Auditor in 1991, losing his primary race. However, later he then ran for State Senate and won. He talked me into this endeavor due to my statewide positive reputation as a candidate in my previous races. I had the reputation for running clean campaigns, being a hard fighter, and being free of any political scandals. As soon as I signed the filing papers, I felt uneasy about this campaign. I really did not know anything about Virgil Moore's personal political beliefs, etc. He had been in the State Senate for almost twelve years. Therefore, he should be a decent fellow.

His spouse was a nice lady, and he had a college degree, retiring from the US Army after twenty years. After being around him more and more, I began to doubt his ever having enough sense to be an Army major, plus, having a college degree. After a few weeks in the campaign, I began to be embarrassed to be seen with him on the campaign trail. He talked me into attending his church with him one Sunday, in Leitchfield, KY. Alas, to my amazement, he introduced me to the congregation as his running mate. I wanted to crawl under the bench that I was sitting on. I did not believe that partisan politics should be brought into a church. This, in my world, was 100 percent a no-no. After this incident, I made up my mind to get out of this race, ASAP. I wrote a letter to the Kentucky Secretary of State's office, telling them to remove me from this race, as a lieutenant governor running mate with Senator Moore. I demanded that I wanted nothing to do with this campaign.

At this point, I completely stopped any association with Virgil Moore. However, he did not want a divorce. He would not leave me, alone. He and his campaign manager, who was a large fellow from Texas, would knock the front door at my residence unexpectedly. I always invited them in, and we would go to our living room, where Virgil would attempt to persuade me to continue as his running mate. They stopped by more than once, and this made me feel very uncomfortable. Knowing what I had learned about that idiot, I never knew what to expect from him. The stupid SOB went so far as to attempt to persuade a Franklin County Circuit Judge to issue an order demanding that I remain on the ticket as his lieutenant governor running mate. While he was in the courtroom, I received a phone call from one of my friends, a well-known TV news reporter, who was also in the same courtroom on other business. He advised me what Moore was attempting to do. However, Moore was not successful. My request to the Secretary of State's office arrived two days too late to have my name removed from the May primary race ballot. So on Election Day, here was my name on the ballot listed as Senator Virgil Moore's lieutenant governor running mate. My name will forever be listed as Moore's running mate on the Kentucky election records in the state archives. Obviously, we did not win.

I hung up my political spikes, with absolutely no desire to ever be a candidate for a political office again. I felt satisfied with myself knowing that I did my part in helping our political system. I never realized that Senator Virgil Moore was so disliked by both Republicans and Democrats in the State Senate. A long-time friend of mine told me later that I should have never associated myself with Virgil Moore. I asked him why in hell he did not tell me sooner. Believe, me, I saw firsthand the dark side of politics. As I have previously stated, if your feet are not totally grounded, both mentally and financially, you should never become a candidate for political office. As a candidate, you must dodge many political zingers coming at you. A potential candidate should be in a position to never have to depend completely on the income from the elected office. These "wanna-be" campaign volunteers will attach themselves to your campaign, in order to enhance their selfish political ambitions. This happened to me more than once. I felt like I had done my share to improve our political system.

As I have previously stated, I believe the most perfect political party platform would be to take the best issues from each party and combine them. There are good issues in both parties. I was a candidate in ten races, which included four primary races. I never lost a primary race. I can honestly say that I became extremely familiar with the state of Kentucky. I believe that I earned as much, or more, political experience than anyone else in the United States. Remember, as a Secret Service agent I observed presidential races for twenty years. During those years, as I have previously stated, I never, under any circumstances, even thought about partisan politics.

During the period of time that I was a candidate for various political offices in the state of Kentucky, I met many candidates who would literally sell their soul to the devil in order to get elected. Many candidates that won their race, would shortly, thereafter, develop this sense of false importance and almost immediately get divorced from their spouse for a more attractive and richer person. I saw this happen on all levels. In other words, their spouse from back home that helped get them to their current political position was not good enough for them after their were elected to their office.

# Bell on stage with Bush

Don Bell's congressional campaign will get a leg up from Texas Gov. George W. Bush today.

Republican Bell, challenging Democratic incumbent Ken Lucas for Northern Kentucky's seat in Congress, will be on the platform with Bush at a 5 p.m. rally at Devou Park in Covington.

"I would rather have that than $200,000," said Eric Deters, Bell's campaign manager.

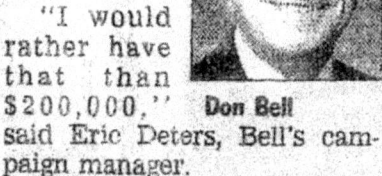

The event will help create the connection to Bush that Bell had hoped for since his campaign started. Since winning the May primary, Bell has said he envisions the battle for the 4th Congressional District as "George Bush and Don Bell vs. Ken Lucas and Al Gore."

Bell's campaign also said this week Lucas, the Democratic incumbent, has agreed to three debates – one on local cable TV, another on KET and a third in Eastern Kentucky, in September or October.

Sen. Mitch McConnell, R-Ky. of Louisville, will address the National Republican Convention Monday. Chairman of the National Republican Senatorial Committee, he will discuss key races and introduce several senatorial candidates.

A celebration honoring Willie Mathis Jr., longtime commonwealth attorney for Boone and Gallatin counties, will be from 4 to 6 p.m. Monday at 2252 Burlington Pike. He officially retires Tuesday

*Don Bell*

My race for Congress 2000 unknown newspaper article.

The one person who helped me get where I am, today, was a Democrat US Congressman, Frank Albert Stubblefield. I was introduced to him by a friend of mine, when I was a nineteen-year-old kid, making less than $4,000 a year, in Washington, DC. At that time, I was a registered Republican, and this did not matter to him, because he and his spouse were extremely decent people. I registered as a Republican because his future son-in-law, who worked for Republican US Senator, John Sherman Cooper, went with me to register to vote, there, in DC.

# LIFE AFTER BEING A CANDIDATE FOR POLITICAL OFFICES

I realized that that there was more to my life than being a Secret Service agent, or being a candidate for political offices. As a Secret Service agent, I always attempted to present the most professional image that I thought a Secret Service agent should present. I never wanted to appear overweight, or dress poorly. Today, I have seen too many agents who do not present the image that I feel a Secret Service agent should present. Neatness, along with the proper physical image, should always be a top priority for an agency such as the Secret Service. The perfect image of what a Director of the Secret Service should look like was James J. Rowley. He was the director when I came on board in 1968. I realize that a female director could not look like Director Rowley, but she could present a professional look, also.

Since Director Rowley, for example, the Secret Service has had only one or two lousy directors. I believe that a director should be someone who has been on board long enough to retire before that person becomes the director of the Secret Service. Also, a very well respected individual from the outside could possibly be appointed director. The director should finish off his/her career as the director, not some young whipper snapper, inexperienced, "ninety-day wonder agent" type. In addition, far too many public scandals involving Secret Service agents have taken place in recent history. Some of these agents, along with their personal appearance and behavior, have been a total embarrassment to the decent agents. One of my pet peeves is to observe one of our agents chewing gum while on duty in the presence of the president of the United States. However, all agencies have their bad apples, including the FBI and other agencies. I realize that it is impossible for all human beings to be perfect, at all times. All of us cannot look like Clint Eastwood or Cindy Crawford, but we should do the best we can, with what we have to work with.

# LIFE IN FLORIDA

"I am a part of all I have met." I am become a name, for always roaming with a hungry heart. Much have I seen and known—cities of people and manners, climates, councils, governments. Myself, not least, but honored of them all—and drunk delight of battle with my peers, far on the ringing plains of windy Troy.
—Ulysses by Alfred Lord Tennyson.

With President George H. W. Bush taken at the White House, 1990, while I was a candidate for Kentucky State Senate.

One of my campaign cards taken with Presidential candidate George W. Bush, 2000.

Me with Abraham Lincoln taken at a campaign event.

# DON BELL

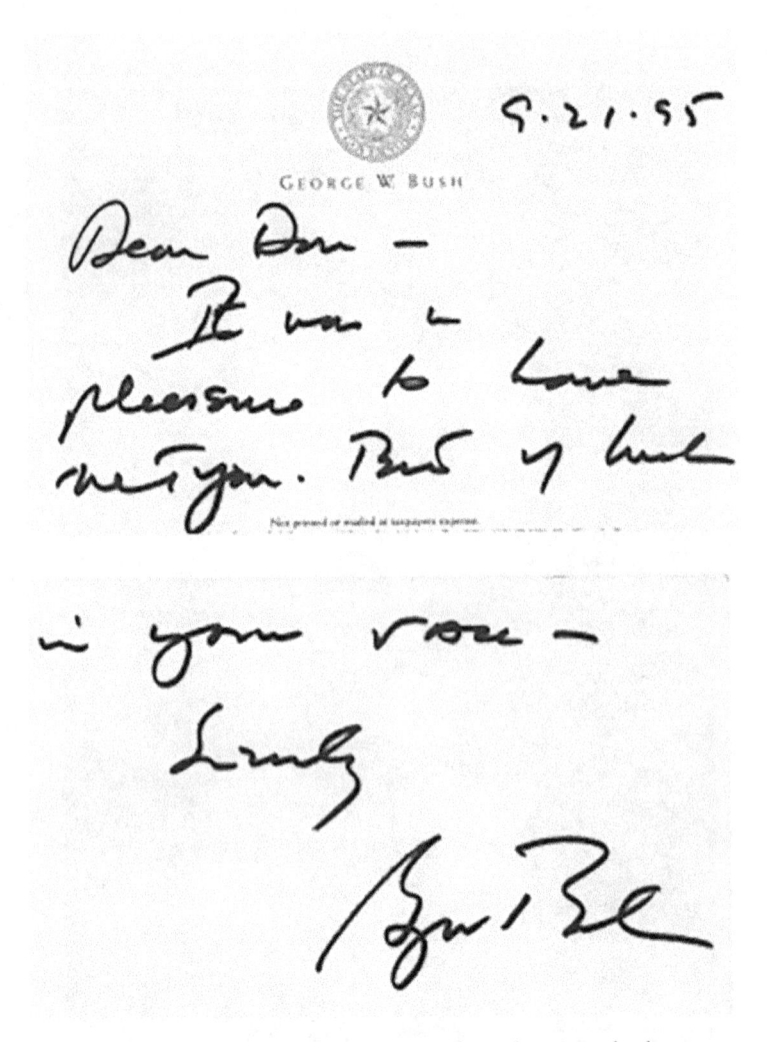

Letter from Governor George W. Bush wishing me luck in my race for Kentucky State Auditor during his visit to one of our campaign events in a private home in northern Kentucky.

# STRUGGLE TO ZERO

**President**
L. RAY SMART
1002 Hillwood Avenue
Falls Church, Virginia
JEfferson 2-3736

*Vice President—Membership*
MRS. CHARLES CHANCE
208 Massachusetts Avenue, N.E.
Washington, D. C.
Lincoln 6-4100

*Vice President—Entertainment*
JUDGE J. GREGORY BRUCE
5524 Pembrook Road
Bethesda, Maryland
OLiver 2-5615

*Vice President—Special Events*
LELAND HOWARD
3835 Lorcum Lane
Arlington, Virginia
JAckson 2-5895

1961 - 1962

## Kentucky Society
## of
## Washington

**Secretary**
MRS. BEN G. CROSBY
1204 Burtonwood Drive
Marlan Forest, Alexandria, Va.
SOuth 8-8832

*Treasurer*
RAY H. HAMILTON
7200 Hawthorne Street
Hyattsville, Maryland
SPruce 3-2067

*Sergeant-at-Arms*
CHARLES CHANCE
208 Massachusetts Avenue, N.E.
Washington, D. C.
Lincoln 6-4100

*Honorary Vice Presidents*
GOVERNOR BERT THOMAS COMBS
JUSTICE STANLEY F. REED
SENATOR JOHN SHERMAN COOPER
SENATOR THRUSTON B. MORTON

March 26, 1962

Dear Friends,

It is Cherry Blossom Time again....... and in keeping with the spirit of the season your Kentucky Society of Washington is honoring its Princess, Miss Barbour Lee Perry, at a Reception on Wednesday evening April 4, 1962, from 5:30 to 7:30 p.m., in the Public Works Committee Hearing Room # 1302 (third floor), New House Office Building.

Admission to the Reception will be by Membership Cards and guests will be charged the usual fee of $1.00 each.

Plan to be present and make this another enjoyable evening in the Society's calender of social events. Please bring your friends.

Tickets are still available for the conference of State Societies Princesses Ball at the Sheraton Park Hotel on Tuesday evening April 3, 1962.

Sincerely yours,

L. Ray Smart,
President

Letter from the Kentucky Society of Washington, to me, requesting my presence at a reception honoring that year's Cherry Blossom Festival Queen.

DON BELL

# DON BELL
## STATE AUDITOR

Cartoon of me drawn by a member of the Lexington Herald-Leader newspaper, during my editorial Board interview as a candidate for Kentucky State auditor.

Campaign photo of me at a dinner while a candidate for Kentucky State Auditor, 1995.

US Congress race photo of myself and Stephanie, fall 2000.

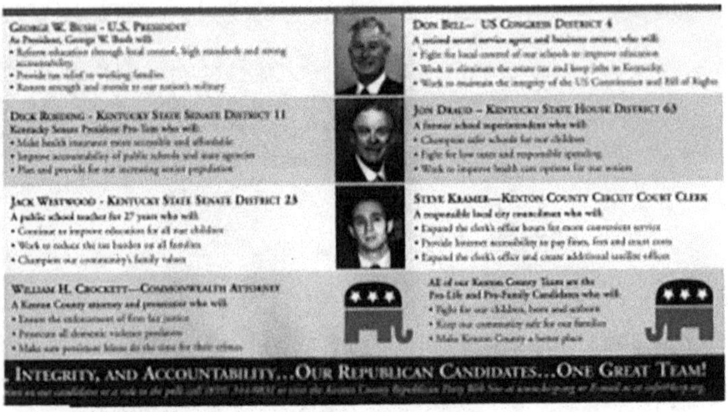

# DON BELL

Political mailer.

# STRUGGLE TO ZERO

State Senate campaign parade with all members of my family, 1990.

Myself and Stephanie with US Congressman Gene Snyder at his home. The freeway around Louisville is named after Congressman Snyder.

# DON BELL

GOP Kentucky Governor's race in 2003 indicating
the chaos in the Primary Race.
My running mate and I are in the center-far right.

Myself and Stephanie with US Senator Jim Bunning,
and his spouse Mary Bunning, at the resident of US
Congressman Gene Snyder, Pee Wee Valley, KY.

STRUGGLE TO ZERO

## State Board of Elections
## Frankfort, Kentucky

June 9, 2000

The undersigned, a Board for examining the returns of a primary election held on Tuesday the 23rd of May 2000 for Nomination for the office of

## United States Representative (Republican)
## Fourth District

Commonwealth of Kentucky, do certify that

## Don Bell

received the required number of votes given for that office, as certified to the Secretary of State, and is, therefore, declared to be a nominee for said office, to be voted for as such at the regular election to be held on November 7, 2000.

_____
Chairman

_____
Member

_____
Member

_____
Member

_____
Member

_____
Member

Today, I reside in Vero Beach, Florida, with Stephanie and our youngest child, Brian. During 2003, prior to relocating to Florida from La Grange, KY, we built a new vacation home in The Villages, Florida. The Villages currently has fifty thousand to sixty thousand, homes, and approximately four hundred new homes are built each month. I believe that it is the largest fifty-five and over development in the world. We sold this home in 2010 and moved full-time to Vero Beach. The Villages is TOTAL living with a beautiful hospital and doctors everywhere, to include 2,500 social clubs and forty golf courses. A person could stay there without ever having to leave even after death because you can be buried there. It is truly unbelievable in every sense. However, for me, the life there sort of reminds me of the life in the movie, *The Stepford Wives*. Many of the residents would become very angry if you happen to criticize anything about The Villages.

As for me, this whole HOA (Home Owners Association) thing is similar to living under Communist rule. Everyone and everything is supposedly equal. I do not like it because a homeowner can get into situations where your neighbor or board members can be son of bitches. I prefer to deal with the city or county government instead of these HOA boards, in general. Also, I always felt that I had one foot in the grave, while residing there in The Villages. Finally, I do not want to be around all those old people all the time. I am one of those "old" people, myself, but I enjoy looking at and associating with younger people sometimes. However, I soon learned that these "old" people knew how to party and have sex. A halfway-decent looking man could literally commit sex suicide if he wanted to, as a homeowner in The Villages. This is due to the fact that men are really outnumbered by women.

Currently, I am here in Vero Beach residing in our four bedroom middle class home that we built new in 2005. It is located on the "poor" side of the bridge from the ocean. Also, we own a condo located on the "rich" side, on Ocean Drive, directly across the street from the ocean. I never mention this in my conversations.

At this stage of my life, I am still reminded of the saying that "no good deed goes unpunished." For example, I loaned my 1964

Murray State University yearbook to a member of a respected family here in Indian River County. This particular yearbook was the one that I wanted to keep forever. Would you believe that it has been a few years since I loaned this book to this individual, and he has not returned it. This could have been a totally honest, forgetful oversight. His spouse wanted to make a photo of this person from his photo in MY yearbook due to the fact it was a great photo. I really want this item back.

One of my mistakes that I have made over the years is that I have given human beings too much credit as it relates to honesty, commitment, trust, and morality, etc. However, I have come to the realization that far too many human beings are not honest and trustworthy. I always seemed to have these dishonest leeches drawn to me for whatever reason. This was especially true in the political arena. Some of those, "helpful" volunteers latch on to your campaign in order to further their own political ambition. I came in contact with an individual in my church who deceived me into thinking he was okay.

The first occurred when one of our church employees escorted a neatly dressed man with his Bible into my Sunday school classroom. I was lead to believe that this person had been somewhat "vetted" in some manner. After the class was over this man approached me with a sob story about how much he needed money. He caught me in a weak moment and I ended up giving him $40. I did not think too kindly of this situation. I was beginning to think that an illegal alien in San Francisco has more sanctuary than my own church. I realize that I have always given human beings more credit than they deserve, due to the fact they are HUMAN BEINGS. This has been one of my weaknesses. I guess I will never learn. I know there are certain human beings that cannot be salvaged under any circumstances. However these poor souls must be taken care of, as to food, medical care, and shelter. Therefore, we MUST attempt to salvage those that are salvageable. Remember, we need three categories for all living things— human, animals, and OTHER. Certain human beings are so awful and totally beyond help that they do not deserve to be called human beings. Therefore, they need to be in the OTHER classification.

Another situation occurred while at one of our annual civic club Christmas dinners. I was sitting next to one of our elderly, long time members who had severe physical problems, such as not being able to sit up by himself in his chair. Mind you, his fifty-ish-year-old son was sitting right next to him on the other side. During the dinner, the man continually fell over in my lap, and I would continually sit him up in his chair. One time he almost fell completely out of his chair, but I managed to catch him before he hit the floor. This scene for whatever reason reminded me of movie WEEK END AT BERNIE'S. Would you believe that his son just sat there like a knot on a log and never helped me prevent his father from falling out of his chair? My dinner was totally not enjoyable, plus, I had to practically carry the gentleman to his car after dinner. I did my duty by helping the nice elderly man in view of the fact that his son sat there like a potted plant and did nothing in preventing his father from falling out of his chair.

   My physical fitness routine consists of walking a total of three miles up and back from Humiston Park to Jaycee Park, on Ocean Drive, in Vero Beach, FL. Humiston Park is located right on the beach. After one of these walks, I entered the men's restroom there in Humiston Park. After entering, I heard a man's voice from one of the stalls in the rear. He was stating over and over in a loud voice, "help me, please help." Well, I was the only other person in the restroom (damn it), and due to my "inquiring mind needs to know" syndrome, I went back to the stall and faced this elderly person who could have been between eighty to one hundred years of age sitting on the crapper with his shorts and underwear below his knees. He could not get up! At that point I REALLY wanted to turn around and leave, but my conscience said otherwise.

   Anyway, as I was standing there looking down on this poor soul sitting on the crapper, I was trying to figure out the best way to lift him up. First, I tried pulling him up with one hand and then with his two hands, rocking him back and forth. That did not work. His whole body was totally dead weight. He had no physical strength at all. Well, the only thing left to do was to pull him up by putting both my arms under his arm pits, thus, with all my strength, rocking him

# STRUGGLE TO ZERO

back and forth and lifting his whole body off that damn shitter. This worked. After stabilizing him on his feet along with his walking cane, I pointed him toward the front entrance. He took off like a young bird on its first flight from the nest. This man was dressed nicely, and was not a pan handler or a homeless person, but he was either too embarrassed or ill-mannered to thank me. He just wanted to get out of that restroom and disappear into the beach crowd. The first thing that I did after entering my home was to take a good, soapy shower. I really felt dirty after this incident. Again, I truly did not want to help this poor soul, but I guess my kindness and respect for human beings made me help him. I kept thinking that this could have been my elderly father, if he was still alive. I realized that if I had not helped this man, he would have sat on that crapper all day long, or until the park cleaning staff came in at the end of the day to clean the bathroom. At least, my conscience was clear and I did feel better about myself.

Another situation that I became involved in occurred in 2011, when myself, and another member of my civic club traveled to New Orleans, LA, to attend the annual club International Convention, which lasted for one week. The elderly, nice, and gentle gentleman had an obsession with one of our club causes. He truly believed in this cause, and he convinced me to travel with him in my car to New Orleans for this convention, due to the fact no one else would go with him. The trip was eleven hours straight driving time, one way, interstate all the way. Well, he listened to a book on CD all the way, which was played on my car sound system. The book was about a frontier family moving from one location to another, etc. It was really boring. We get to New Orleans and checked in at the convention and immediately sat up his Songs for Peace booth. He became so obsessive in making certain that I said the proper things in a certain programmed way to the visitors stopping by our booth that he would become angry if I deviated from the norm.

I could not even enjoy my lunch because he did not really want me away from the booth. I realized that he was probably in bad health when a couple of religious types from Texas stopped by and chatted with my fellow club member. After chatting, they put their arms around him and started praying. It was obvious that he had some type of health problem. Later, as we left the convention and while on our way back to our hotel in the French Quarter, my pal could hardly walk one block without stopping to rest. The next morning as we had a cup of coffee in the small restaurant across from our hotel, he told me that during the night he could not breathe and that he thought he would not make it.

In addition, he was drinking some red liquid from a smaller bottle. He told me the medication was for his prostate cancer. It was apparent that he was miserable and in bad shape. Also, he appeared to have a heart attack during the previous night in view of the fact that he had great difficulty breathing. I tried to convince him that we should pack up and go home, but he would have nothing to do with that idea. I was very concerned that he may pass away before we got back home. He was so obsessed by the Songs for Peace project that it appeared he was willing to take his chances by not leaving. The week was totally miserable for me, but I kept on trucking. On the way home, he continued to listen to the book on the CD. Throughout the trip he did not talk or want to stop to eat. I only stopped for gas. What a miserable trip for me. After we got back, and at the next club meeting I told one of his children that he appeared to have a heart attack, and that he should see a cardiologist. This gentleman was a kind, nice person who had something to believe in, very strongly.

I do not believe in royalty, political dynasty's, worshiping any human being, or treating anyone better than they deserve. I respect and honor ACCOMPLISHMENTS and KINDNESS in human beings. Many people mistake kindness for weakness. I cannot believe how many poor weak souls worship celebrities, politicians, kings and queens. FINALLY, JUST REMEMBER…SHOW ME A PERSON WITH NO ENEMIES AND I WILL SHOW YOU A PERSON WHO HAS DONE NOTHING IN THEIR LIFE. So here I am, doing my thing in Vero Beach, Florida, hoping that I can escape any more "no good deed goes unpunished" situations. I just hope that I will not meet the Grimm Reaper before my time. Today, I am more cautious about making new friends due to the fact that once I become your friend, I WILL be your friend forever, and will go the extra mile to help you. I will never desert you. OTHER THAN MY FAMILY, my most personal satisfying moment/accomplishment during my life was when I learned that I passed the comprehensive exam which earned me my master's degree from George Washington University, Washington, DC. I will always be very grateful to that University. Going from earning a high school diploma, from a school located next to a corn field, in western Tennessee, with eighty students in the whole school, to earning the Master's Degree from George Washington University, continues to give me a good personal feeling even today.

Just remember, I have been told by several in the medical profession that all human beings take their last breath then soil their pants, regardless of their title, financial accomplishments, or their believing how great thou art. One common theme in all those who are truly great human beings that I have come in contact with during my life (which have been many) is that they have humility, kindness, and never thought of themselves as being better than anyone else. In other words, they never need to boast about their accomplishments due to the fact their success is evident by their kind and respectful actions.

Sometimes I believe that life can be similar to a series of hurdles, in that it seems we must deal with one crisis or hurdle on a continuous basis. Some are small, but some are HUGE. I have gone through a bout of colon cancer, and my spouse Stephanie has survived breast cancer and a heart attack. However, the latest hurdle that I am currently attempting to overcome is my daughter's very aggressive breast cancer. We were advised very recently that Becky had a very large aggressive tumor in her breast. This was totally unexpected due to her being what seemed to be a very healthy person. She is currently under an aggressive treatment plan, but I am very concerned about her due to the nature of this cancer. Upon returning home after a recent two-week visit with her, my appetite has diminished for some reason. As I come to the end of my story, and as you can see, it seems that our lives are a series of hurdles, and we must face each one with a level headed, clear mind, in order to prepare for the next hurdle/crisis.

So here I am sitting in my condo on Ocean Drive in Vero Beach, FL, on February 13, 2018. I am having flashbacks about our past presidential election. There is one thing for certain, whomever becomes our next president will definitely seem boring compared to Donald J. Trump, or even Andrew Jackson. We are watching a reality show every day.

# SUMMARY

I want my life story to be told mainly for my children and grandchildren in order to let them know and understand how one person can be born into an economic lifestyle that was definitely below the zero economic scale, which made me struggle every day to just make it to zero in order to have an even playing field with everyone else.

My journey starts from my place of birth, Parnell, Kentucky, and takes me throughout my life to age eighteen, when I left home for a clerical job with the Federal Bureau of Investigation in Washington, DC. I remained in Washington from 1958 to 1962, when I left to attend Murray State University, Murray, Kentucky. After earning my bachelor of science degree in August 1965, I joined the US Marine Corps Reserves in Memphis, Tennessee. After six months on active duty, I returned to Memphis and fulfilled my military obligation, receiving an honorable discharge during 1969. While in Memphis, during this period of time, I was employed by the First National Bank, Memphis, and from 1966 to 1968, I was employed in a non-agent position in the Memphis FBI Field Office. On December 16, 1968, I became a United States Secret Service agent. I remained in the Memphis Secret Service Field Office until June 1971, when I was transferred to Secret Service Headquarters in Washington, DC, myself and family remained there until 1977, leaving for my assignment in our Louisville, Kentucky Field Office. I remained in our Louisville Office until I retired on December 31, 1988.

As a Secret Service agent, I observed our federal political system up close and personal, due to my duties protecting the president of the United States and numerous others who were involved in our political system, such as major presidential candidates. I developed this strange urge to run for political offices, in Kentucky. Today, as I look back, the knowledge that I acquired by getting involved in the political arena cannot be overestimated. I saw a side of humanity that I never knew existed. My eyes were opened in many, many directions. I probably have the same or more firsthand experience in the political arena as any other American. I never lost a primary race, but also, never won a race due to the fact my political party was grossly outnumbered in registered voters. I did this mainly for the challenge, knowing that I probably would never win. I have attempted to go into detail in describing my races, but I left out names of certain individuals due to the fact their children are still living. Everything I have described is definitely factual.

One accomplishment that gives me probably the most satisfaction, other than my family is earning a master of arts degree from George Washington University, Washington, DC. In order to earn this degree, I had to keep my hand on the throttle and my eye on the rail at all times. I was employed full-time, and had a spouse and two children.

Also, I want to emphasize the fact that a United States Secret Service Special agent has numerous duties other than protecting the president of the United States, and others. The Secret Service was created on April 14, 1865, to investigate the counterfeiting of the US currency, not protecting the president. The first president we protected was President Theodore Roosevelt in 1901. In other words, our agents were criminal investigators first, then later, becoming involved in protection duties.

Today, I reside in Vero Beach, Florida, with my family, continuing to swim around the great white sharks in life and waiting for the next hurdle/crisis to happen and hopefully, overcome.

February, 25, 2018, as I think of the recent horrible high school massacre in Broward County, Florida, I am reminded of my extensive experience in predicting dangerous behavior as a Secret Service agent who specialized in these type of investigations as they related to threats to kill the President of the United States and others. I believe the most important FIRST BABY STEP that we, as a society, should take is to deal with our mental illness situation. Our health insurance companies need to treat mental illness the same as physical illness, in regards to financial coverage. The brain is the most important part of our body and needs to be healed the same as any other body part, sometimes more. Our mentally/emotionally ill citizens must have the same access to treatment as the physically ill patients. This FIRST step must come from the health insurance companies by treating them the SAME. I realize this will not solve all our problems in this area, but DAMN IT, this could be just the FIRST BABY STEP.

President Nixon and William P. Rogers, Secretary of State, 1969–1973, having a confidential conversation on the White House grounds.

This photo of Japanese Emperor Hirohito was taken in 1971 with President and Ms. Nixon at the White House during the Emperor's visit to the United States.
It was given to me by a White House staff member.

Frank Albert Stubblefield.